The Law and Elderly People

Aled Griffiths, Y Coleg Normal, & School of Sociology and Social Policy, University College of North Wales, Bangor.
Richard Grimes, Partner, Watson Esam & Co, Solicitors.
Gwyneth Roberts, School of Sociology and Social Policy, University College of North Wales, Bangor.

Despite the growth in the number of elderly people in Britain of recent years the law as it relates to elderly people is a relatively neglected field.

This is the first book devoted to the examination of the law as it affects the elderly. Concerned for the independence and autonomy of both the young elderly and the old elderly, the book covers employment and income, accommodation and housing, community and residential care, health provision and delivery, and family relationships, to provide an invaluable guide to the most important legal issues.

The Law and Elderly People will be of practical help to all those concerned with the welfare of the elderly and to undergraduates and lecturers in social work, law, and gerontology.

THE LAW AND ELDERLY PEOPLE

Aled Griffiths, Richard H. Grimes, and Gwyneth Roberts

First published 1990
Reprinted 1991
by Routledge
11 New Fetter Lane, London EC4P 4EE

Printed in Great Britain by Billing & Sons Ltd, Worcester

British Library Cataloguing in Publication Data

Griffiths, Aled
   The law and elderly people.
   1. Great Britain. Old persons. Legal aspects
   I. Title II. Grimes, Richard H. III. Roberts.
Gwyneth
344.102'87

ISBN 0-415-00517-5

Parrys 6807 /35 · 9·91

CONTENTS

TABLE OF CASES

xvi

TABLE OF STATUTES

xviii

Housing Act 1985 (HA 1985)

TABLE OF STATUTORY INSTRUMENTS

LIST OF ABBREVIATIONS

AAU	Attendance Allowance Unit
ABU	Agencies Benefits Unit
AJC	Allocation Joint Committee
CABx	Citizens Advice Bureaux
CCG	Community Care Grant
CGT	Capital Gains Tax
CHC	Community Health Council
CNS	Community Nursing Service
CTT	Capital Transfer Tax
DCP	District Community Physician
DEB	Dental Estimates Board
DGH	District General Hospital
DGM	District General Manager
DH	Department of Health (after July 1988)
DHA	District Health Authority
DHSS	Department of Health and Social Security (up to July 1988)
DMP	Delegated Medical Practitioner
DP	Disability Premium
DSS	Department of Social Security (after July 1988)
EAT	Employment Appeal Tribunal
EC	European Community
EPA	Enduring Power of Attorney
FP	Family Premium
FPC	Family Practitioner Committee
FPS	Family Practitioner Services
FSAVC	Free Standing Additional Voluntary Contributions
GDM	General District Manager
GMC	General Medical Council
GMP	Guaranteed Minimum Pension
GMS	General Medical Services
GOS	General Opthalmic Services
GP	General Practitioner
HAS	Health Advisory Service
HB	Housing Benefit
HBS	Housing Benefit Supplement
HDP	Higher Disability Premium

HPP	Higher Pensioner Premium
HSC	Health Services Commission
ICA	Invalid Care Allowance
IHT	Inheritance Tax
ILF	Independent Living Fund
IS	Income Support
MHAC	Mental Health Act Commission
MHRT	Mental Health Review Tribunal
MOD	Ministry of Defence
MOH	Ministry of Health
MSC	Medical Services Committee
NAHA	National Association of Health Authorities
NHS	National Health Service
NISW	National Institute of Social Work
OPAS	Occupational Pensions Advisory Service
OPB	Occupational Pensions Board
PP	Pensioner Premium
RAC	Rent Assessment Committee
RADAR	Royal Association for Disability and Rehabilitation
RGN	Registered General Nurse
RHA	Regional Health Authority
RMO	Regional Medical Officer
SDA	Severe Disability Allowance
SDP	Severe Disability Premium
SEN	State Enrolled Nurse
SERPS	State Earnings-Related Pension Scheme
SHA	Special Health Authority
SSAFA	Soldiers, Sailors and Airmen's Families Association
SSAT	Social Security Appeal Tribunal
TP	Transitional Payment
UM	Unit Manager
WO	Welsh Office
YTS	Youth Training Scheme

In memory of

Stewart Pritchard

a much missed colleague and friend

PREFACE

The purpose of this book is to examine aspects of the law which are of particular significance to elderly people. The six main subject areas discussed here are: employment and income; accommodation and housing; community care; residential care; health provision and its delivery; family relationships and personal autonomy.

The law as it relates to elderly people is a relatively neglected field, with existing material scattered throughout a number of different sources. This book, therefore, attempts to provide a more comprehensive view of the field than is currently available.

Any discussion which refers to elderly people needs to take account of the fact that 'old age' can cover a span of 30 or more years. There may well be significant differences between the lives of many of those in the 'young elderly' age group (that is, those between 65 and 74 years of age) and the lives of those who are 'old elderly' (that is, 75 years of age and over). Whereas issues relating to employment and retirement may be of relevance to the former, they will be less so for the latter. Similarly, issues relating to dependency and vulnerability are likely to be more important as people become very old. References to the elderly in this book are made with that proviso.

Our hope is that the text will provide a useful guide to some of the more important legal issues, and that it may contribute, in some small way, to enabling people to enjoy, for as long as possible in old age, independent, self-fulfilling and autonomous lives.

ACKNOWLEDGEMENTS

Many people have helped, directly or indirectly, in the production of this book. We would particularly like to thank Freda Mainwaring and other members of the Law Department, University of Keele; Gwyneth Walsh and staff of Y Coleg Normal, Bangor, and members of the School of Sociology & Social Policy, University College of North Wales, Bangor. The Librarian and staff of the library at UCNW gave us much assistance. We would also like to acknowledge the help given in various ways by Delyth Murphy, John Llewelyn Jones and Jaswant Chanay. Clive W. Parr, editor of *The Family Practitioner Services,* readily agreed to the use of material from that journal, and we are grateful to him. Finally, our very special thanks and greatest debt are owed to Angela Rowlands and Geraldine Roberts whose tremendous enthusiasm, commitment and skill were invaluable in producing various versions of this book, including the final one. Responsibility for the final text remains with us. We have tried to state the law as it stood in England and Wales on December 31, 1988, but have taken into account major statutory changes to come into effect early in 1989.

Aled Griffiths
Richard H. Grimes
Gwyneth Roberts

31st December, 1988

Chapter One

EMPLOYMENT, INCOME AND RETIREMENT

1.1.1 ECONOMIC ACTIVITY

Of recent years, there has been a considerable decline in the number of those of retirement age still at work. Only 50 years ago, more than half the male population over 65 was in some form of employment but by 1986, the figure had dropped to as little as 7.5 per cent.[1] The economic activity rate of women over 60 has always been low. At present, it stands at 6.5 per cent and is similarly declining.[2]

1.1.2 A disturbing feature of this decline in economic activity is that giving up work is often involuntary. Hunt's survey revealed that almost half the men and women in her sample would have liked to continue working beyond the age at which they gave up. Over half the males still at work and over a quarter of the females had been compulsorily retired, but had then taken up other employment. Over 90 per cent of employed respondents enjoyed working and hoped to carry on for as long as possible.[3] Several studies have shown people of retirement age possess the necessary capacity to acquire new skills. Contrary to the general view that elderly people are rigid and dogmatic, it has been shown that people of 70 and 80 are as flexible in their attitudes as younger respondents of similar educational backgrounds.[4] Current trends indicate a further decline in the economic activity rate of those of retirement age, and that earlier retirement will also become more common. The evidence suggests a sharp decline in economic activity among men between 60 and 64 years of age; and it is projected that only some 50 per cent of this age group will be in employment in 1991. Although not so dramatic, there has been a similar decline in economic activity among women aged 55 and over. This contrasts with the trend towards increased economic activity among females generally.[5] As Midwinter has observed: 'As the actual quantity of work available decreases, we talk of raising the school leaving age and lowering retirement age for those two straps of the labour force concertina'.[6] Changes in the make-up of Britain's population mean, however, that fewer young people are entering the labour market, a trend which will continue until the end of this century. It seems likely that the government may introduce incentives to persuade those over the existing retirement age to remain in employment.

1.1.3 This is not to argue that pensionable age should be raised for everyone. Research findings suggest that for some people, retirement improves health. According to recent American literature, studies carried out in the 1960s, which suggested that imposed retirement had a negative effect on self-image, gave grossly exaggerated results. Loss of work may not be nearly as devastating to the individual as was once assumed.[7] The status of older people may also be enhanced by the legitimization of leisure.[8] The argument here is simply that individuals should be allowed greater choice whether or not they continue to work beyond pensionable age.

1.2.1 EMPLOYMENT PROTECTION

Issues of particular importance for employees approaching the end of their working life, as well as for those wishing to continue to work after reaching normal retirement age, relate to unfair dismissal, redundancy, and frustration of the contract of employment. It also seems that jobs done by elderly workers are typically of a lower socio-economic status than that of the population as a whole. Townsend found that the gross earnings of one third of fully employed pensioners was below half the mean for their sex, compared to six per cent only of men, and 22 per cent of women, in their forties and fifties. Three-quarters of the pensioner sample, compared with only a half of men aged 40 to 59, spent their time at work standing, or walking about, indicative, perhaps of low occupational status.[9] For this reason, the law relating to wages protection is also of importance to this group.

1.2.2 PARTICULARS OF THE CONTRACT OF EMPLOYMENT

Where a dispute arises over the terms of a contract, particularly in relation to rights arising on its termination, it may be important for the employee to be able to ascertain its contents. It is still common practice for many contracts of employment to be entered into orally, or both orally and in writing. In accordance with s.1 of the Employment Protection (Consolidation) Act 1978 (EP(C)A 1978), most employees - the major exceptions being Crown employees, including those employed in the NHS - are entitled to receive a written statement from their employer setting out the terms of the contract not later than the end of the thirteenth week after commencement of employment. The existence of the contract will not, however, be affected should no statement be issued. In such circumstances, the terms of the contract will be deduced from custom, practice or by implication. The statutory statement itself is not conclusive evidence of the terms of the contract although it can help to establish what those terms are.

The statement must include the terms and conditions which relate to hours of work; holiday entitlement; sick pay (if any); pension rights; the length of required notice; any relevant disciplinary rules; and whether a certificate of contracting-out of the state pension scheme is in force. Should no written statement be provided or should the one which has been provided, be incomplete, an employee can ask an industrial tribunal to determine what should be included in it.

1.2.3 WAGES PROTECTION

In some trades where no voluntary machinery for negotiating collective agreements exists, the task of securing and enforcing agreement on wages is undertaken by wages councils. The Wages Act 1986 (WA 1986) curtailed the powers and operation of existing wages councils, and prohibited the establishment of new bodies of this kind. The Agricultural Wages Boards, which have similar powers, are, however, unaffected. In 1985, 26 wages councils were in existence covering over two and a half million workers, primarily in the retailing, catering and hairdressing industries. Approximately two-thirds of protected employees were part-timers, and 80 per cent were women.[10] The powers of the

3

wages councils have now been limited to setting a single minimum basic rate (that is, to making wages orders) and to setting a single overtime rate for all those employed within their sphere of operation. Wages councils can also limit the amount which the employer can charge for accommodation supplied as part of the contract of employment. Where a wages council order exists, workers are entitled to regard the statutory minimum wage as replacing any lower contractual figure. An employer who refused to pay the difference between the two amounts would be liable to prosecution. An order can also allow for arrears to be paid for up to two years prior to the date of the offence. An alternative option is for the employee to sue for breach of contract. A civil action may be more appropriate where the underpayment was for a period longer than the statutory two years.[11]

1.2.4 The WA 1986 repealed the Truck Acts 1831 to 1940 and other statutes imposing control over the manner in which employers were permitted to pay their workers. In practice, probably the most important restrictions which remain are those relating to cash deductions from the wages of workers in retail employment. The basic rule is that deductions cannot exceed ten per cent of the gross wages payable on a pay day.[12] This protection relates only to retail workers, and to deductions made on grounds of cash shortages or stock deficiencies only. It does not extend to deductions from pay made for any other reason, such as absenteeism.

1.3.1 DISABLED EMPLOYEES

The majority of disabled people are over pensionable age. Legislation exists to protect the disabled at work, although it is somewhat ineffective. Formerly, if an employer wished to pay a disabled person below the rate established by a wages council, he/she had to obtain a special permit. The WA 1986 abolished that provision so that there is now no special statutory protection in respect of disabled persons.[13] To register as disabled under the Disabled Persons (Employment) Acts 1944 and 1958 (DP(E)A 1944, 1958), a person must be substantially handicapped in obtaining or keeping employment, or in undertaking work on his/her own account, of a kind which apart from his/her injury, disease or deformity would be suited to his/her age, experience, and qualifications.[14] It must also be shown that the disability is likely to persist for at least twelve months.

Employers with more than 20 employees must ensure that three per cent of their labour force consists of registered disabled persons. Where a firm is below quota, it must take on a suitable registered disabled person to fill a vacancy, unless permitted by the Employment Service, (within the Department of Employment), to engage someone who is not disabled. Companies which, on average, employ more than 250 employees throughout the year, are obliged to include a statement in their annual report setting out the company's policy with regard to the employment, training and career development of disabled persons.[15] A code of good practice has been published by the Manpower Services Commission.

Some hazardous industries are exempt from the provisions of the DP(E) Acts. An employer can also apply for special exemption if the quota of disabled persons cannot be filled because no suitable candidate has come forward, or because the work is not suitable. Breach of these provisions is an offence, but prosecutions are seldom brought.[16] Registration as a disabled person should not be regarded as futile, however, since a degree of protection has been established at common law. In *Kerr v. Atkinson's Vehicles Ltd [1974]*[17] it was held that an employer should not expect a normal standard of work or output from a disabled person. Dismissal would be fair only if it could be shown that the standard of a person's work was below that which could reasonably be expected from him/her. An employer would also need to show the case had been given special consideration and that the needs of the business made dismissal necessary.[18] Failure to show need of this kind might be sufficient to establish dismissal as unfair.[19]

1.3.2 Registration as a disabled person under employment legislation is distinct from registration with social services authorities under the Chronically Sick and Disabled Persons Act 1970 (CSDPA 1970). (see Chapter 3 at paras. 3.8.1-3.8.4) Those meeting the relevant criteria can register under both Acts.

1.4.1 MINIMUM NOTICE PERIODS

Except where there is serious misconduct, a person is entitled to be given notice for the period set out in his/her contract of employment. A contract for a fixed term does not require notice since it is brought to an end automatically by passage of time.[20] Where there is no express provision for notice in the contract, reasonable notice must be given. What is regarded as reasonable will vary, depending upon the position held by the employee. It has been held that a senior engineer was entitled to more than a month's notice, and that reasonable notice in such circumstances could have been anything between six months and one year.[21] Whatever the contract provides, the length of notice cannot be shorter than the minimum required by statute. This varies according to length of service. After four weeks, an employee is entitled to one week's notice, until he/she has been engaged for up to two years. The employee is then entitled to one week's notice for each completed year of service up to a maximum of twelve weeks.[22] A person employed for seven years or over, for example, would be entitled to seven weeks notice.

Where an employee is given notice, but is asked to work until the notice has expired, dismissal will not be effective until the end of that period. In effect, should an employee leave earlier, he/she will be regarded as having brought the employment to an end rather than having been dismissed.[23]

1.4.2 An employee must give a minimum of one week's notice of termination of employment, but the contract of employment can stipulate a longer period.[24] In theory, an employee who failed to work out his/her period of notice could be sued for breach of contract. This is unlikely in practice.

1.5.1 FRUSTRATION OF THE CONTRACT

Where performance of a contract of employment is rendered impossible by some intervening event, it will be brought to an end automatically by operation of law. In legal terms, the contract is said to have been 'frustrated'. The most common causes of frustration are probably sickness or injury. An accident may be so serious that it is apparent that the employee is no longer able to perform his/her part of the contract.

Prolonged periods of sickness could also result in the employer claiming the contract of employment no longer existed. Relevant considerations are the length of employment; how long it could have been expected to continue were it not for the illness or injury; the nature of the work; the type of employment and the employer's need to have the work done; the terms of the contract, including the provision of sick pay; and whether, in all the circumstances, a reasonable employer could be expected to give the employee more time to return to work.[25] Where an occupational sick-pay scheme exists, the contract will normally continue until such time as payment under the scheme comes to an end but this is not always the case. The contract may come to an end earlier where sickness or injury is so serious that there is no prospect, in the foreseeable future, of the employee returning to work. It should be stressed, however, that absence from work, even for a long period of time, does not necessarily mean that the contract has been frustrated. In *Maxwell v. Walter Howard Designs Ltd [1975]*[26] the employee had been sick for nearly two years. It was held that the post did not need a permanent replacement and that the contract of employment had not, therefore, been frustrated. Where the contract has been frustrated, the employer need not dismiss the employee, but could do so, and claim the dismissal to have been fair. (see para.1.6.2 below).

1.6.1 UNFAIR DISMISSAL

Under the EP(C)A 1978, protection against unfair dismissal extends to most employees who can show they have been in continuous employment for 104 weeks and for not less than 16 hours per week (or for not less than eight hours per week after five years of employment).[27] A person of normal retiring age is outside this protection. In occupations where there is no established age for retiring, the normal retirement age will be 65 for both men and women. (see para. 1.8.2 below) Where dismissal is on the grounds of an employee's membership of a trades union (or his/her intention to join one) it is not necessary to show that there has been continuous employment for the requisite period. The same rule applies where a person has been dismissed because of refusal to join a trades union.

1.6.2 UNFAIR DISMISSAL AND NORMAL RETIRING AGE

'Normal retiring age' is not necessarily identical with 'pensionable age'. 'Pensionable age' is simply the age at which an employee is entitled to retire on a pension but not necessarily obliged to do so. It would be an example of unfair dismissal, therefore, to compulsorily retire an individual who had not yet reached normal retiring age but who was beyond pensionable age. Although those over 65 are excluded from the terms of the EP(C)A 1978, this does not bar the making of a claim for unfair dismissal on the basis that a person could have continued to work after 65. In *Wood v. Louis Edwards Ltd [1972]*[28] a 62 year old manager was awarded compensation on the grounds that he would not have retired until he was 70. Anticipated overtime earnings can be taken into account when assessing a compensatory award.[29]

Normal retiring age is not necessarily the retirement age specified in the contract of employment either, although there is a strong legal presumption that the two are identical. The presumption can be rebutted, however, if there is some other age at which employees are regularly retired. If the contractual retiring age has been abandoned, so that employees retire at a variety of ages, then there is no retiring age and the exclusion, at the age of 65, operates. In *Waite v. GCHA [1983]*[30] the House of Lords indicated that in cases of dispute, the primary question was the employee's reasonable expectation at the relevant time. This test was also applied in *Whittle v. Manpower Services Commission [1987]*,[31] a case which concerned a civil servant who had been dismissed when he was 63. Until 1984, the contractual age for retirement was 60, although, in practice, most employees worked beyond that age, about half of them working until they were 65. As a result of cutbacks it was decided, in 1984, to retire all those aged 64. Twelve months later, this age was reduced to 62, and a Circular to that effect was issued. The applicant became compulsorily retired under the new policy and then claimed he had been unfairly dismissed. He failed at the initial tribunal hearing and also on appeal. The Employment Appeal Tribunal (EAT) held that the Circular had the effect of altering the reasonable expectation of those in the applicant's position so that they would normally expect to retire at 62. Sixty-two, therefore, became the normal retiring age and since the applicant was beyond that age when dismissed, he was not entitled to bring an action for unfair dismissal. On the evidence available, the fact that some of the applicant's colleagues had continued in employment after the age of 62, so as to accumulate full pension rights, was abnormal, and did not affect normal retiring age.

1.6.3   FAIR DISMISSAL ON GROUNDS OF INCAPACITY

Section 57 of the EP(C)A 1978 sets out the grounds upon which dismissal is fair. These include the employee's conduct and capability. 'Capability' includes any assessment of skill, aptitude, health or other physical or mental quality. Dismissal on grounds of sickness might, therefore, be fair. It is for the employer to show that he/she acted reasonably. An important, though not necessarily crucial, consideration in this context, is whether or not the employer has consulted the employee about his/her state of health and future work prospects. In *Polkey v. A E Dayton Services Ltd [1987]*[32] the House of Lords held that where consultation had not taken place, and where this was not the result of obdurate behaviour on the employee's part, there would be a *prima facie* case for holding the dismissal unfair. Other factors would need to be taken into consideration, however, in determining whether the employer's action was reasonable, including the business needs of the firm. Risk of future illness cannot be used as grounds for fair dismissal unless the employment is of such a nature that the risk makes it unsafe for the employee to continue in the post. In *Coverform (Darwen) Ltd v. Bell [1981]*[33] the applicant was a works director who had been absent from work as the result of a heart attack. He recovered, but his employers refused to allow him to return to his post because they thought there was risk of another attack. It was held that his dismissal had been unfair.

It is possible, however, for dismissal to be fair even where the period of sickness was brief. In such cases, it is normally necessary for the employer to have warned the employee that unless his/her attendance record improves then he/she will be dismissed.[34]

1.6.4   REINSTATEMENT AND RE-ENGAGEMENT

When an industrial tribunal decides an employee was unfairly dismissed, it has discretionary powers to order reinstatement or re-engagement. If an order is for reinstatement, the employer must treat the employee in all respects as if he/she had not been dismissed. The tribunal can specify the arrears of pay due to the employee, for example, and any other rights or privileges, including rights of seniority and pension. An order for re-engagement requires an employer to re-engage the employee in a post comparable to that from which he/she was dismissed. It is often deemed impracticable for tribunals to make such orders and the aggrieved employee will simply receive compensation.

1.6.5   AGE ELIGIBILITY

The age at which employees cease to be eligible to claim unfair dismissal is the same for men and women, that is, 65. This is the result of an amendment to s.64 of the EP(C)A 1978 by s.3 of the Sex Discrimination Act 1986 (SDA 1986) introduced in response to the decision of the European Court in *Marshall v. Southampton & South-West Hampshire Area Health Authority (No 152/84) [1986].*[35]

The government, however, decided not to amend s.82(1) of the EP(C)A 1978, which distinguishes between male and female employees as to the age at which they cease to be entitled to bring an action for redundancy, which is 65 for men and 60 for women.(see para. 1.7.3 below)   A differential age entitlement for statutory redundancy payments therefore remains. It has been suggested that a woman over 60, selected for redundancy, may be eligible to claim she had been unfairly dismissed, although not eligible to receive statutory redundancy pay.[36]
Claims for unfair dismissal would not, however, be possible where there was a normal retirement age of 60 for both men and women. Section 73 of the EP(C)A 1978 provides for a taper in the basic compensation award for an employee unfairly dismissed in the last year before retirement age, which is 64 for both men and women.

1.7.1 REDUNDANCY

For the purposes of s.81(2) of the EP(C)A 1978, an employee is dismissed by reason of redundancy if dismissal can be attributed wholly or mainly to

a) the fact that the employer has ceased, or intends to cease, to carry on the business for the purposes for which the employee was employed by him/her, or has ceased, or intends to cease, to carry on that business in the place where the employee was so employed, or

b) the fact that the requirements of that business for employees to carry out work of a particular kind, or for employees to carry out work of a particular kind in the place where he/she was so employed, have ceased or diminished or are expected to cease or diminish.

Redundancy can, therefore, arise in two principal circumstances, that is, where the whole business closes down; or where the business carries on, but the need for the services of a particular employee ceases or diminishes. Where the change in an employee's work situation is sufficient to change the nature of the employment, an employee who is unwilling or unable to perform the new function could claim that he/she has been made redundant.

1.7.2 Three issues, in particular, warrant consideration here. First, to what extent is an employee obliged to move location with his/her firm? A person approaching retirement might not wish to be uprooted and might prefer to be treated as redundant. An employee's obligations will depend upon the nature of his/her contract of employment. The question of law is whether or not the employer has authority, under the terms of the contract, to order the move, so that the words 'in the place where the employee was so employed' can be said to include the place where he/she could be obliged to work under the terms of the contract of employment. It is, therefore, a question of construction in each case. Where a contract contains a specific term to that effect, legal authority to require a move to another location exists.[37] A term in the contract which merely allows the employer to require the employee to travel will not necessarily satisfy this legal requirement.[38] In the absence of an express term, the relevant evidence will have to be examined so as to determine whether or not a term can be implied into the contract.[39] The question whether an employee can be required to move will depend, therefore, upon the terms of the contract. Even where there is no express or implied contractual term, the employee may be obliged to accept any suitable alternative employment offered by the employer. The fact that the alternative employment is at a different location does not necessarily render it unsuitable. Even where an offer of work elsewhere is regarded as 'suitable', however, an employee will not lose his/her right to redundancy payment if refusal to move can be seen as 'reasonable'. 'Reasonableness' in this context is subjective, and depends upon personal matters, such as health, family commitments, or retirement plans. Such factors may make it reasonable to refuse what, at first sight, might have appeared suitable alternative employment.

1.7.3   Secondly, what is the basis upon which an employee can properly be selected for redundancy?   Unfair selection for redundancy could amount to unfair dismissal.

Where a particular selection is contrary to an agreed procedure, or to customary arrangements, and no special reasons exist justifying departure from that agreement or arrangement, dismissal will be unfair.[40]   In a recent case, it was held that the phrase 'last in, first out, subject to exceptions' was sufficiently certain to constitute a 'customary arrangement'.[41] In another case, it was held that customary arrangements on the basis of 'last in, first out', without further specification, referred to continuous, not cumulative, service.[42]   An employee who has longer continuous service should, therefore, usually be given preference over an employee with more overall service, but shorter continuous service.   Selection on the basis of 'last in, first out' usually discriminates in favour of older workers, but indirectly discriminates against women, and could be contrary to the provisions of the Sex Discrimination Act 1975 (SDA 1975). In situations which are unfair to women, the employer would need to satisfy a tribunal that the selection arrangements were necessary.

The qualifying conditions for redundancy pay are largely the same as apply to unfair dismissal (see para.1.6.1 above) save that men over 65, and women over 60, are excluded from redundancy payment schemes. The reason for the continued existence, in relation to redundancy, of a lower age limit for women, is that, in the government's opinion, the EC Social Security Directive[43] permits different age limits to be set. A detailed discussion of the issues is beyond the scope of this book. Simply put, however, the point at issue is whether redundancy pay is a matter of employment protection or of social security entitlement. Were the courts to decide that entitlement to redundancy pay is a matter of employment protection, it would be incumbent upon the government to give effect to the 'equal treatment' principle in relation to redundancy as well as unfair dismissal. It is difficult not to conclude[44] that the government is at odds with guidelines set out by the European Court of Justice in *Marshall v. Southampton & South-West Hampshire Area Health Authority (No 152/84) [1986].* (see para. 1.10.1 below) The government's position is therefore open to challenge. It might be deemed legal to discriminate with respect to age differences *per se* but not as regards the quantum of benefits.[45] It was held in *Hammersmith Queen Charlotte's Special Health Authority v. Cato [1987][46]* that redundancy payments, progressively reduced for men after they reach 64 and for women after they reach 59, are discriminatory under Article 119 of the Treaty of Rome (equal pay) and probably under the Equal Treatment Directive. (see discussion at para. 1.12.1) In fact, the government has conceded, in the light of this decision, that the redundancy law in the United Kingdom needs amending so as to remove discrimination on grounds of sex.[47]

1.7.4 Thirdly, what are the legal consequences of a person volunteering for redundancy? Should that happen, those affected may still qualify for redundancy payments.[48] This situation can be compared with that in which the employer and employee come to a mutual agreement to part company, because, for example, of the possibility of redundancies at a future date.[49] In such situations, employees are not deemed to have been dismissed by reason of redundancy. The essential question, therefore, is by whom was the contract of employment brought to an end?[50]

Harsh decisions are still made by the courts however. In the recent case of *Scott v. Coalite Fuels and Chemicals [1988][51]* the employees were given notice of redundancy. During the period of their notice, they were offered, and subsequently accepted, early retirement as an alternative. On leaving employment, they received lump sums under the pension scheme and reduced pensions. In deciding to accept this offer, the employees were influenced by the fact that if, according to rules of the pension scheme, they had accepted redundancy and a frozen pension, there would have been no survivor's benefit if they died before reaching the age of 65. The question at issue, therefore, was whether the employees had converted their prospective redundancy dismissals into termination of the contract by mutual consent. The EAT upheld the decision of the tribunal that the contracts had been terminated by mutual agreement. It has been argued elsewhere[52] that this decision seems at odds with the approach adopted in the earlier case of *McAlwane v. Broughton Estates Ltd [1973].*[53] In that case it was suggested that a situation such as this would give rise to termination by consent on rare occasions only. Sir John Donaldson said '... it would be a very rare case indeed in which we properly found that the employer and the employee had got together and, notwithstanding that there was a current notice of termination of the employment, agreed mutually to terminate the contract, particularly when one realises the financial consequences to the employee involved in such an agreement'.[54]

It can only be hoped that the EAT's decision in the Scott case will not be followed[55] or that it will be held to be one of those 'very rare cases' where termination by consent is possible. In other words, it might be authority only 'on its actual facts'.[56]

1.8.1 OCCUPATIONAL PENSIONS

Occupational pension schemes can be provided by employers to give pension and life assurance benefits to employees, quite separate from the benefits provided by the state. An occupational pension is payable, therefore, regardless of entitlement to a state pension. Nevertheless, eligibility for an occupational pension can affect entitlement to state benefits.

In 1983, the number of male employees in occupational pension schemes was 7.8 million, and the number of females was 3.3 million. Only 37 per cent of women then in employment were entitled to an occupational pension on retirement, although over half of all employees in full-time work were covered in this way.[57] A research report, published in December 1984, based on a sample of one hundred schemes, found that part-timers were entirely excluded from 62 per cent of the schemes, and that, in a further 15 per cent, only those who worked for a stated minimum number of hours were eligible to join.[58] Full-time employees contemplating a reduction in working hours towards the end of their working life should give careful consideration to the possible implications of doing so.

1.8.2 Since 1978 there has been a statutory obligation upon employers to provide equality of access to occupational pension schemes for both men and women. Section 53(2) of the Social Security (Pensions) Act 1975 (SS(P)A 1975) provides that approved schemes should be:

> open to both men and women on terms which are the same as
> to the age and length of service needed for becoming a
> member.

Where inequality of access persists, a complaint can be made to an industrial tribunal under the Equal Pay Act 1970 (EPA 1970). On receiving a complaint, the tribunal can order an employer to stop discriminating against an employee, and to back-date membership in the scheme for a period of up to two years. Schemes imposing special conditions on part-time workers could give rise to a complaint of discrimination under the SDA 1975.[59] The employer would be in breach of the Act unless it could be established that such conditions were justified by reasons other than sex.

1.8.3 Some schemes make provision for part-time employees. Their terms and conditions will vary but might include provision for doubling part-time hours for the purposes of calculating pension rights. Free, independent, and confidential advice on such matters is available for older people from the Occupational Pensions Advisory Service (OPAS).[60] Assistance may also be available from the Occupational Pensions Board (OPB), set up under the Social Security Act 1973 (SSA 1973), which is responsible for advising the Secretary of State on occupational pension matters. One of the Board's responsibilities is to ensure that pension schemes meet the statutory requirements, such as providing equal access to men and women as well as the preservation of pension benefits for those leaving particular employment. Although the OPB can advise, it will not intervene in a particular dispute. Disputes can be resolved only by the members and the trustees of the scheme in question. A member of a pension scheme is entitled to receive information about it from the trustees, and if information is withheld, can request the OPB to make representations on his/her behalf. Alternatively, a member can apply to the County Court for an order directing the trustees to provide the information which has been requested. The rules relating to entitlement to information are set out in the Occupational Pension Scheme (Disclosure of Information) Regulations 1986.[61] Under the regulations, the rights of pension scheme members, and other specified parties, are not limited to receiving basic information only. They are also entitled, on making a written request, to an actuarial valuation and statement, for which a reasonable charge may be made.

1.8.4 Although equal access is now a requirement of the law, it does not always give protection against discrimination in respect of the terms of a pension scheme. Research shows that occupational pension schemes often discriminate between men and women as to the terms and conditions upon which benefits are offered, and as to the amount of benefit provided.[62] Attempts at remedying this injustice through the European Court of Justice have so far been unsuccessful. In *Newstead v. Department of Transport and H M Treasury [1988]*[63] it was held that the Equal Treatment Directive applies only to those occupational pension schemes which can be regarded as supplementary to the state scheme rather than as substituting for it. About 90 per cent of occupational pension schemes in the United Kingdom are 'contracted out' schemes[64] and so classified as 'substitutes' for the state scheme. Most schemes are not, therefore, governed by the Equal Treatment Directive. It seems doubtful, however, whether the Newstead decision will be upheld for long, particularly since the European Court of Justice is not bound by precedent, and is free to depart from its previous decisions. It has been suggested that the European Court should review this decision in order to ensure that members of occupational schemes receive the equal treatment they deserve.[65]

The Social Security Act 1986 (SSA 1986) provides equality of treatment in one instance. Under s.9(3), contracted-out occupational schemes must provide benefits for widowers on the same basis as benefits for widows, except where a wife had died before April 6, 1989.

1.8.5 Another important change introduced by the SSA 1986 is the requirement that after two years membership, all schemes must preserve a member's benefits rather than refunding the contributions made. Previously, this rule applied only where membership had lasted for five years.[66] The most controversial change, however, is that an occupational pension scheme can be administered on a money purchase basis as well as on a final salary basis. Final salary occupational pension schemes provide the employee with a pension based on a percentage of his/her final salary. A lump sum is often payable as well. Usually the employer and the employee both pay an agreed proportion of the employee's salary into the pension fund. The pension is normally protected against inflation under the terms of the Pensions (Increase) Act 1971 (P(I)A 1971), as amended. Final salary schemes are also required to provide guaranteed minimum pensions (GMPs) for members and surviving spouses.[67] From 1988/1989, however, a GMP will be based on 20 per cent of relevant earnings, and not 25 per cent, as was the case previously.[68]

In contrast, money purchase schemes do not guarantee the level of the final pension. Employer and employee contributions are paid into a fund which, on retirement, is used to purchase a pension. The level of the pension will depend entirely upon the size of that fund. Some protection exists, however, in that money purchase schemes must be approved by the OPB. Minimum contributions are also required as a pre-condition of contracting-out of the state scheme. Members of both types of occupational pension have a statutory right to pay additional, voluntary contributions so as to increase their pension entitlement on retirement.[69]

1.8.6 Employers can no longer insist upon employees becoming members of an occupational pension scheme. Employees have the right to opt out and may, instead, choose to take out a personal pension, (see para. 1.9.1 below) or participate in the state earnings related pensions scheme (SERPS). (see para. 1.17.1 below) Deciding upon the best course of action can be difficult. Some of the issues are referred to briefly below at paras. 1.18.1-1.18.3.

1.9.1   PERSONAL PENSIONS

Personal pensions are a new form of pension introduced under the provisions of the SSA 1986 and the Finance (No 2) Act 1987 (F(No.2) A 1987).[70] Since July 1988, personal pensions are the only pension scheme available to the self-employed, replacing retirement annuity contracts which were previously the major form of provision for this group. With the exception of married women, and widows paying national insurance contributions at a reduced rate,[71] employees have the right, under the SSA 1986, to choose a personal pension in preference to membership of an occupational pension scheme.

1.9.2   A personal pension scheme is defined in s.18 of the F(No.2)A 1987 as a scheme whose sole purpose is the provision of annuities or lump sums under arrangements made by individuals in accordance with the scheme. As with occupational pensions, personal pension schemes must be approved by the OPB. A Memorandum containing guidance notes on the social security and contracting-out requirements is available.[72] Approved personal pension schemes can vary between issue of an insurance policy, or annuity contract; a unit trust scheme set up solely for the purpose of providing personal pensions; or an investment of contributions in shares or deposits with a building society or an interest account with a bank.[73] Personal pensions are thus provided by insurance companies, unit trusts, building societies, or banks.

1.9.3   As an inducement to invest in a personal pension scheme, employees can exercise a 'contracting-out' option. This is available only for those paying Class One national insurance contributions (see para. 1.11.1 below) and does not apply to the self-employed. 'Contracting-out' of the state scheme is possible, however, only if a minimum number of contributions are made to the personal pension scheme. This is then paid over by the Department of Social Security (DSS) to the body providing the personal pension. From 1988 to 1993, this payment will be increased by a bonus from the state representing two per cent of the employee's earnings used to calculate the SERPS element, or £1 per week, whichever is the greater.[74]

Employees can decide to pay contributions into a pension plan which is entirely separate from any occupational pension scheme.

Payments of this kind are known as 'free standing additional voluntary contributions' (FSAVC). Contracting-out may also be possible in such circumstances if the additional voluntary contributions provide a sufficiently substantial pension.

1.9.4 Tax approval for FSAVC schemes is given under the provisions of the Finance Act 1970 (FA 1970), as amended, and not the F(No.2)A 1987. As a result, members of FSAVC schemes cannot obtain tax relief on minimum contributions. Tax relief for other appropriate schemes is available and is paid automatically at the basic rate of tax. The DSS claim the tax from the Inland Revenue.

The F(No 2)A 1987 provides for tax relief on personal pension schemes up to a maximum of 17.5 per cent of net relevant earnings up to age of 50. For individuals over the age of 50 on April 6, 1988, this may be increased to 20 per cent; for those aged 56-60 to 22.5 per cent; and for those aged 61 and over to 27.5 per cent.[75]

1.9.5 Concern has been expressed that a spouse's financial situation could be unfairly prejudiced if an employee elected for a personal pension. During the Act's Parliamentary stages, the Opposition unsuccessfully sought to amend the Bill so as to ensure that such decisions would need confirmation by the spouse. It also sought to have a provision inserted for a 'cooling off period' which would allow the employee to change his/her mind.[76] The right to cancel membership within 21 days and have contributions (if any) returned, has been provided for in certain schemes, and in other schemes may be protected by the terms of the Financial Services Act 1986 (FSA 1986).[77] Regulations also require personal pension schemes to make provision for 'qualifying' widows and widowers. In order to qualify a widow or widower must either be 45 years of age or over, or caring for a child under 18 in circumstances which are specified.[78] In the first case, the pension will be paid until the widow or widower dies, or remarries while under pensionable age.[79] In certain circumstances, a pension can be paid after the death of the widow or widower.[80]

1.9.6 Regulations also require personal pension scheme rules to specify that the rate of payment will be determined without regard to the sex or marital status of the member.[81]

1.10.1 DISCRIMINATORY MANDATORY RETIREMENT

Section 2 of the SDA 1986 makes provisions relating to retirement unlawful if they involve discrimination against a woman in relation to a job offer, or the way she is afforded access to opportunities for promotion, transfer or training, or in relation to dismissal or demotion. Dismissing a woman on grounds of age, when a man in a comparable position would not be dismissed, is unlawful. It would, for example, be unlawful to make a woman over 60 ineligible for promotion if a similar rule relating to men referred to 65 as the relevant age.[82] The SDA 1986 applies to those engaged in partnerships as well as to those who are employees.[83]

Section 2 was introduced following the decision of the European Court of Justice in *Marshall v. Southampton & South-West Hampshire Area Health Authority (No 152/84) [1986].*[84] It was decided that the dismissal of a woman solely on the grounds that she had attained the qualifying age for a state pension, when that age was different for men and women under national legislation, constituted discrimination on the ground of sex, contrary to Article 5(1) of the Equal Treatment Directive No. 76/207. It was also held that the Equal Treatment Directive applied directly to state, but not to private, employees. In other words, it could be relied on by state employees without further legislation within the member state. The major practical effect of s.2, therefore, is to extend protection to those employed other than by the 'state'.

1.10.2 The SDA 1986 does not affect rules on eligibility for a state pension. By virtue of Article 7 of the EC Directive on Social Security, member states of the European Community are free to decide for themselves at what age state pensions are payable. This freedom also applies to other qualifying conditions.

1.10.3 'State' employees dismissed before the decision in Marshall may be able to rely on it since an EAT has subsequently held the case to be declaratory of existing law.[85] Those not employed by the state, however, can claim protection only from February 1988.[86] at which date s.2 came into force. The distinction between 'state' employees and others is, therefore, important and to be determined by the national courts. In

Foster v. British Gas [1987][87] an industrial tribunal decided
that British Gas was not a 'state' authority but a 'public'
authority. To be a state authority, it was necessary that the
employer should exercise powers of the state either as principal
or agent. The difference remains unclear and further litigation
seems inevitable.

1.11.1 STATE PENSIONS

In general, state pensions are paid on the basis of contributions made by the claimant into one or more of the relevant
contribution classes.[88] Class 1 national insurance contributions
are paid both by employers and employees. These entitle the
employee to receive all contributory benefits, including a
pension. Class 2 contributions are paid by self-employed persons
and give entitlement to all contributory benefits, except
unemployment benefit. Class 3 contributions are voluntary and
are paid either by non-employed persons, or by those who
contribute to the first two categories, but whose contribution
record is insufficient to meet the benefit criteria. Such
contributions might, for instance, qualify a person to receive a
retirement pension. Class 4 contributions relate to a self-
employed person who has earned profits above a stipulated amount
and give no entitlement to benefit. Those over pensionable age
are exempt from paying into the contribution scheme.[89] Some of
the more relevant benefits are discussed below.

1.11.2 Requirements as to contributions vary depending upon the
benefit which is being claimed. Some general points only will
be made here. First, married women who, before 1977, chose to
pay reduced contributions into the national insurance scheme
fall into a special category with limited entitlement to
long-term benefits.[90] Secondly, a claimant may be entitled to
more than one benefit. If benefits overlap, the usual rule is
that the claimant is entitled to receive the benefit which is
paid at the highest rate.[91] Thirdly, a claimant may only be
entitled to benefit at a reduced rate where the contributions
record falls short of the full requirement.[92] Finally, claims
must be made within specified time limits which are strictly
adhered to, and which will be extended only where good cause can
be shown.

Ignorance of the law is not of itself good cause for delay but, in *C1/147/1986*, it was recognised that the complexity of the law could excuse delay. The Social Security Commissioner suggested that the crucial question was whether the person concerned had done or omitted to do that which could reasonably be expected, having regard to rights and duties under the social security scheme. Relying on advice from social security officials was held to be a sufficiently good cause. Regulations now give the Secretary of State discretion to treat any written letter, or even a claim for another benefit, as a valid claim. This discretion applies to all national insurance benefits.[93] Even where an earlier communication is not treated as a valid claim, or where 'good cause' cannot be shown, the right to benefit is not necessarily lost permanently. A claim might still succeed, although the claimant will usually lose out because there is only a limited right to receive back-dated benefit. The time limit for retirement pensions, unemployment benefit, and invalidity benefit (the three contributory benefits discussed below) is one year, the day for which a claim is made, and one month respectively.[94]

1.11.3 PENSION LEVELS

Those who rely upon state pensions as their main source of income cannot be regarded as financially well-off. Only one pensioner in ten has an income above the average for working families, whereas only a fifth of working families receive an income below average pensioner income.[95] In April 1987, the basic retirement pension for a single person was 21 per cent of gross male earnings.[96] If the basic retirement pension had grown in line with the overall rise in earnings since 1978, it would now be worth £47.10, compared with its actual value of £41.15.[97] The 'earnings link' was broken by the government in 1980. Since then the level of the state pension has been raised only in line with a rise in prices. As a result its value has fallen, in relation to average earnings, by some 13 per cent.[98]

1.11.4 TYPES OF PENSION

The state pension scheme consists of two elements. The first is the basic state pension which is a flat rate benefit paid to all those fulfilling the contribution conditions. There are four categories. Category A pensions are based on an individual's own contribution record. Category B pensions are paid to married women, widows and some widowers. Entitlement to these usually depends upon contributions having been paid by the pensioner's spouse but qualifying conditions differ for the various categories of claimant. Some widows and widowers will be entitled to a pension even if they do not meet the contribution conditions, providing they were receiving invalidity benefit immediately before they reached retirement age. Category C pensions are non-contributory pensions payable to those already over pensionable age on July 5, 1948. (see above at para. 1.11.1) In certain circumstances, this pension is also payable to the wives, widows, or divorced partners of those qualifying for the pension. Category D pensions are paid to those over 80 years of age who do not qualify for any other retirement pension.

1.11.5 As indicated above, (see para. 1.10.1) it is still possible, in relation to state pensions, for qualifying conditions to discriminate between men and women since they need not conform to EC rulings in this respect. The point can be illustrated by *R(P)3/88.* The claimant, who was married, claimed an increase in her Category A pension with respect to her dependant husband. Section 45A(1) of the Social Security Act 1975 allows for qualifying conditions to vary as between claimants. For a woman to qualify for an increase in entitlement to a pension, she would have to be entitled to an increase in unemployment, sickness or invalidity benefit for an adult dependant in the period immediately preceding the claim. No such requirement is imposed upon men. The Social Security Commissioner held that the statutory provision placed women in a less favourable position than men in relation to an increase for an adult dependant in retirement and was therefore discriminatory. Nevertheless, the provision was not in breach of the European Social Security Directive 79/7 which allows, *inter alia*, for men and women to be treated differently in relation to increases of old age benefit for a dependant spouse.

1.12.1 PENSIONABLE AGE AND RETIREMENT

Entitlement to the two contributory pensions, (Categories A and B), depends upon the claimant having attained 'pensionable age' which is 65 for men and 60 for women.[99]

The requirement as to age has given rise, in some circumstances, to the problem of proving the claimant has reached the requisite age. Where no birth certificate is available, other evidence may suffice. In *R(P)1/75,* which concerned an immigrant from a district of Pakistan where there was no register of births, medical evidence was held to be admissible.

Entitlement also depends upon an 'act of retirement'. In this context, retirement has a technical meaning which is nowhere defined in the legislation. Section 27(3) of the SSA 1975, however, sets out the circumstances in which a person can be treated as retired even though he/she may continue in some form of employment. It provides that:

> a person may be treated as having retired from regular employment at any time after he has reached pensionable age -
>
> a) whether or not he has previously been an earner;
> b) notwithstanding that he/she is, or intends to be, an earner if -
>
>   (i) he/she is or intends to be only occasionally or to an inconsiderable extent, or otherwise in circumstances not inconsistent with retirement, or
>   (ii) his/her earnings can be expected not to exceed, or only occasionally to exceed, the amount any excess over which would, under section 30(1) below (earnings rule) involve a reduction of the weekly rate of pensions.

For this purpose, employment includes self-employment or any other gainful employment, such as activity as a local authority councillor.[100] Entitlement will depend upon the amount of work being undertaken, the degree of responsibility and the extent of income.[101] Fewer than twelve hours employment per week is normally regarded as 'inconsiderable', but there is no maximum limit to the hours worked. The phrase 'not inconsistent with retirement' gives scope for arguing against disqualification where the applicant has failed to meet the alternative tests of 'occasional' or 'inconsiderable' employment and the rule regarding earnings. Among matters which might be seen as relevant are the lightness of the duties being performed or the fact that the work is of a type usually carried out by retired people. Establishing retirement will clearly be more difficult where an individual continues in his/her former employment, unless it can be shown that what is being undertaken is light employment, taken up originally in anticipation of retirement.[102] This provision can apply also to a person whose earnings are in excess of the limit fixed by the earnings rule. (see below at para. 1.13.1)

1.12.2 RETIRING AGE

Section 27(5) of the SSA 1975 provides that a person not previously retired from regular employment shall be deemed to have retired on the expiration of five years from attaining pensionable age. The statutory retiring age is thus 70 for a man and 65 for a woman. The distinction between 'pensionable age' and 'retiring age' is of considerable practical importance. On attaining retiring age, a person is entitled to a pension irrespective of whether he/she actually retires or what he/she earns.

1.13.1 THE EARNINGS RULE

The earnings of an individual over pensionable age but below retiring age can affect entitlement to a pension. As indicated above (at para. 1.12.1), earnings above a stipulated statutory limit may result in a person being regarded as in regular employment and not, therefore, entitled to a pension. Even if the earner is deemed to have retired (despite his/her employment) the pension will, nevertheless, be reduced where the weekly amount is above the statutory limit. At present this limit is set at £75 per week (1988/89). A basic pension will be reduced by 5p for each 10p of the first £4 in excess of the limit and by 5p for every 5p above that. Thus, earnings of £81 per week would result in a reduction in pension of £4.00 per

25

week. Earnings in this context are the amount earned before tax but after expenses.[103]

The earnings rule does not apply to graduated retirement pensions, to SERPS (see below at para.1.17.1) or to contracted-out occupational pensions. (see above at para. 1.8.4) The earnings of a dependent adult cannot reduce an individual's entitlement to basic pension but could affect any increase in pension that would otherwise have been received in respect of that person. The earnings limit for an adult dependant is currently £32.75 (1988/89).

1.14.1 DEFERRED RETIREMENT

Schedule 1 of the SSA 1975 has the effect of increasing the rate at which Categories A or B retirement pensions are paid where retirement has been deferred by a person who has attained pensionable age. The increase is assessed by reference both to the basic, and to the SERPS component of the pension. (see para. 1.17.1 below)

A widow will benefit from her late husband's deferred retirement providing she does not re-marry before reaching pensionable age, that is, 60. A widower is similarly entitled to any increase based upon his late wife's deferred pension, provided he is over pensionable age, that is, 65 or over, at the time of her death.[104]

1.14.2 NOTICE OF RETIREMENT

Until a person reaches retiring age, he/she will be treated as retired only if notice of retirement has been given in accordance with the regulations.[105] The regulations require notice to be given to the Secretary of State in writing, specifying the retirement date. Notice can be given up to four months in advance. If it is given after retirement, however, the claim can be backdated for three months, or twelve months if good cause for the delay is shown. It is clear from *R(P)2/85* that the requirement as to notice, and the limit upon back-dating, are strict. An earlier claim or enquiry is not sufficient unless it includes notice of retirement. A claim form is normally sent by the DSS some four months in advance of the date upon which an individual reaches pensionable age. If no form has been received, a claimant would be well advised to write to the DSS requesting one.[106]

1.14.3 CANCELLING RETIREMENT

Those over retirement age cannot move into or out of retirement more than once.[107] On the second occasion, there will be no entitlement to defer retirement and gain pension increments.

A man whose wife is entitled to a Category B retirement pension by virtue of his contributions cannot elect to cancel retirement unless his wife consents or withholds her consent unreasonably.[108] In *R6/60(P)* it was held that it is for the husband to show his wife has acted unreasonably. Examples of unreasonable behaviour would be pique, or spite, or a desire to stand in the husband's way. On the facts, it was held that the wife had acted reasonably; she had refused consent because cancelling retirement would have resulted in substantial financial loss.

1.15.1 HOME RESPONSIBILITY PROTECTION

The rights of those not paying national insurance contributions are sometimes protected if they are caring for another person. The number of years during which this task is carried out is deducted from the number of years during which they would otherwise have had to make contributions.[109] Protection relates both to retirement pension and to widow's pension. Home responsibility protection is available if, during a complete tax year, child benefit has been received in respect of a child under 16; or income support (IS) has been received without the person being required to be available for work since he/she is looking after an invalid person; or spends at least 35 hours a week looking after someone receiving attendance or constant attendance allowance.[110]

A person could qualify for home responsibility protection if he/she has not paid sufficient national insurance contributions for retirement pension purposes in a particular tax year. Loss of attendance allowance for a period of less than four weeks because of hospitalization does not affect the protection available to the carer of the person in hospital.

1.15.2 Married women and widows who had originally elected to pay national insurance contributions at a reduced rate, can benefit from the home responsibility protection scheme should they elect to pay contributions in full.[111] Those likely to spend more than two years out of employment would be well advised to elect to do so since the right to pay reduced contributions terminates at the end of the second year. Other married women may also benefit from paying full Class 1 national insurance contributions. This issue is discussed more fully elsewhere.[112]

1.16.1 ADMISSION INTO HOSPITAL

The effect of admission into hospital on entitlement to retirement pension and other non-means tested benefits depends upon two factors: the length of stay; and the existence or otherwise of a dependent relative. A dependant is defined in the regulations to include, *inter alia*, the other spouse when the couple are retired pensioners who normally live alone.[113]

Where there are no dependent relatives, the pension will be reduced by £16.50 per week after six weeks in hospital. Only half this amount is deducted when there are dependent relatives. When a person becomes a long-stay patient, that is, remains in hospital for longer than 52 weeks, a further reduction is made. If there are no dependent relatives, the pension is reduced to £8.25 per week, but where there is a dependent relative, the pension is reduced by £16.50 per week. The patient who has a dependant is entitled to receive directly only the same amount as patients with no dependants, that is, £8.25 per week. The remainder of the pension, together with any increase for a dependant to which entitlement exists, is paid to the dependant.[114] Provision is more generous for those receiving war pensions or war widows pensions. A war pension is not reduced on admission to hospital. It will be increased, in fact, if treatment is for a war injury.[115] A war widow's pension is paid at the full rate for the first 52 weeks and reduced only subsequently.

A long-term patient may lose entitlement even to a reduced pension (or have it further reduced) if he/she is unable to act for him/herself and the pension is paid directly to the hospital authorities. The medical officer in charge of the patient must certify that he/she is not capable of appreciating the money or the comfort that could be bought with it.[116] Entitlement is, therefore, at the medical officer's discretion. Where a patient spends days outside hospital, he/she is then entitled to have the pension fully restored on a pro-rata basis. It is also worth noting that, for this purpose, hospital admission and discharge days are regarded as 'home' days. Indeed, where persons regularly spend weekends with carers the latter might be entitled to the full rate of Invalid Care Allowance (ICA), since that is a 'weekly benefit' and not one paid on a daily basis.[117] It also needs stressing that only a full 'day' in hospital gives rise to a reduction in entitlement. Where a patient spends part of the day in hospital and part of it away, the pension should be restored in full for that day.[118] A patient spending part of a day attending a social services day centre as a prelude to discharge, for example, should have the pension restored for those days.

1.17.1 ADDITIONAL STATE PENSIONS

The second element of the state pension scheme is earnings-related. Participation in SERPS depends upon whether the employee pays Class 1 national insurance contributions and is not contracted-out of SERPS. Contracting-out of SERPS is possible where the employee opts for an occupational pension or an approved personal pension. Where contracting-out has occurred, the employer and employee pay reduced national insurance contributions and contribute instead to the cost of alternative provision.

1.17.2 The rules for calculating SERPS are complicated but depend, basically, upon the claimant or his/her spouses's 'earnings factor' in the 'relevant' years.[119] Widows and widowers can receive two additional pensions, one based upon their own contributions, and another based on the contributions of the deceased spouse.[120] A useful example of the way in which these are calculated is available elsewhere.[121] Those who wish to plan ahead can enquire of the DSS how much additional pension they are likely to receive. A special form for doing so is available.[122]

1.17.3 The provisions of the SSA 1986 will change the method of calculating SERPS but will not affect persons reaching pensionable age before April 6, 1999. The intention and net effect of these provisions will be to reduce the cost of the scheme from an estimated £25.5 billion in the year 2033 to around £15 billion.[123] Section 18 makes such savings possible by basing the calculation on average life earnings rather than on the basis of earnings for the best 20 years, as in the past. Another reduction in cost has been achieved from 1988/89 onwards by calculating the SERPS element on 20 per cent rather than 25 per cent of earnings, as previously. Some transitional protection is provided, however, for those reaching pensionable age between April 6, 1999 and April 5, 2009 when the basic percentage will be increased by 0.5 per cent for each complete tax year in which the claimant has reached pensionable age before the tax year 2009/10. Section 19 also amends existing legislation so that where a husband dies after April 5, 2000 the widow will be entitled to only half the amount of the spouse's pension, rather than to the whole of it as at present.

1.17.4 Those paying Class 1 national insurance contributions between April 1961 and April 1975 contributed to a graduated pension scheme. Those participants are entitled to a pension supplement calculated on the number of graduated pension units purchased during the period of the scheme's operation. A widow is entitled to half the graduated pension earned by her late husband, as well as to any graduated pension earned on her own contributions. The additional pension can be paid to someone not entitled to the basic retirement pension[124] and is not affected by the earnings rule. It is increased if retirement is deferred. In 1986, there were 788,000 receiving graduated pensions of £2.60 or over.[125] The maximum entitlement, at present, is around £3.88 a week for women and £4.64 for men.[126]

1.18.1 CHOICE OF PENSIONS

Legislative changes have been introduced which aim at encouraging individuals to turn either to occupational pension schemes or to personal pension schemes in preference to remaining in SERPS. Over 50 per cent of employees are already members of occupational pension schemes with a large majority of these in contracted-out schemes. Given the reduction in entitlement to SERPS, referred to above, the only practical choice for those already in an occupational scheme is between remaining in membership or opting for a personal pension scheme. The government has promoted personal pensions by giving bonus incentives but only those who have been in occupational pension schemes for less than two years will qualify. There are other reasons for suggesting that, as a general rule, those who are members of occupational schemes would be well advised to remain in them, rather than take out a personal pension scheme.

First, under an occupational pension scheme, the employer is obliged to contribute towards the pension. On average, an employee pays about five per cent of his/her earnings into an occupational pension scheme with the employer paying between five and 20 per cent. By comparison, there is no requirement for an employer to make any contribution to a personal pension scheme, and evidence suggests most employers are reluctant to do so.[127] Secondly, occupational pensions usually provide a degree of financial security for the families of those employees who die, or who are forced to retire from work early because of ill health. The benefit payable from a personal pension scheme, however, would depend upon the size of the fund accumulated at time of death, or forced retirement.[128] Financial security for the families of those in personal pension schemes may need to be safeguarded by arranging additional assurance, at extra expense. Thirdly, occupational pension schemes are usually 'final salary' schemes in comparison with personal pension schemes which are of the money purchase type and therefore vulnerable to stock market fluctuations. Fourthly, the administrative costs of personal pension schemes are likely to be higher whereas the collective nature of occupational schemes provides scope for discount.

1.18.2 There are arguments on the other side which would favour personal pension schemes, but they do not seem particularly convincing. It has been suggested, for instance, that personal pensions facilitate employment mobility, and that members of occupational pension schemes could be discouraged from changing employment since frequent changes might adversely affect pension rights.[129] The difficulty of transferring between occupational pension schemes may, however, be exaggerated. Legislative changes include provision for ensuring easier transfer of accrued pension rights and benefit entitlement under occupational pension schemes.[130] Those adversely affected by a change in employment could, in any case, top up their occupational pension entitlement by contributing to a FSAVC scheme. Another argument in favour of personal pension schemes is that they are more tax efficient since, as previously mentioned, they provide greater tax relief, especially for older contributors. There may be little by way of financial advantage to the employee, however, since the employer need make no contribution to the cost of a personal pension. The situation would be considerably different should the employer agree to contribute to the costs of providing a pension. Personal pensions also allow members to draw a pension at 50, without necessarily giving up work. Some investment schemes offer to re-invest money released from a pension fund, but those contemplating such action may be in danger of not making proper provision for their retirement. It may also be the case that better financial returns can be achieved by leaving a personal pension undisturbed.[131]

1.18.3 Where no occupational schemes exist, employees are faced with one choice only, whether to remain in SERPS or take out a personal pension scheme. In spite of the incentive bonus which is available for those taking out personal pension schemes, it would seem that men over 50, and women over 45 would, usually, do better to remain within the state scheme since the cost of providing equivalent benefits in a private pension scheme are higher at these age levels.[132] Consideration should similarly be given to topping-up state provision by taking out a personal pension.

1.18.4 Employees face having to make crucial decisions over pensions. Changes to the relevant legislation will mean lower pensions for those relying upon SERPS. Those most affected will be the ones least able to afford an additional personal pension. They include individuals disabled during their working lives, women, employees with fluctuating earnings, and those suffering long spells of unemployment.

1.19.1 EARLY RETIREMENT

Those who leave employment 'voluntarily' and 'without just cause' may be disqualified from unemployment benefit for a period up to 26 weeks.[133] If they are compulsorily retired, or take voluntary redundancy, they cannot be disqualified, however, although it remains important for employees to be dismissed and not simply to resign or retire.[134] Disqualification can also be avoided by showing there was 'just cause' for leaving employment. The onus is on the claimant, and the 'just cause' must relate to his/her personal circumstances. In *R(U)2/81* a school teacher was encouraged to take early retirement but failed in his attempt to show 'just cause' for leaving the employment. His unsuccessful submission to the tribunal was that the public interest would be served by the savings accruing to the education budget, and by his making way for younger members of the profession.[135] Among the submissions which have successfully shown 'just cause' have been loss of confidence by the claimant in his/her mental or physical ability to perform essential duties, and pressing domestic or personal circumstances.[136]

1.19.2 Since redundancy payments are a form of compensation for the loss of a job, they ought not to affect a person's right to unemployment benefit. Employees sometimes receive an additional lump sum payment as an incentive for them to retire from employment early. The effect of such payments upon an individual's entitlement to unemployment benefit will depend upon whether the sum represents compensation for loss of job, or compensation for loss of earnings. If the former, entitlement to benefit will not be affected. If the latter, entitlement will be temporarily lost. Consequently, a lump sum which includes payment in lieu of notice, disqualifies a claimant from entitlement to unemployment benefit for the period during which he/she is deemed not to be unemployed.[137] It is advisable, therefore, to ensure that payments of this kind should not be directly referable to rates of pay, or period of notice. This is best achieved by the payment being rounded up, and presented as an *ex-gratia* payment.[138]

1.19.3 Men retiring at 60 can be credited with Class 1 national insurance contributions so as to satisfy contribution conditions for receipt of a retirement pension.[139] Thus, a male employee retiring at 60 can be credited with full contributions for the five years preceding pensionable age. Credits are not available for women wishing to retire five years before attaining pensionable age, that is, at 55 rather than at 60. Women who choose to continue working after the age of 60, however, need not pay national insurance contributions.

1.19.4 Those retiring early because of incapacity arising from a specific disease, or as a result of some bodily or mental disability, may qualify for invalidity benefit.[140] What is relevant, in this context, is the person's capacity for work, not the nature of the employment market in the area where the claimant resides. A claimant will qualify for invalidity benefit if he/she can work only with extra help and support. The 'capacity' test relates to current, not contingent, circumstances. For example, a person whose ability to work is contingent upon having premises suitably adapted for his/her needs would be deemed incapable of work for the purposes of invalidity benefit.[141] An intermittent disability could result in a person being incapable of work. In *R(S)9/79*, the claimant succeeded because it could be shown he was capable, on average, of working on three days only out of five.

Those already receiving invalidity benefit can elect, on reaching pensionable age, to continue receiving it for a further five years rather than opting for a retirement pension as long as they remain incapable of work. There are two advantages in electing to do so. First, it enables the claimant to qualify for the higher pensioner premium under the Income Support (IS) or housing benefit (HB) provisions. (see below at paras. 1.24.1; 1.24.15) The second advantage is that invalidity benefit is tax free whereas retirement pensions are taxable. This could be important where, for example, a person was also entitled to an occupational pension. On the other hand, choosing invalidity benefit has the disadvantage of reducing the amount a person is able to earn without affecting his/her benefit entitlement. A person receiving invalidity benefit can earn up to £27 per week by way of 'therapeutic earnings'.[142] For those receiving a retirement pension, the earnings rules are more generous. (see above at para. 1.13.1)

Invalidity benefit is paid at the same rate as a retirement pension; where a person is not entitled to a full retirement pension, invalidity benefit will be reduced proportionately. It should not be reduced, however, where incapacity is the result of an industrial accident or disease.[143]

1.20.1 SEVERE DISABILITY ALLOWANCE

Severe disability allowance (SDA) is another benefit which is payable to those incapable of work. In this case, however, entitlement is not dependent upon having paid a sufficient number of contributions. The benefits discussed below - mobility allowance, attendance allowance, and invalid care allowance - are also non-contributory.

1.20.2 SDA is payable where a person's national insurance contributions are insufficient to enable him/her to qualify for invalidity benefit. The only qualifying condition is that the claimant has been incapable of work for at least 196 days.[144] First time claimants must, in addition, be 80 per cent disabled. By April, 1987, some 16,500 SDA claims had been disallowed because the claimants did not meet the 80 per cent disablement test.[145] The extent of a person's disability is sometimes calculated on the basis of the fixed disability percentages adopted under the industrial injuries scheme. A person who is totally deaf, for example, is assessed as 100 per cent disabled, whereas someone who has lost an arm is assessed as 80 per cent disabled.[146] A person unable to use his/her arm as the result of a stroke or severe arthritis could also be assessed in this way.[147] Some individuals, including those already receiving an attendance allowance, or a mobility allowance, or who are registered blind or partially sighted, are deemed to have satisfied the disablement test.[148]

1.20.3 To claim SDA, a man must normally have qualified before he reaches pensionable age.[149] The position of women is less certain. Section 36(4)(d) of the SSA 1975 provides that a person will not be entitled to SDA if he/she

> has attained pensionable age and was not entitled to a severe disablement allowance immediately before he attained it.

For women, 'pensionable age' is 60. In *CS/98/1987*, the Commissioner held that the provision was at odds with EC Social Security Directive 79/7 which provides, *inter alia*, that men and women should be treated equally within any statutory scheme which provides protection against invalidity. It was held that the claimant, who had become incapable of work after reaching the age of 60, was entitled to SDA, providing she satisfied the medical and other conditions before she reached the age of 65. It is not known, at time of writing, whether an appeal against this decision is in the offing, but it is submitted that the decision makes good law.

1.20.4 Entitlement to SDA can be of advantage to married couples particularly since, like invalidity benefit, it is not taxable. A married woman whose husband retired after reaching pensionable age could benefit financially from remaining on SDA rather than claiming a Category B pension based on her husband's contribution. The amount of weekly entitlement would be the same in both cases, except that the pension would be taxable.[150]

1.20.5 For the first five years after reaching pensionable age, a person claiming SDA must continue to meet all the qualifying conditions, including incapacity for work and 80 per cent disablement. On reaching retiring age, however, it no longer becomes necessary to satisfy these requirements. The qualifying conditions are, therefore, relaxed for men at the age of 70 and for women at the age of 65. Should the logic of the decision in *CS/98/1987* be extended to cover this provision it cannot be predicted what the outcome might be. (see para. 1.20.3 above) It might be that the qualifying condition which currently applies to men would be relaxed.

Those qualifying for SDA upon reaching retiring age will remain qualified to receive it for the rest of their lives, whether or not they remain incapable of work.[151]

1.21.1. MOBILITY ALLOWANCE

Mobility allowance is also tax-free. The benefit is available for those under 80 years of age who are physically disabled and unable to walk, to help them become mobile. It must be shown that the disability is likely to persist for at least twelve months, and that the claimant could benefit from 'enhanced facilities for locomotion'.[152] It is intended that it should be spent upon outdoor mobility, but, in practice, the allowance can be spent in any way the recipient wishes. The allowance cannot be paid, however, to those with an invalid car supplied by the NHS or who are receiving a private car allowance under the pre-1976 vehicle scheme. Those receiving assistance under the previous schemes can be transferred to the mobility allowance scheme, in which case the age limits discussed below do not apply.[153]

1.21.2 A person between 65 and 80 years of age can receive mobility allowance only if he/she was entitled to it immediately before reaching the age of 65, and if, in addition, he/she had made a claim before reaching the age of 66.[154]   Section 37A(5) (aa)(ii) of the SSA 1975 has the effect of allowing a claimant twelve months grace to make the claim after reaching 65 years of years of age as long as he/she satisfies the specified physical conditions before having reached that age. In *R(M)4/86* a claim for mobility allowance was made after the age of 66 had been attained. An earlier claim, made before the age of 65, had been turned down because the claimant had failed to satisfy the required medical conditions. The question at issue, therefore, was whether a claim, once made, continued to be effective. The tribunal, in rejecting the claim, confirmed that, once dismissed, a claim cannot continue in existence. It is not necessary to make a fresh application, however, where a person's physical condition is deteriorating while the appeal is in progress.

An allowance can be awarded from a date later than the original claim. The rules permit the condition to be satisfied for up to three months later than the date of the claim, notwithstanding that, at the date of the claim, the claimant did not satisfy the conditions.[155] Those refused mobility allowance, either on appeal or otherwise, are in any case entitled to make a fresh application whenever they believe their condition to have deteriorated further.

1.21.3 Issues relating to the grant of mobility allowance have given rise to considerable litigation, much of which concerns a claimant's partial but restricted capacity to walk. The Mobility Allowance Regulations 1975 provide that:

A person shall only be treated, for the purposes of s.37A, as suffering from physical disablement such that he is either unable to walk or virtually unable to do so, if his physical condition as a whole is such that, without having regard to circumstances peculiar to that person as to place of residence or as to place or, as to the nature of, employment -

a) he is unable to walk; or
b) his ability to walk out of doors is so limited, as regards the distance over which or the speed at which or the length of time for which or the manner in which he can make progress on foot without severe discomfort, that he is virtually unable to walk; or
c) the exertion required to walk would constitute a danger to his life or would be likely to lead to a serious deterioration in his health.[156]

The regulations, therefore, introduce four basic tests. First, is the person unable or virtually unable to walk? Second, does the inability to walk stem from physical disability? Third, where ability to walk exists, does walking cause severe discomfort? And, fourth, does the exertion necessary in order to walk, endanger the claimant's life or lead to a serious deterioration in health? It is clear from the decision of the House of Lords in *Lees v. Secretary of State for Social Services [1985]* that the disability in question must relate directly to the claimant's ability to walk. That case concerned an application for mobility allowance by a visually handicapped woman. It was established that the claimant required the help of another person to guide her from place to place. Disallowing her claim, the House of Lords held that a person could qualify for mobility allowance only if his/her physical ability to walk was impaired.[157]

A person is considered able to walk even when an artificial aid must be used.[158] The test, however, is whether or not a person can walk out of doors. Difficulties with pavements or in balancing upon uneven surfaces would, therefore, be relevant.[159] There is no set walking distance which would make it possible to distinguish between those who can, and those who cannot, walk. If such a test existed, there would be little point in the legal requirement to have regard to the speed and manner of walking.[160] The cause of incapacity to walk must be physical, not mental. Down's Syndrome has been held to constitute a physical condition, whereas agoraphobia has not.[161] A somewhat disturbing development in this context is the decision in *CM 228/87*, in which a child was disqualified on the grounds that refusal to walk could be overcome by his being pulled.

Where a person suffers 'severe discomfort' when walking outdoors, any extra distance covered after the onset of the discomfort should be disregarded. In *R(M)1/83* 'severe discomfort' was said to include 'pain' and 'breathlessness'. It should also be stressed that the term is given a subjective meaning: people have different pain threshholds and show pain in different ways.[162] If the exertion needed in order to walk constitutes a danger to life, it is not necessary that any serious deterioration in health, which might also occur, should be permanent or long-lasting.[163]

It has been suggested[164] that recent decisions will mean that mobility allowance will become available almost exclusively for those with heart, chest or orthopaedic complaints. It should be remembered, however, that the allowance can be claimed by people in hospital or living in residential homes, as well as by people who normally live in their own homes. To be eligible, it would seem that a person need not be interested in, or enjoy, going out. The requirement is simply that it would be beneficial for him/her to do so.[165]

1.22.1 ATTENDANCE ALLOWANCE

There are no upper age restrictions upon claiming attendance allowance, nor is it necessary for the claimant to have satisfied the qualifying conditions before attaining the age of 65. The allowance can be claimed for the first time after retiring. In March 1987, there were 630,000 individuals in receipt of this benefit,[166] the majority of whom were elderly.[167] The allowance is a weekly benefit paid to those who need a legally prescribed level of care and attention from someone else. They must also have been in need of care for at least six months.[168] The allowance is not necessarily paid to the carer. Indeed, it is not strictly necessary for the person to be receiving care. The only legal requirement is that the claimant is in need of attendance.[169]

The allowance is paid at two rates: a lower rate when the care is required either during the day, or during the night; and a higher rate when attendance is required during both day and night. The conditions relating to eligibility for the allowance differ significantly, according to whether the claim is for daytime or night-time attendance.

1.22.2 The legal requirements for claiming attendance allowance are set out in s.35(1) of the SSA 1975 as amended by s.1(2) of the Social Security Act 1988 (SSA 1988).Section 35(1) provides:

A person shall be entitled to an attendance allowance if he satisfies prescribed conditions as to residence or presence in Great Britain and either -

a) he is so severely disabled physically or mentally that, by day, he requires from another person either -

(i) frequent attention throughout the day in connection with his bodily functions, or
(ii) continual supervision throughout the day in order to avoid substantial danger to himself or others; or

b) he is so severely disabled physically or mentally that, at night -

(i) he requires from another person prolonged or repeated attention in connection with his bodily functions, or
(ii) in order to avoid substantial danger to himself or others he requires another person to be awake for a prolonged period or at frequent intervals for the purpose of watching over him.

1.22.3 In spite of the fact that 'residence' or 'presence' in Great Britain is required, the allowance continues to be payable where the resident is temporarily abroad for up to six months.[170] Persons who meet one of the 'day' conditions and one of the 'night' conditions will qualify for the higher allowance. Section 35(1)(b) is a new provision introduced by the government in response to the decision of the Court of Appeal in *Moran v. Secretary of State for Social Services (1987)*.[171] Under previous legislative provisions, there was no need for the claimant to show that he/she required 'another person to be awake for a prolonged period or at frequent intervals for the purpose of watching over him/her'. It merely required 'continual supervision throughout the night'. It was held in the *Moran* case, which concerned a person suffering from epilepsy, that the requirement for continual supervision could be satisfied if a person's need for supervision was unpredictable, and where the consequence of having no supervision would be grave. It confirmed that a person standing-by to intervene if necessary, was exercising supervision. The latter could be adequately achieved even if, for some of the time, the supervisor was asleep. The case was regarded as having established a particularly useful precedent which could apply to people who were mentally alert but nevertheless vulnerable during 'attacks'. The purpose of the recent legislative change is to close the door on this development. There are no reported cases under the new provision and it is not clear how the courts will interpret it. A number of points are worth noting, however.

1.22.4 First, it needs stressing that the new provision applies to night-time attendance only. The *Moran* case remains good law for those requiring continual supervision throughout the day. The meaning of 'throughout the day' was explained in *CA/1140/1985*. The claimant had total visual handicap and needed help with bathing and laying out his clothes, and in cutting up his food at mealtimes. He also needed help in walking up stairs and in walking outside his home. The claim was rejected on the basis that the claimant's needs for attention in connection with bodily functions[172] were confined 'in the main' to the beginning and the end of each day and that he did not satisfy the requirement for frequent attention throughout the day. The Chief Commissioner reversed the decision, stressing that refusal of the claim could not be justified on the basis that there were gaps in the supervision. The evidence relating to the day must be looked at as a whole, where the need for care was naturally connected. It is also clear from *CA/97/1987* that the scope of the precedent established in *Moran* is not limited to 'mental attacks'. The claimant suffered from multiple myelomatosis (that is, thinning of the bones which makes them liable to fracture with minimal pressure) and successfully appealed against the decision of the delegated medical practitioner (DMP).[173] The

DMP had decided that, because the claimant was mentally alert, and could be expected to avoid situations where he would be at risk unless supervised, continual supervision was not necessary. The Social Security Commissioner reversed the decision, concluding that the requirement for continual supervision had to be considered in the context of the supervision needed by a person who, by a simple movement, could cause him/herself a spontaneous fracture. It would be surprising if a similar argument could not be put in respect of those suffering from other physical complaints.

1.22.5 Secondly, although the night supervision test is harder to satisfy, it should be remembered that in *R. v. Social Security Commissioner, ex parte Connolly [1986]*[174] the Court of Appeal suggested that in determining a person's need for attention, the essential consideration was what he/she 'reasonably required' and not what was 'medically required'. The significance of the distinction is illustrated by *R(A)3/86*. The claimant had a mental handicap and suffered from grand mal epilepsy. She was incontinent at night and received attention for 15 minutes twice per night in order to change night clothes and sheets. The DMP considered that, if adequate padding were used, there would be no medical need for repeatedly changing the bed. It was held that, since that decision was based upon medical considerations only, it was erroneous in law.

1.22.6 Those refused attendance allowance can ask for a Review. Excellent practial advice on the process is available in a publication from the Disability Alliance entitled *Attendance Allowance - going for a Review*. The basic requirement is to show that the original decision was faulty in that it was made in ignorance of, or based upon a mistake as to, a material fact, or that there has been a relevant change of circumstances since that decision was reached.[175] In 1987, 66 per cent of people who asked for a review, after initially being refused attendance allowance, were successful. It should be noted that the right to a review also applies to those who have been awarded the lower rate of allowance but who believe themselves entitled to the higher rate. The success rate is again high at 83 per cent, but it must be stressed that those who request a review, in such circumstances, run the risk of losing the allowance entirely.[176]

1.22.7 The provisions relating to attendance allowance also allow for a change in circumstances which might result in a person no longer being entitled to receive it. Where a person's health improves, he/she should write to the Attendance Allowance Unit (AAU) which will arrange a review.[177] The regulations allow for flexibility where a person's condition improves but he/she suffers a relapse later. In such circumstances, the claimant need not satisfy the six months qualifying period on the second occasion.[178]

1.22.8 For elderly people, the financial significance of receiving attendance allowance cannot be overstated. First, it can be paid to each member of a family who qualifies for it. Secondly, it is not taxable. Thirdly, it can be paid additionally to other national insurance benefits such as invalidity benefit, SDA, and mobility allowance. Fourthly, it is usually ignored for the purposes of assessing IS and HB.[179] Entitlement to attendance allowance is also one of the ways of qualifying automatically for the higher pensioner premiums under the IS scheme. Fifthly, it is usually disregarded, for the purposes of IS, when a person enters a residential care home or nursing home in the independent sector.[180] It can also be used to fund respite care in local authority homes.

Entitlement to attendance allowance comes to an end after 28 days residence in a local authority home. It will not be lost if the claimant returns home within the period of 28 days and remains in the community for a further period in excess of 28 days. A useful explanation of how attendance allowance can be used to help fund respite care is to be found elsewhere.[181]

1.23.1 INVALID CARE ALLOWANCE

In contrast to attendance allowance, invalid care allowance (ICA), is payable to the carer and not to the disabled person. It is relevant to the financial and social well-being of elderly people for three distinct reasons. First, it may encourage and enable individuals to provide elderly people with the support and the care which they need. Second, as providers of care, they will themselves sometimes qualify for the allowance, although, as a general rule, those over pensionable age will have no entitlement.[182] Claimants entitled to the allowance immediately before reaching pensionable age, or who would have been except for overlapping benefit provisions, retain their entitlement providing they continue to satisfy all the qualifying conditions.[183] Third, the rules provide for those receiving the allowance when they reached retiring age to continue receiving it, even if they are no longer caring for another person.[184] In effect, it becomes a non-contributory pension.[185]

1.23.2 Following the case of *Drake v. Chief Adjudication Officer [1986]* the previous restrictions upon the payment of ICA to a married woman, or to a woman cohabiting with a man as his wife, are no longer relevant.[186] In March 1988, there were 95,000 people in receipt of the allowance.[187] No less than 89,000 married and cohabiting women had received ICA within some twelve months of this legal change.[188]

1.23.3 Section 37 of the SSA 1975 sets out the qualifying condition for the receipt of ICA. The section provides that an individual will be entitled to ICA if he/she is regularly, and substantially, engaged in caring for a severely disabled person, and is not in gainful employment. It is not necessary, however, to have given up work in order to become the carer[189] nor need the claimant have ever been in gainful employment.

1.23.4 An operational definition of the phrase 'regular and substantial care' is given in the regulations.[190] A person will be deemed to have satisfied the requirement if he/she provides, 'or is likely' to provide care for at least 35 hours a week. A person who provides less than 35 hours regular care can never be deemed to be providing 'substantial' care. The act of 'caring' is nowhere defined in the legislation or regulations. The probable legal effect of including the phrase 'is likely to be ... engaged' in the regulations is to allow for temporary absences by the carer over and above the period of absence allowed for in the regulations.[191]

The regulations allow for absences of up to a total of four weeks in every 26 week period, without any loss of entitlement.[192] As with attendance allowance, the claimant does not necessarily lose entitlement on going abroad, but for ICA there is usually a limit of four weeks. The four week limit will not apply, however, if the claimant continues in the caring role.

Should the claimant go away unaccompanied, he/she can continue to receive ICA but the person providing substitute care during that time will receive no additional payment.[193] Even under normal circumstances, only one person is entitled to ICA. Where two people are involved as carers, one of them may be entitled to home responsibility protection. (see para. 1.15.1)

1.23.5 In the context of claiming ICA, a 'severely disabled person' is a person in receipt of attendance allowance, constant attendance allowance under the industrial injuries, or the war disablement scheme.[194] A person is not to be treated as 'gainfully employed' unless his/her earnings exceed £12 per week.[195]

1.23.6 The financial impact of ICA is not as great as that of other benefits referred to above. This is because of the rules relating to overlapping benefits.[196] Between June 1986 and November 1987, 2,270 claims for ICA, from married and co-habiting women, were disallowed because the claimants were receiving other social security benefits which equalled or exceeded the weekly rate of ICA.[197] ICA can, however, be received at the same time as mobility allowance and attendance allowance. Where other national insurance benefits are being claimed, such as invalidity benefit or SDA, the receipt of ICA will result in the claimant not being entitled to claim an allowance for the carer. He/she will no longer be treated as a 'dependant'. ICA is a taxable benefit, but can be offset against a married woman's earned income allowance. This may help reduce a couple's liability for income tax, particularly on reaching pensionable age.[198] Entitlement to IS is also affected since it will be reduced by the amount of ICA being received. Where a carer is receiving ICA, the person being cared for could lose the right to severe disability premium under the IS scheme. (see para. 1.24.11 below)

1.24.1 INCOME SUPPORT

Income support (IS) is a new benefit which replaced supplementary benefit/pension as from April 11, 1988. As with supplementary benefit, IS is intended as a safety net. Those whose income falls below a level prescribed by Parliament, or who have no other income, are entitled to it. In other words, it is means-tested. Entitlement to IS is a passport to other assistance such as HB (see below at para. 1.24.15), free dental treatment, and vouchers for glasses. (see Chapter 5 at para.5.7.3) Once entitlement to IS has been established, no further means-testing is required in order to claim other benefits.

1.24.2 The importance of means-tested benefits for elderly people, as a group, is clear. Some 20 per cent of those who are elderly were receiving supplementary benefit in 1987/8.[199] The take-up rate of supplementary benefit remained low, however, with a case-load take-up rate of only 76 per cent in 1983, the last year for which statistics are available.[200] The position is unlikely to improve with the advent of IS, given the paltry sum spent on advertising it. While £41 million was spent on trying to persuade individuals to buy shares in British Gas,[201] only £55,400 was spent on publicising IS.

1.24.3 THE QUALIFYING CONDITIONS

The SSA 1986 provides that a person will be entitled to IS (and HB) if

    a) he is over 16
    b) he has no income or his income does not exceed the applicable amount;
    c) he is not engaged in remunerative work and, if he is a member of a married or unmarried couple, the other member is not so engaged; and
    d) except in such circumstances as may be prescribed -

        (i) he is available for employment;
        (ii) he is not receiving relevant education.[202]

1.24.4 The term 'applicable amount' means the sum which it is stipulated a person needs to live on.[203] In this context, remunerative work means work that a person is engaged in, on average, for not less than 24 hours a week, being work for which payment is made or which is performed in expectation of payment.[204] The regulations provide, however, that persons are not to be treated as engaged in remunerative work where, *inter alia*, they are engaged in voluntary work for a charity or voluntary body; or as a childminder in their own home; or as carers for a person who receives, or has applied for, attendance allowance; or if earning capacity has been reduced by physical or mental disability to 75 per cent or less than they would otherwise be capable of earning.[205]

1.24.5 'Unmarried couples' are those 'living together as husband and wife'.[206] The definition is important not only in relation to qualifying for IS but also in relation to the amount of benefit payable. The 'applicable amount' for a couple is less than for two single claimants. To denote two people as an 'unmarried couple', it is necessary to show more than that they are living together in the same household. Elaborate guidelines, based on case-law, had been established under the supplementary benefit scheme[207] but difficulties still arose as can be seen from the following cases. *CSSB/145/1983* concerned disabled persons living in sheltered housing, who moved into a flat so as to share expenses and provide each other with mutual support. There was no sexual relationship between them although there had been only one bedroom in the flat. The Social Security Appeal Tribunal (SSAT) decided that the situation was no different from that of a married couple where one partner had a serious disability. The Social Security Commissioner, however, rejected the SSAT's approach, concluding that the sharing of expenses and mutual support need not, of themselves, amount to living together as husband and wife. In *R(SB) 35/85*, the claimant shared her bungalow with a widower, who needed care and help. She did the cooking and expenses were shared. The Social Security Commissioner held that the SSAT, in finding the claimant and the widower to be living together as husband and wife, had taken the wrong approach. The SSAT had failed to recognise that the existence of a common household was only one of the matters to be considered. The Commissioner, quoting earlier case-law,[208] emphasised that it was impossible to categorise all the various kinds of available explanation as to why two people might be sharing a household, apart from living together as husband and wife.

1.24.6 Persons aged 60 and over are not required to be available for employment.[209] Those who are within ten years of pensionable age can be exempted from the requirement to be available for work if they have been unemployed for ten years and there is no prospect of employment.[210]

1.24.7 CAPITAL LIMIT

Where a person's savings plus other capital totals more than £6,000, there is no right to IS. Some capital assets, notably the value of a dwelling occupied as a home, and personal possessions (other than those acquired with the intention of reducing capital in order to secure entitlement) are disregarded. A list of disregarded capital assets is set out in the regulations.[211] Capital between £3,000 and £6,000 is treated as producing a notional 'tariff' income. Each block of £250 (or part thereof) is deemed to produce a weekly income of £1.[212]

Assessing a person's capital resources can give rise to complex legal problems. It is first necessary to establish that the capital belongs to the claimant. In *R(SB)49/83*, for instance, the claimant had bought a house, but argued it had been bought on behalf of his son, who was repaying the loan. The Social Security Commissioner held that it was possible, in such circumstances, to regard the claimant as holding the property on a resulting trust for the benefit of a third party. Where it can be established that the claimant is a trustee, the asset cannot be regarded as forming part of the claimant's capital resources.[213]

1.24.8 TRUST PROPERTY

The treatment of capital and income to which a person is entitled under a trust fund, is complicated. Where a person's interest is 'reversionary' (that is, arising only when some specified event occurs, such as the death of another person) the capital value must be disregarded.[214] Similarly, where a person's interest in a trust fund, or property held on trust, constitutes a life interest under which he/she is entitled to income, then the capital value of the interest is ignored.[215] It may be different, however, where the terms of the trust enable the trustees to encroach on capital. In *R(SB)13/87* the claimant had a life interest in her husband's residuary estate.

The terms of the trust gave the trustees a discretionary power to make use of capital if the income was insufficient for the claimant's suitable maintenance. The Social Security Commissioner confirmed the need to consider the value of the claimant's interest in the capital of her husband's estate, because of the trustee's power to use the capital for the claimant's benefit.

1.24.9 A DWELLING

The most frequent problems are probably those which arise over the treatment of a dwelling as a capital asset. As indicated above, the value of a dwelling occupied as the claimant's home is disregarded. Nevertheless, problems can arise on purchase or sale of premises, or where the claimant leaves his/her former home to stay with relatives, for instance, or to enter a residential home. The capital disregard, which applies to one dwelling only, can relate to premises acquired for occupation which the claimant intends to occupy as a dwelling within 26 weeks of acquisition, or such longer period as is reasonable in the circumstances.[216] This also applies to proceeds held as a result of the sale of premises where it is intended to use the capital for the purchase of other premises to be occupied within a similar period of time.[217] The effect of leaving a dwelling in order to live with relatives or to enter a residential home depends upon four factors: first, whether a partner or relative continues to occupy the premises; secondly, the intention of the claimant; thirdly, the availability of the premises; and, fourthly, the period of absence from the premises. The regulations provide for premises to be disregarded if occupied, in whole or in part, by:

a) a partner or relative of any member of the family where that person is aged 60 or over or is incapacitated;

b) the former partner of a claimant where the claimant is not to be treated as occupying a dwelling as a home; but this provision shall not apply where the former partner is a person from whom the claimant is estranged or divorced.[218]

A 'partner' includes the other member of an unmarried couple.[219]
The statutory definition of a family also takes account of
unmarried couples.[220] A 'relative' need not, therefore, be
related to the claimant; but, unlike a partner, a relative must
be over 60 years of age, or incapacitated. Where neither a
partner, nor a relative, remains in occupation, the dwelling
will be treated as capital unless it is the claimant's intention
to return. The regulations provide that:

A person shall be treated as occupying a dwelling as his
home for a period not exceeding 52 weeks while he is
temporarily absent therefrom only if

a) he intends to return to occupy the dwelling as his
home; and
b) the part of the dwelling normally occupied by him has
not been let or, as the case may be, sub-let; and
c) the period of absence is unlikely to exceed 52
weeks, or, in exceptional circumstances, (for
example, where the person is in hospital or otherwise
has no control over the length of his absence) is
unlikely substantially to exceed that period.[221]

Where the intention is to give up the home permanently, the
disregard does not apply. Where no such intention exists, the
disregard will normally apply for 52 weeks. A longer period may
be allowed in exceptional circumstances, where the person has no
control over the length of absence. The Secretary of State has
also announced a further disregard is to be introduced, which
will allow the value of premises which have ceased to be the
claimant's home for six months, or longer, to be disregarded in
exceptional circumstances. No regulations have been published to
date, but they could possibly have the effect of extending the
period of disregard to 18 months, or longer, in exceptional
circumstances. The new disregard will apply 'if that is
reasonable in the circumstances'. It applies to persons who have
entered residential accommodation or hospital permanently, and
to those who have had to leave the matrimonial home because of
marital breakdown. Decisions will be made by Adjudication
Officers and, therefore, carry the normal right of appeal to an
SSAT. Local DSS offices can make payments as if this relaxation
to the rules had been in force since April 11, 1988.[222]

1.24.10 THE APPLICABLE AMOUNT

IS can be paid if a person's income does not exceed the 'applicable amount'. (see para. 1.24.3 above) The term 'applicable amount' refers to four elements: a personal allowance, which is the basic scale rate for a single claimant or for a couple; a dependant's allowance, which is the basic scale rate for each dependant child of the family; a client group premium, which is a flat-rate additional payment where the claimant satisfies specified conditions; and certain housing costs. These last two elements can give rise to difficulty.

1.24.11 THE PREMIUMS

Premiums, to supplement personal allowances, can be paid to claimants with special needs. There are seven premiums, five of which are of particular relevance to those who are elderly. These are:

	Single	Couple
Family premium (FP)	£6.15	
Disability premium (DP)	£13.05	£18.60
Pensioner premium (PP)	£10.65	£16.25
Higher pensioner premium (HPP)	£13.05	£18.60
Severe disability premium (SDP)	£24.75	

A claimant may qualify for more than one premium; but, in general, he/she will be entitled to one only, that is, the premium which gives the highest benefit.[223] There are three exceptions to this rule, two of which are of particular importance here.[224] The first exception is that a family premium (FP) can be paid in addition to any other premium which the claimant is receiving. An FP is payable to claimants who are responsible for children who live within the same household.[225] Secondly, the severe disability premium (SDP) can be paid at the same time as the disability premium (DP) or higher pensioner premium (HPP).

1.24.12 A PP is payable to a claimant who is, or whose partner is, 60 years of age.[226] To qualify for HPP, the claimant must satisfy one of these four conditions.[227] First, either the claimant or his/her partner must be aged 80 or more. Second, one of them must satisfy the disability conditions which apply in respect of entitlement to DP, that is, he/she must be registered blind, or be receiving attendance or mobility allowance; or be continuing to receive assistance under the pre-1976 vehicle scheme. (see para. 1.21.1 above) Third, the claimant must have been entitled to IS plus DP because of his/her deemed incapacity for work immediately before (that is, within eight weeks of reaching) his/her sixtieth birthday.[228] It is incumbent upon the claimant to show entitlement to IS has continued, although the regulations allow for a break of up to eight weeks once it has been established that HPP is applicable.[229] Fourth, if the claimant was entitled to DP within eight weeks of his/her sixtieth birthday because his/her partner satisfied the disability conditions which entitle a person to receive DP, eligibility will be established. The eight week limiting rules are arbitrary. Individuals can be unlucky and lose entitlement to HPP simply because they failed to qualify for IS during the eight weeks preceding their sixtieth birthday. A bequest or other capital gift received during this critical period could deprive the claimant of entitlement to HPP until he/she reaches 80, unless he/she could claim a disablity benefit and so qualify along that route.[230]

1.24.13 The number qualifying for SDP is likely to be small since the eligibility criteria are difficult to satisfy. Those unable to meet them might, however, qualify for assistance from the newly established Independent Living Fund (ILF). (see para. 1.27.1 below) To qualify for SDP the claimant must be receiving attendance allowance. Where the claimant is one of a couple, both must be receiving it.[231] The implicit assumption, therefore, is that a partner should accept responsibility for caring for the disabled person, unless he/she is also disabled. Second, there must be no adult non-dependants aged 18 or over, residing with the claimant. Certain co-residents, such as boarders or temporary visitors are disregarded.[232] Third, no one should be receiving ICA for caring for the claimant. Where both partners are receiving attendance allowance, the right to SDP will be preserved where ICA is paid to a carer in respect of only one of them. Where no one is receiving ICA with respect to either claimant, both will be entitled to the premium.[233] A carer cannot be forced to claim ICA.[233] Conversely, neither can a carer be prevented from making a claim. Where no claim for ICA is made, however, and the carer him/herself is receiving IS, or some other similar state benefit,[234] the risk exists that he/she may be credited with notional income, equivalent to the amount of ICA which would be available.[235]

1.24.15 HOUSING COSTS

The costs which can be claimed in relation to housing are set out in the regulations. They include mortgage interest payments; interest on loans for repairs and improvements to the dwelling occupied as the home; payments by way of rent and other analogous payments.[236] Where the claimant or his/her partner is over 60, 100 per cent of mortgage interest payments can be claimed.[237] Where both the claimant and his/her partner are under 60, only half of the mortgage interest payments can be met by IS during the claimant's first 16 weeks of entitlement. Where a claimant is temporarily absent, and living at a residential home, the housing costs can be met until such time as he/she is no longer deemed to be occupying the dwelling. (see para. 1.24.9 above)

1.25.1 SOCIAL FUND

The Social Fund was established to help people with exceptional needs which are difficult to meet from regular income. It replaced the system of single payments, most urgent needs payments, as well as maternity and death grants available under the supplementary benefits scheme. The Social Fund can also provide budgeting loans (for people on IS); crisis loans (for people without resources, whether or not they are on benefit); Community Care Grants (CCGs) (for people receiving or entitled to IS) and payments towards funeral costs (for people on IS or HB). The SSA 1988 also provides the Secretary of State with power to make regulations in respect of assistance with heating expenses in cold weather.[238] (see para. 1.25.3 below) The payment of funeral costs is discussed in Chapter 7 at paras. 7.11.1 - 7.11.3. Discussion here will, therefore, be limited to outlining the purpose for which CCGs can be used and the eligibility conditions which apply.

1.25.2 COMMUNITY CARE GRANTS

A CCG is available to meet four types of expenditure. First, it can be paid to assist a person move out of institutional care and become re-established in the community. Secondly, payment can be made to assist a person remain in the community. A grant could be made, for example, towards heavy laundry costs, 'specialist' furniture, or extra warmth for the household.[239] Thirdly, payment can be made to ease exceptional pressures on an individual and his/her family. Fourthly, grants are available to assist with travel expenses within the UK so as to enable the recipient to visit someone who is ill, ease a domestic crisis, or move into suitable accommodation.[240] Eligibility depends upon the applicant being either in receipt of IS at the date of the application, or likely to become entitled to it on discharge from residential or hospital care.[241] A claim can be made six weeks prior to discharge but payment may be deferred until two weeks beforehand.[242] The fact that payment of the grant can be delayed almost up to the time of discharge may lead to difficulties in accomplishing a planned discharge.[243]

Not only do applicants have to qualify for IS but a grant will be reduced by the amount of any savings in excess of £500 held by the applicant.[244] The Social Fund Manual specifies certain groups as having priority for certain grants. Elderly people are included in the priority list, particularly if they have restricted mobility, or difficulty in performing personal tasks.[245] The suggested maximum grant is £500 for a single person and £750 for a couple.[246] Amendments to the Social Fund Manual suggest that where a person has applied for a CCG but is found to be ineligible, the application should be treated as one for a budgeting loan.[247]

Recent regulations specify the manner in which applications can be made.[248] They must be in writing on an approved form, or in writing in a form which the Secretary of State accepts as sufficient. Where an application is sent on someone's behalf, that person must indicate his/her consent in writing, unless the applicant is an appointee of the Secretary of State.

1.25.3 COLD WEATHER PAYMENTS

The power to award additional cash to help with the cost of fuel during periods of cold weather is contained in s.32(2A) of the SSA 1986. From November 7, 1988, non-discretionary social fund cold weather payments have been available to certain people on IS, to cover 'periods of cold weather'. The £5 a week payments are available only to claimants who get income support for at least one day during the period of cold weather. Claimants must also be entitled to one of the following premiums: disability; pensioner; higher pensioner or severe disablity premium.

A period of cold weather is defined as a period of seven consecutive days during which the average of the mean daily temperature for that period is equal to or below O° celcius. The mean daily temperature means the average of the maximum and minimum temperature recorded for that day.

Once a person has claimed a cold weather payment successfully he/she will automatically receive payments for later periods of cold weather that occur until the end of April 1989, while he/she remains on IS and provided he/she continues to satisfy the above conditions. A claimant may make a claim up to three months after the start of the period of cold weather.[249]

1.26.1   HOUSING BENEFIT

Housing benefit is a means-tested benefit which assists people on low income with payment of rent and/or general rates. The scheme is administered by local authorities and the benefit is calculated in a similar, though not identical, manner way to IS. Those receiving IS are not subject to a further means-test on making a claim for HB, although a formal claim must, nevertheless, be made.[250] Only the more important differences between IS and HB are discussed here.

1.26.2 The major conditions governing entitlement to HB are set out in ss.20-22 of the SSA 1986. These are:

a) that a person is liable to make payments in respect of a dwelling in Great Britain which he/she occupies as his/her home;

b) that there is an appropriate maximum housing benefit in his/her case;[251]

c) that he/she has no income or his/her income does not exceed specified limits above the appropriate amount in his/her case;

d) that his/her capital does not exceed prescribed limits; and

e) in the case of a family, that no member of his/her family is already entitled to the housing benefit.

1.26.3 CAPITAL LIMIT

On April 27, 1988, the Secretary of State announced that the capital limit for HB would be raised from £6,000 to £8,000.[252] The change was put into effect on June 1, 1988. The tariff system remains unchanged, however. As a result capital over £3,000 is treated as producing a notional income of £1 for every £250 (or part thereof) of capital above £3,000. A person with £8,000 will, therefore, be deemed to have a notional income of £20.[253] This may result in many claimants losing their entitlement.

1.26.4 HB TRANSITIONAL PAYMENTS

A new transitional payments scheme (TPs) was introduced in April 1988.[254] TPs are an important part of the new IS scheme, providing some protection for claimants entitled to SB at the time of the changeover to the IS system so as to ensure their entitlement to benefit under the new scheme is not less than it would have been under the former scheme.

It is precisely because some HB claimants lost out by more than £2.50 a week that TPs have been made available. The details of the scheme are to be found in DHSS Circulars.[255] Since these TPs are extra-statutory payments there is no right of appeal against a refusal to award one. Applicants must have been receiving HB under the previous scheme; must have less than £8,000 in capital; and must qualify for an HB premium,[256] or be receiving a 'qualifying benefit'. The latter includes war disablement pensions, industrial injury benefits, widow's pension, and war widow's pensions. Protection is to be extended, in due course, to those receiving IS.[257] The amount of weekly TP is calculated by a 'before and after' benefits comparison, although not every loss can be taken into account. An excellent illustration of the way in which calculations are made is set out elsewhere.[258]

TPs must be claimed, and a special application form exists.[259] It is not known for how long these particular TPs will be available, but possibly for no longer than two years. At present, there is no deadline for submitting claims.

1.26.5 Those pensioners in receipt of Housing Benefit Supplement (HBS) may qualify for transitional protection along an alternative route. HBS was introduced in 1983 to protect claimants adversely affected by certain legislative changes.[260]

In April 1988, the final provisions of the SSA 1986 came into force and the government's intention was to abolish HBS before the new scheme came into effect. It appears that there were procedural irregularities, and one SSAT came to the decision that regulations providing for the payment of HBS remained in force.[261] The practical effect of this decision, unless over-ruled, is that TPs are extended to those receiving HBS when the April changes occurred. It is not known, at present, whether the DHSS intends to appeal against this decision. In the meantime, those formerly entitled to HBS should appeal against any decision not to pay it for the week beginning April 4, 1988, the 'first benefit week'. The transitional additions, which some claimants could receive, might result in extra weekly income for several years to come, possibly an extra £10 for almost half a million claimants.[262]

1.26.6 ELIGIBLE HOUSING COSTS

HB is payable in respect of eligible housing costs only. The qualifying conditions are set out in the regulations.[263] For instance, fuel charges are not generally to be treated as part of eligible rent, except if they relate to communal areas. Service charges, too, are usually outside the scheme with some being specifically excluded. These include meals, laundry (except for the provision of a laundry room where the claimant can do his/her own laundry); and the cleaning of rooms and windows (unless no one in the household is able to do it). The regulations contain a number of exceptions so that those liable to service charges might qualify for HB, despite the general rule. TPs are available for those receiving assistance with fuel charges and assistance towards the cost of service charges before April 1988.[264]

1.27.1 THE INDEPENDENT LIVING FUND

The ILF is a trust fund, recently established by the government in conjunction with the Disabled Income Group and the Disabled Income Group Scotland. Broadly, the fund will be available to severely disabled people on low incomes who receive attendance allowance. The aim is to:

> provide help to some severely disabled people who need domestic support if they are to live in their own homes. The aim will be to prevent such people having to enter residential care if they cannot afford the support; and to enable people in residential care, who are capable of living independently, to do so.[265]

1.28.1 DISCRIMINATORY PRACTICES

Those who are elderly often face discriminatory practices in relation both to employment and to social security provision. Age-restrictive polices in the workplace sometimes force individuals into involuntary premature retirement when they might have preferred to go on working. The law relating to the termination of the contract of employment is, therefore, of particular importance to those approaching retirement age. Having retired, many find themselves having to manage on low incomes with little by way of financial support for those with special needs. The disparity between individuals who have to rely on state provision, and those benefiting from membership of an occupational pension scheme highlights the inequality which exists between different groups of elderly people, to the point that it is possible to speak of 'two nations in old age'.[266]

Notes

1. CSO (1982) *Social Trends*, Table 7.8; (1988) *Social Trends*, Table 4.5 (HMSO).
2. CSO (1988) op.cit., at p.68.
3. Hunt, A. (1976) *The Elderly at Home* (HMSO).

4. Angleitner, A. (1975) 'Faktorenonlytisch untersuchungen Zym. Koncept der Rigidat' *Archiv fur Psychologie* vol.125 at pp.73-104. See Johnson, M. (1975) 'Old Age and the Gift Relationship' *New Society* March 13, at p.640.

5. CSO (1988) op.cit., at p.68.

6. Midwinter, E. (1983) 'Ten Million People' the *Listener*, April 14, 1983 at p.9.

7. Ekerdt, D. J. et al. (1983) 'Claims that Retirement Improves Health' *Gerontologist,* vol.38, no.2 at pp.231-7.

8. Pampel F. C. (1981) *Social Change and the Aged: Recent Trends in the United States* (Lexington Books).

9. Townsend, P. (1979) *Poverty in the United Kingdom* (Penguin Books Ltd) at pp.805-6.

10. Consultative Document on Wages Councils (1985) (HMSO) at paras. 4 and 5.

11. Wages Act 1986, s.14. See also White, R. A. (1986) 'The Wages Act' *Legal Action* October 1986, at p.130.

12. s.2.

13. Wages Act 1986, Sched 5.

14. Disabled Persons (Employment) Act 1944, s.1.

15. Companies (Directors' Reports) Employment of Disabled Persons Regulations 1980 S.I. 1980 No.1160.

16. Selwyn, M. (1988) *Law of Employment* (Butterworth) at p.122.

17. *IRLR 36.*

18. *Pascoe v. Hallen & Medway [1975] IRLR 116.*

19. Robertson, S. (1988) *Disability Rights Handbook* (Disability Alliance), at p.87.

20. But note that failure to review a fixed term contract may amount to unfair dismissal, as in *Terry v. East Sussex Council [1977] 1 All ER 567.*

21. *Hill v. C. A. Parsons & Co Ltd [1971] 3 All ER 1345, CA.*

22. Employment Protection (Consolidation) Act 1978, s.49(1).

23. *Walker v. Cotswold Chine Home School [1977] 12 ITR 342.*

24. Employment Protection (Consolidation) Act 1978, s.49(2)

25. *Egg Stores (Stamford Hill) Ltd v. Leitovici [1977] IRLR 376.*

26. *IRLR 77.* See also: *Garricks (Caterers) Ltd v. Nolan (1980) IRLR 259.*

27. Employment Protection (Consolidation) Act 1978, s.64, as amended.

28. *IRLR 18.*

29. *Mullet v. Bush Electrical [1977] ICR 829.*

30. *2 All ER 1013.*

31. *IRLR 441.*

32. *3 All ER 974.*

33. *IRLR 195.*

34. Robertson, S. (1988) op.cit., at p.86.

35. *1 CMLR 688*

36. Hansard, H. L. vol.481, no.161, col.971.

37. *Rank Xerox v. Churchill (1988)* the *Daily Telegraph,* May 27, 1988.

38. *Lister v. Fran Gerrard [1973] IRLR 302.*

39. *O'Brien v. Associated Fire Alarms Ltd [1969] 1 All ER 93.*

40. Employment Protection (Consolidation) Act, 1978 s.59(1)(b).

41. *Suflex v. Thomas [1987] IRLR 435.*

42. *Crump v. Chubb and Sons Lock & Safe Co Ltd [1975] IRLR 293.*

43. Directive 79/7 *Equal Treatment in Social Security Matters.* For the government's views, see Report of Standing Committee A, July 1, 1986.

44. Fitzpatrick, B. (1987) 'The Sex Discrimination Act 1986' *Modern Law Review* vol.50, at p.973.

45. Friedman, S. (1986) *The Sex Discrimination Act 1986.* Current Law Statutes Annotated, at 59/5.

46. *IRLR 338.*

47. Fitzpatrick, B. (1988) 'Exit Offers: A British Perspective' *Exchange on Ageing,* Bulletin No.1, Summer 1988 (International Federation on Ageing, European Office).

48. *Burton, Allton & Johnson Ltd v. Peck [1985] ICR 193.*

49. *Morton Sundour Fabrics v. Shaw [1966] 2 ITR 84.* But compare *Caledonian Mining Co Ltd v. Basset and Steel [1987] ICR 425.* It was held in the later case that in reality it was the employer who had terminated the contracts by 'inveighling' the employees into resigning.

50. *Martin v. MBS Fastenings Glynwed Distributions Ltd [1983] IRLR 198. C.A.*

51. *IRLR 131.*

52. Bourn C. 'Employment protection rights' *New Law Journal* vol.138 August 12, 1988, at p.581.

53. *2 All ER 299.*

54. op.cit., at p.302.

55. EATs are not bound by previous decisions. See Smith, I. T. and Wood, J. G. (1986) *Industrial Law* (Butterworths) at p.223.

56. See Williams G. (1982) *Learning the Law* (Stevens) at p.77.

57. CSO (1988) *Social Trends* (HMSO) at p.100.

58. McGoldrick, A. (1984) *Equal Treatment in Occupational Pension Schemes: A Research Report* (Equal Opportunities Commission).

59. i.e. direct or indirect discrimination. See the Sex Discrimination Act 1975, s.1.

60. Room 327, Aviation House, 129 Kingsway, London WC2B 6NN.

61. S.I. 1986 No.1046.

62. McGoldrick, A. (1984) op.cit., at p.iv.

63. *1 All ER 129, European Court of Justice, (Case 192/85).*

64. Government Actuary, (1987) *Occupational Pension Schemes: Review of Certain Contracting Out Terms,* Cmd.110. (HMSO) March 1987.

65. Fitzpatrick, B. (1988) Recent Cases, *Journal of Social Welfare Law,* 1988 at p.210.

66. Social Security Act 1986, s.10.

67. s.6.

68. s.9.

69. ss.12-14.

70. Finance (No 2) Act 1987, s.54.

71. Social Security Act 1986, s.1.

72. Memorandum No. 92, Joint Office of the Inland Revenue Superannuation Funds Office and the Occupations Pensions Board, January 1988.

73. ibid., at para. 10.

74. Personal and Occupational Pension Schemes (Incentive Payments) Regulations 1987, S.I. 1987 No.1115.

75. Finance (No 2) Act 1987 s.32.

76. See Current Law Statutes (1986) vol.3 (Sweet and Maxwell) at 50/6. Annotations by Keith Ewing and Douglas Brodie.

77. See Memorandum No 92 op.cit., at para.247.

78. Personal Pension Schemes (Personal Pension Protected Rights Premiums) Regulations 1987 S.I. 1987 No.1111, reg 3(2). Personal and Occupational Pension Schemes (Protected Rights) Regulations 1987 S.I. 1987 No.1117 reg 10(1).

79. A scheme may, however, provide for the pension to continue after the widow or widower ceases to satisfy the specified requirements.

80. S.I. 1987 No. 1117, op.cit., reg 10.

81. reg 4(2).

82. Casty, H. (1987) 'The Sex Discrimination Act 1986: Equality or Employment Deregulation?' *Journal of Social Welfare Law* May 1987, at p.177.

83. Sex Discrimination Act 1986, s.2(2).

84. *ICMLR 688.*

85. *Parsons v. East Surrey Health Authority (1986) 10 Equal Opportunities Review 35.*

86. *Duke v. GEC Reliance Ltd (1988) The Times*, February 12, 1988.

87. *ICR 52.*

88. Ogus, A. I. and Barendt, L. M. (1988) *The Law of Social Security* at p.185. Rowland, M. (1988) *Right Guide to Non-Means Tested Social Security Benefits* (CPAG) at p.144.

89. Social Security Pensions Act 1975, s.4

90. Ogus, A. I. and Barendt, L. M. (1988) op.cit., at p.51.

91. Social Security (Overlapping Benefits) Regulations 1979. S.I. 1979 No.597, reg 4(5).

92. Rowland, M. (1988) op.cit., at p.153.

93. Social Security (Claims and Payments) Regulations 1987 S.I. 1987 No.1968, reg 4(1). See also reg 9(1).

94. reg 19 and Sched 4. Note also that the time limits will vary according to the circumstances. For instance, the limit for claiming invalidity benefit will depend on whether or not it is a first claim.

95. Feigehan, G.V. (1986) 'Income After Retirement' in C.S.O. *Social Trends* (HMSO) at p.16.

96. Hansard, H.C. Written Answers, June 30, 1987, col.71.

97. Hansard, H.C. Written Answers, April 22, 1988, col.602.

98. *Disability Rights* Summer 1988 (Disability Alliance) at p.19.

99. Social Security Act 1975, s.27(1).

100. *R(P)2/76.*

101. Bonner, D., Hooker, I., Smith, P., and White, R. (1988) *Non-Means Tested Benefits: The Legislation* (Sweet and Maxwell) at p.55.
102. Rowland, M. (1988) op.cit., at p.l78.
103. Social Security Benefit (Computation of Earnings) Regulations 1978 S.I. 1978 No.1698.
104. Social Security Pensions Act 1975, Sched 4, as amended.
105. Social Security (Claims and Payments) Regulations 1979, S.I. 1979 No.628 Sched 3, para.4.
106. Robertson, S. (1988) op.cit., at p.170.
107. Social Security (Widow's Benefit and Retirement Pensions) Regulations 1979 S.I. 1979 No.642, reg 2.
108. Social Security Act 1975, s.30(4).
109. Sched 3, para. 5(6).
110. Social Security Pensions (Home Responsibilities and Miscellaneous Amendments) Regulations 1978 S.I. 1978 No.508, reg 2(2).
111. The right only applies to those who elected to pay reduced national insurance contributions before April 5, 1977.
112. Rowland, M. (1988) op.cit., at p.157. Robertson, S. (1988) op.cit., at p.145.
113. Social Security (Hospital In-Patients) Regulations 1975, S.I. 1975 No.555, reg 2(3).
114. or someone else on his/her behalf.
115. DHSS Leaflet MPL 110 *Treatment Allowances for the War Disabled.*
116. S.I. 1975 No.55 op.cit., reg 16.
117. See Robertson, S. (1988) op.cit., at p.161.
118. See *R(S)4/84.*
119. See Rowland, M. (1988) op.cit., at p.130.
120. Social Security Pensions Act 1975, s.9(3). Social Security (Maximum Additional Component) Regulations 1978 S.I. 1978 No.949, reg 2. The right is qualified in the sense that no one is allowed to receive more that the maximum payable to one individual.
121. Rowland, M. (1988) op.cit., at p.131.
122. Leaflet MP 38 *Your Future Pension.*
123. DHSS (1985) *Reform of Social Security - Programme for Action* Cmnd. 9691 (HMSO) para. 2.1.
124. Because of insufficient contributions.
125. DHSS (1987) Social Security Statistics Table 13.46. (HMSO).

126. Robertson, S. (1988) op.cit., at p.168.

127. Bourke, L. (1988) 'Employees face crucial decisions on pensions' the *Independent*, April 9, 1988.

128. Chatterton, D. (1988) 'The reform of pensions into the 21st century: A Critique' *New Law Journal* April 1, 1988 at p.227.

129. Because a personal pension is a personal contract between an individual and the pension company, there is no difficulty when the individual changes employment.

130. Health and Social Services and Social Security Adjudication Act 1984 s.19 as amended by the Social Security Act 1985, s.2.

131. Wright, D. (1988) 'Be wary of early pensions' the *Sunday Times*, August 21, 1988.

132. Robertson, S. (1988) op.cit., at p.164; Bourke, L. (1988) op.cit.

133. Social Security Act 1975, s.20(1)(a).

134. s.20(3A). See also Rowland, M. (1988) op.cit., at p.40.

135. See also *Crewe v. Anderson (National Insurance Officer) (1982) The Times*, May 3, 1982.

136. Ogus, A. I. and Barendt, E. M. (1988) op.cit., at p.102.

137. *Chief Adjudication Officer v. Brunt (1988) The Times* March 4, 1988.

138. Rowland, M. (1988) op.cit., at p.36.

139. Social Security (Credits) Regulations 1975 S.I. 1975 No.556, reg 9A as amended.

140. Social Security Act 1975 s.15, s.15A, s.17(1)(a)(ii).

141. *R(S) 6/85*.

142. Robertson, S. (1988) op.cit., at p.77.

143. Social Security (Unemployment, Sickness and Invalidity Benefit) Regulations 1983, S.I. 1983 No.1598, reg 3(5).

144. Social Security Act 1975, s.35 (as amended).

145. Those who previously qualified for non-contributory pensions need not satisfy the disability test. The same applies for those who become incapable of work before their twentieth birthday. For the latest statistics on SDA see Hansard, H.C. April 22, 1988, col.602.

146. Social Security (General Benefit) Regulations 1982 S.I. 1982 No.1408, Sched 2.

147. See Robertson, S. (1988) op.cit., at p.83.

148. Social Security (Severe Disablement Allowance) Regulations 1984 S.I. 1984 No.1303 reg 10.

149. It is possible to make a claim at any time within twelve months of passing pensionable age if good cause is shown for the delay.

150. See Robertson, S. (1988) op.cit., at p.167.

151. S.I. 1984 No.1303, op.cit., regs 5 and 20(3).

152. Social Security Act 1975, s.37A as amended.

153. See Robertson, S. (1988) op.cit., at p.111.

154. There is no upper age limit, however, for war pensioners' mobility supplement.

155. Social Security Act 1986, s.71.

156. Mobility Allowance Regulations 1975 S.I. 1975 No.1573, reg 3.

157. *2 All ER 203.*

158. S.I. 1975 No.1573, op.cit., reg 3(2).

159. Rowland, M. (1988) op.cit., at p.95.

160. Robertson, S. (1988). op.cit., at p.108.

161. Rowland, M. (1988) op.cit., at p.94.

162. Robertson, S. (1988) op.cit., at p.108.

163. *CM/23/85.*

164. Wise, R. (1988) 'Able to Walk' *Adviser* July 1988 at p.66.

165. *CM 6/86.*

166. *Disability Rights* Spring 1988 (Disability Alliance) at p.16.

167. Rowland, M. (1988) op.cit., at p.88.

168. Social Security Act 1975, s.35(2)b.

169. Bonner, D. et al. (1988) op.cit., at p.61.

170. The Secretary of State may sanction a longer period abroad if for treatment. See Social Security (Attendance Allowance) (No.2) Regulations 1975, S.I. 1975 No.598, reg 2(2)e.

171. *The Times,* March 14, 1987.

172. For a definition of bodily functions see: *R. v. N.I. Commissioners, ex parte Secretary of State for Social Services [1974] 1 WLR.* Note, however, that bodily functions do not include cooking.

173. i.e. the doctor who takes the decision as to eligibility. The DMP is not necessarily or usually the doctor who visits the applicant.

174. *1 WLR 421, CA.*

175. Social Security Act 1975, s.106.

176. Robertson, S. (1988) op.cit., at p.99.

177. Attendance Allowance Unit, DHSS, North Fylde Central Office, Norcross, Blackpool FY 53TA.

178. S.I. 1975 No.598 op.cit., reg 5A.

179. for the exceptions, see reg 4.

180. except where charges above the national rates are imposed.

181. Robertson, S. (1988) op.cit., at p.100.

182. See Chapter 3 at para. 3.14.1.

183. Social Security Act 1975, s.37(5).

184. Social Security (Invalid Care Allowance) Regulations 1976, S.I. 1976 No.409, reg 11.

185. Bonner, D. et al. (1988) op.cit., at p.67.

186. *3 CMLR 43*.

187. Hansard, H.C. Written Answers, March 22, 1988 col.86.

188. Hansard, H.C. Written Answers, November 30, 1987, col.469.

189. Bonner, D. et al. (1988) op.cit., at p.66. The authors point out that advice contained in the DHSS pamphlet 'Which Benefits' is misleading in this respect.

190. S.I. 1976 No.409 op.cit., reg 4(1).

191. Bonner, D. et al. (1988) op.cit., at p.356.

192. S.I. 1976 No.409 op.cit., reg 4(2).

193. Social Security Act 1975, s.37(7).

194. s.37(2).

195. S.I. 1976 No.409 op.cit., reg 8.

196. For details, see Robertson, S. (1988) op.cit., at p.102.

197. Hansard, H.C. Written Answers, November 23, 1987 col.2.

198. Age Concern (1988) *Your Taxes and Savings 1988-1989* (Age Concern England) at p.17.

199. 'Social Security Facts and Figures' *Disability Rights* Spring 1988 (Disability Alliance), at p.17.

200. ibid. p.10. The 'case-load take-up rate' is that proportion of eligible claimants actually receiving the benefit.

201. Hansard, H.C. Written Answers, April 28, 1988 col. 249. See also 'Updates and Corrections' *Disability Rights* Summer 1988 at p.16.

202. Social Security Act 1986, s.20(3).

203. s.21.

204. Income Support (General) Regulations 1987 S.I. 1987 No.1967 reg 4. The Secretary of State, has announced that transitional protection is to be provided for disabled people, and pensioners who were receiving supplementary benefit but who

are not entitled to IS because of the changes in the rules. Under the previous rules claimants were allowed to work for up to 30 hours per week. See *Disability Rights: Update and Corrections* Summer 1988.

205. S.I. 1987 No.1967 op.cit., reg 6, that is, a voluntary worker is a person who only receives expenses. Note also that a carer can qualify if he/she receives invalid care allowance. See Sched 1 at para. 4.

206. Social Security Act 1986 s.20(11).

207. DHSS (1984) *The Supplementary Benefit Handbook* at para.2.13.

208. *Butterworth v. SBC [1982] 1 All ER 498.*

209. S.I. 1987 No.1967 op.cit., Sched 1, para.14

210. para.13.

211. Sched 10.

212. reg 53.

213. For other examples, see Mesher, J. (1988) *CPAG's Income Support, The Social Fund and Family Credit: The Legislation* (Sweet and Maxwell) at pp.93-95.

214. S.I. 1987 No. 1967 op.cit., Sched 10, para.5.

215. para. 13.

216. para. 2.

217 para. 3.

218. para. 4.

219. reg 2(1).

220. Social Security Act 1986, s.20(11).

221. S.I. 1987 No.1967 Sched 3, para. 4(8).

222. Hansard, H.C. April 27, 1988 col. 359.

223. S.I. 1987 No.1967 Sched 2, para. 5.

224. A disabled child premium can also be paid.

225. i.e., persons under 16, or under 19 if in full-time non-advanced education (up to A Level).

226. S.I. 1987 No.1967 Sched 2, para.9.

227. para. 12.

228. The claimant must have been incapable of work for 28 weeks.

229. S.I. 1987 No.1967 Sched 2, para. 10(3)(a). Sub-para. 3(b) allows a gap of eight weeks if it straddles the sixtieth birthday.

230. Citizens Rights Office (1988) *Welfare Rights Bulletin 83* April 1988 (CPAG) at p.10.

231. S.I. 1987 No.1967 Sched 2, para. 13 (2)(b). For the purposes of SDP, a person shall be treated as receiving attendance allowance, even though his/her attendance allowance, or that of the person for whom he/she is caring, has stopped because he/she, or that person, has been in hospital for more than four weeks, para. 13(3A). This provision does not apply to DP and HPP claimants.

232. para. 13. See also reg 3(2) and 3(3) for a definition of a 'non-dependant'.

233. Robertson, S. (1988) op.cit., at p.14.

234. for example, Family Credit or Housing Benefit.

235. S.I. 1987 No.1967 reg 42.

236. Sched 3, para. 1.

237. para. 7.

238. Social Security Act 1986, s.32A, inserted by Social Security Act 1988, Sched 3, para. 2.

239. DHSS (1987) *The Social Fund Manual* paras. 6387, 6388, and 6382.

240. ibid., direction 4.

241. ibid., direction 35.

242. ibid., para. 6054.

243. Hudson, B. (1987) 'Granted on condition' *Health Service Journal* November 19, 1987, at p.1354.

244. DHSS (1987) op.cit., direction 27. Also para. 6097.

245. The list is not exhaustive, nor is it in rank order, see para. 6025.

246. This is for a start-up grant.

247. ibid., para. 6057, as amended.

248. Social Fund (Applications) Regulations 1988 S.I. 1988 No.524.

249. Housing Benefit (General) Regulations S.I. 1987 No.1971, reg 72.

250. There is a ceiling on the total benefit any person may receive for housing costs, for example, 100 per cent for eligible rent, and 80 per cent for eligible rates.

251. S.I. 1987 No. 1971, regs 61,62.

252. Hansard, H.C. April 27, 1988, col.359.

253. 'Housing Benefit Concessions' *Disability Rights* Summer, op.cit., at p.8.

254. Citizens Rights Office (1988) op.cit., June 1988 at p.1.

255. HB(88)7; HB(88)8.

256. See discussion in relation to IS.

257. See Citizens Rights Office (1988) op.cit., August 1988 at p.3.

258. ibid.

259. Leaflet RR4.

260. Social Security and Housing Benefit Act 1982.

261. Citizens Rights Office (1988) op.cit., August 1988 at p.4.

262. Sherman, J. (1988) 'Moore acted illegally in cutting pensioners' benefits' *The Times* June 11, 1988.

263. S.I. 1987 No. 1971, op.cit., reg 8.

264. See leaflet F1G9, August 1988.

265. Press release, 1988.

266. Townsend, P. (1979) *Poverty in the United Kingdom* (Penguin Books Ltd); Midwinter, E. (1982) op.cit.

Chapter Two

LIVING IN THE COMMUNITY

2.1.1 ACCOMMODATION AND THE ELDERLY

The vast majority of people over pensionable age live in non-institutional accommodation. Around 95 per cent live in their own homes or with relatives, with almost one-half of this group occupying property owned either by themselves or their spouse. Approximately 40 per cent are public sector tenants, living in council houses or flats, with a further ten per cent living in privately rented accommodation.[1] This chapter looks mainly at the legal considerations relevant to those living in owner-occupied property, or who hold tenancies in the public or private sectors. Reference is also made, however, to that minority who for a variety of reasons find themselves homeless in old age.

2.2.1 HOMELESSNESS

The homeless, as such, have no legal right to accommodation of any kind. In exceptional circumstances, however, the Housing Act 1985 (HA 1985) places a duty upon local housing authorities (that is, district councils and, in London, the borough councils) to provide or arrange accommodation for certain categories of homeless people. The duty is owed to those with a 'priority need' which includes elderly people deemed vulnerable.[2] 'Vulnerability' is not defined in the Act but the Code of Guidance which accompanies it suggests that everyone above retirement age, and all those approaching that age who are particularly frail, or in poor health, or vulnerable for any other reason, should be treated as having a priority need on account of old age. In *R. v. Lambeth London Borough Council ex*

Living in the Community

parte Carroll (1987) the court was required to consider the meaning of the term 'vulnerable' for the purposes of the Act and to consider the extent of the local authority's duty to enquire into the circumstances of the applicant. The facts revealed that only evidence from the medical officer had been considered. It was held that the local authority had, therefore, failed in its duty to consider the case on its merits. The judge remarked that there were occasions when a medical report would constitute sufficient evidence.[3] In some circumstances, however, additional evidence might be required.

The duty to provide accommodation extends also to those who might reasonably be expected to live with the person to whom the duty is owed. In *R. v. London Borough of Lambeth ex parte Ly [1987]*,[4] the applicant was a 74 year old refugee who had fled from Vietnam with her son and daughter-in-law. The housing authority offered her, and the four elder grandchildren, a four-bedroomed flat, two miles away from the hotel where the rest of the family was accommodated. It was unsuccessfully argued that the housing authority was under a duty to offer accommodation large enough to house the whole family. It was held to be a question of fact for the authority to determine who might reasonably be expected to live with the applicant. It was relevant, in coming to a decision, for the authority to consider the nature and extent of the family unit, as well as the practicability of providing accommodation for such a large group.

An individual's particular circumstances will also need to be considered by the housing authority when deciding the length of time for which accommodation is to be provided.

2.2.2 The duty to re-house is qualified in several important ways. First, there is no right to accommodation where homelessness arose as the result of the homeless person's own acts or omissions, that is, where he/she has become intentionally homeless. Secondly, where the homeless person has a 'local connection' with another housing authority, the primary obligation of the authority to which application has been made, is to refer the applicant to that authority. A temporary housing duty lies with the authority while it is investigating the cause of homelessness, or where a priority need has been established but intentional homelessness is also found. A council need provide accommodation only for long enough to give the person

71

a reasonable opportunity of making other arrangements. Where temporary accommodation is provided, the housing authority may levy a charge for providing it.[5] The HA 1985 is silent as to the type of accommodation to be provided; it would seem that either public or private housing stock can be used. The Code of Guidance to the HA 1985 suggests, *inter alia,* that if an elderly person qualifies for accommodation under the Act and is in need of care and attention, the offer of Part III accommodation under the National Assistance Act 1948 (NAA 1948)(see Chapter 4 at para. 4.4.1), or the offer of other appropriate care, will be sufficient to satisfy the duty under the Act.[6] This is not to imply that a duty to provide Part III accommodation for a homeless person is thereby placed upon a social service authority.

2.2.3 Given these rules, the right to accommodation is limited, and is often dependent more upon the policy of the local housing authority than upon legal entitlement.[7] Ways of challenging such decisions are not readily available.[8] Nevertheless, the government is considering changing the definition of homelessness; a new definition might limit homelessness to 'rooflessness' - in other words, only those actually on the streets would be entitled to priority.

2.2.4 Section 14 of the Housing and Planning Act 1986 (HPA 1986), which amends the HA 1985, deals with the suitability of accommodation offered by a housing authority in discharging its duty towards a homeless person. The HPA 1986 specifies that in deciding what is suitable, the authority must have regard for other provisions in the HA 1985 relating to slum clearance (Part IX) to over-crowding (Part IV) and to houses in multiple occupation (Part XI). The HPA 1986 also provides that a person is not to be treated as having accommodation unless it is such as would be 'reasonable' for him/her to continue to occupy. In other words, it may now be easier for a person to be deemed homeless when he/she has inadequate accommodation. In determining what is 'reasonable', however, the general circumstances relating to housing in the district may be taken into account.

Once accommodation has been acquired, certain rights and responsibilities come into existence. The different types of accommodation and the obligations and entitlements which attach to each are examined below.

2.3.1 PUBLIC RENTED ACCOMMODATION

'Secure tenancies' were first introduced into the public sector by the Housing Act 1980 (HA 1980) so as to give tenants security of tenure similar to that enjoyed by tenants in the private sector under the Rent Act 1977 (RA 1977). (see para. 2.5.2 below). The provisions of the HA 1980 have subsequently been consolidated by the HA 1985, and further amended by the HPA 1986.

2.3.2 A secure tenancy arises whenever a landlord is a pre-scribed public body, that is, either a local authority, an urban development corporation, the Development Board for Rural Wales, the Housing Corporation, a housing trust which is a charity, a housing association, or an unregistered housing co-operative.[9] As a result of these statutory provisions, most, if not all, elderly people living in council or housing association property are secure tenants. The HA 1985 excluded some tenancies from complete security of tenure, but few of them are relevant here.[10] Those relevant to some elderly people include tenancies held in connection with employment, accommodation for homeless persons[11] and tenancies in almshouses. Full security is lost where a secure tenant assigns the tenancy, or sub-lets the whole property. (see below at para. 2.3.5) Legal proceedings must be brought before possession can be gained, however. Where no security of tenure exists, the only defence to any proceedings which are brought is to show that the authority is acting in abuse of its statutory powers.[12] The burden of proving abuse falls upon the tenant.

2.3.3 GROUNDS FOR POSSESSION

Where a tenancy is secure, the onus is upon the public authority landlord to show that granting termination of the tenancy would be justified on one or more of the 16 statutory grounds for possession set out in the HA 1985 (as amended).[13] Grounds 1-7 relate to a tenant's conduct and include non-payment of rent, breach of the tenancy agreement, committing a nuisance, allowing deterioration to the premises or fittings or making false state-ments. Ground 8 applies to any arrangement whereby a dwelling has been made temporarily available to the secure tenant while repair work is carried out on the original dwelling. Where proceedings for possession are based on grounds 1-8, the court must also be satisfied that it would be reasonable for the order to be granted. Thus, where possession against a secure tenant is sought on the basis of rent arrears, it might be deemed unreasonable to grant the order if rent had been withheld because of refusal by the landlord to carry out proper repairs. Similarly, where possession is being sought on the basis of ground 8 it might be successfully resisted if completion of repair work at the original dwelling had taken a considerable time[14] and the tenant was fully settled at the 'temporary' dwelling.

Grounds 9-11 provide for possession to be granted because the dwelling is overcrowded, needed for reconstruction or redevelopment,[15] or, where the landlord is a charity, and the tenant's continued occupation would conflict with the objects of the charity. In such cases, possession will be granted only if the court is satisfied that suitable alternative accommodation will be made available. Where the landlord is not a housing authority, that obligation will be satisfied if the local housing authority produces a certificate confirming that suitable accommodation will be made available. Where no certificate is issued, or if the landlord is a housing authority, the suitability criteria set out in the Act come into play.[16] The list of factors necessary to meet the suitability requirement is not exhaustive.[17] Among them is the distance between the alternative home and a member of the tenant's family where proximity is essential for the well-being of the family member, or of the tenant. The term 'family' is not defined but might be given a broad interpretation.[18]

A court cannot grant an order on grounds 12-16 unless it believes both that it is reasonable to make an order, and is satisfied that suitable alternative accommodation is available. Ground 12 relates to tied accommodation, that is, to a tenancy in property occupied only on the basis of particular employment, whereas grounds 13-15 relate to accommodation for persons with special needs. Ground 13 concerns the possession of properties designed specifically for the needs of disabled people and containing features 'substantially different' from those of ordinary dwellings. To be 'substantially different' the dwelling must have been designed for the special needs of the physically disabled. In *Freeman v. Wansbeck (1983)*[19] it was held that adding a ground floor toilet was not, in itself, sufficient to fulfill this requirement. Possession will be granted on the basis of ground 13 only if it can be shown that no disabled person continues to live in the dwelling, and that it is required for another disabled person. Similar conditions must exist for possession to be granted under grounds 14 and 15. Ground 15 applies where:

> The dwelling house is one of a group of dwelling-houses which it is the practice of the landlord to let for occupation by persons with special needs and -
>
> a) a social service or special facility is provided in close proximity to the group of dwelling houses in order to assist persons with those special needs,
> b) there is no longer a person with those special needs residing in the dwelling house, and
> c) the landlord requires the dwelling house for occupation (whether alone or with members of his/her family) by a person who has those special needs.[20]

Each one of these criteria needs to be satisfied before possession can be granted. It is assumed that should a warden service, provided for a sheltered housing complex, be discontinued, an application for possession under ground 15 might not be successful.

Ground 16 provides for the granting of possession where the tenant is occupying accommodation which is more extensive than he/she reasonably requires. It would not be sufficient to show that the dwelling was too large for the needs of the tenant since the right to possession on this ground applies only where the tenant has 'succeeded' to the tenancy. (see para. 2.3.4 below) This ground will not apply, moreover, where the 'successor' to the tenancy is the former tenant's spouse. It could not be used, therefore, to dispossess the widow/er of a deceased tenant. Furthermore, the statute specifically requires the court to take the tenant's age into account in determining whether an order is reasonable on ground 16. Two other factors must also be taken into account in deciding on the reasonableness of possession procedures. These include the period for which the tenant has occupied the dwelling; and any financial or other support given to the previous tenant by the current tenant of the premises. As indicated above, the burden of proof throughout is on the landlord who must show that, on a balance of probabilities, at least one of the grounds has been made out. In contrast to the situation in the private sector, no mandatory grounds for possession exist here. Even where a court grants a possession order, it has power to stay or suspend execution as long as it thinks fit.[21]

2.3.4 SUCCEEDING TO A TENANCY

Under the provisions of the HA 1985, the spouse of a deceased tenant, or another member of his/her family, including a cohabitee,[22] is entitled to succeed to a tenancy where certain conditions are met. To be entitled, a person must have been occupying the dwelling as his/her principal or only home at the time of the tenant's death. Where the would-be successor is not a spouse, he/she must have lived with the former tenant for a period of twelve months preceding his/her death.[23] In *South Northamptonshire District Council v. Power [1987]*[24] it was held that to succeed to a tenancy a common-law husband or wife must establish cohabitation for at least twelve months in a tenancy in the public sector. In that case, the would-be successor and the deceased tenant had lived together in public sector accommodation for nine months only. The cohabitee failed in an attempt to succeed to the tenancy although the couple had lived together in private accommodation for a number of years.

The statutory provisions allow for one succession only. Where the tenant's spouse has succeeded to the tenancy, a child living in the dwelling will have no further right of succession since a spouse is the preferred successor.[25]

2.3.5 ASSIGNMENT

Since the aim of public housing provision is to meet social need, the general rule is that a tenant cannot assign, that is, transfer, the tenancy to another person.[26] If a secure tenancy is assigned, it ceases to be secure, unless the assignment is the result of a property adjustment order under s.24 of the Matrimonial Causes Act 1973 (MCA 1973)(see Chapter 7 at para. 7.4.3), or is by way of mutual exchange, or is made to a person in whom the tenancy would, or might, have vested by virtue of the succession provisions. (see above at para. 2.3.3) Where assignment takes place in any of those circumstances, the assignee is entitled to full security even where the tenancy agreement contains a prohibition on assignment.[27] Assignments made by way of exchange require the landlord's written consent.[28] Where an assignment benefits a person who would be entitled to succeed to the tenancy on the death of the secure tenant, the assignee need not be the preferred successor. It is sufficient that the assignment is made to a person qualified to succeed. This provision could be used to avoid the 'spouse preference rule' described above, and so ensure that a child of the family, for example, succeeded to a secure tenancy. Such a step might be contemplated by an ageing parent anxious to provide security for a handicapped adult son or daughter living in the household. The provision might be more commonly used, however, by a tenant wishing to prevent a dispute between one of two potential successors, or in order to transfer the tenancy prior to retirement elsewhere. In *Peabody Donation Fund Governors v. Higgins [1983]*[29] the tenancy agreement contained an absolute prohibition on assignment. The tenant wished to retire to Ireland and to transfer the tenancy to a daughter who lived with him. He executed an assignment to her by deed. The court held that a secure tenancy had been validly assigned to the daughter but it was said *obita* that she might be vulnerable to an action for possession for breach of a term of the tenancy. Even so, a landlord could only succeed if it could be shown that he/she had acted reasonably. (see para. 2.3.3 above)

2.3.6 SUB-LETTING AND LODGERS

Tenants may take in lodgers without their landlord's consent but sub-letting the property requires agreement in writing.[30] Failure to obtain consent will not affect the existence of the sub-tenancy, but could make the main tenant liable to possession proceedings under ground 1.[31] In law, a lodger is deemed to be a licensee. In effect, he/she is no more than a paying guest.[32] The distinction between a lodger and a sub-tenant is, therefore, crucial in determining an individual's rights of possession.

Where the occupier is fully integrated into the tenant's household the likelihood is that he/she is a lodger. The usual test is whether or not the occupier has control over the whole of the property although the intention of the parties is also important. The following passage from an earlier judgement by Lord Denning was approved by Lord Templeman in the leading case of *Street v. Mountford [1985]*:

> In all the cases where the occupier has been held to be a licensee there has been something in the circumstances, such as a family arrangement, or act of friendship or generosity, or such like, to negative any intention to create a tenancy.[33]

It is unlikely, therefore, that elderly persons who have been 'boarded-out' under a local authority scheme (see Chapter 3 at para. 3.5.1) with a person who is a tenant; or who moves to live with relatives who are themselves tenants, will thereby become sub-tenants. Where an elderly person is anxious to ensure optimum autonomy, however, a sub-let should be considered. The HA 1985 states that a landlord's consent to a sub-letting must not to be withheld unreasonably.[34] If the whole of the property is sub-let, the tenant's security will be affected.[35] It would not, however, bring the tenancy to an end automatically. To recover possession, the landlord will need to bring the tenancy to an end on contractual or common law grounds.[36]

2.3.7 THE TERMS OF THE TENANCY

Landlords must provide their tenants with information which explains the terms of the tenancy and the provisions of Parts IV and V of the HA 1985 in clear and simple language.[37] The terms will usually continue unaltered until the tenancy is brought to an end in one of the ways described. They can be altered, however, by agreement or by 'notice of variation' served on the tenant by the landlord who must also invite the tenant's comments.[38] This provision ensures that a degree of prior consultation takes place before notice of variation can be served. Prior consultation is not, however, required if the variation applies simply to the rent, or to payment made in respect of services or facilities provided by the landlord, or to payment in respect of rates.[39] In such cases, the terms can be varied by giving one month's notice to the tenant. The only sanction then available to a tenant is to give notice to quit.[40] Where prior consultation is required, however, failure to take a tenant's comments into account would invalidate any variation in the terms of the tenancy. Tenants also have a statutory right to be consulted on matters of housing management, either individually or collectively, through a Tenant's Association.[41]

A tenancy remains secure until possession is granted by a court, or until it is surrendered by the tenant, or disposed of without the consent of the authority or terminated, subject to the right of succession, by the death of a secure tenant.[42]

The rules relating to repair and improvement of property which apply both in the public and private sectors are discussed below at para. 2.7.1. Some, however, apply specifically to secure tenancies and are, therefore, discussed here. A secure tenant may only carry out improvements with the landlord's written consent[43] which cannot be unreasonably withheld. The term 'improvement' is defined widely in this context so as to include any alteration or addition, such as putting up a television aerial or decorating the exterior.[44] A landlord may not increase the rent because of improvements to the property made by the tenant.[45] At the end of the tenancy, the tenant may be reimbursed for any authorised improvements provided the effect is to increase the property's notional market price, or to raise the level of rent at which it can then be let.[46] Reimbursement is limited, however, to the cost of the improvement, off-set by any grants received by the tenant.

2.3.8 As long as they have complied with certain procedural requirements, secure tenants have been entitled, since January 1986, to recover from their landlords the cost of 'qualifying repairs'.[47] 'Qualifying repairs' are repairs, other than to the structure or exterior of a flat, which the landlord is obliged to carry out because of a repairing convenant in the tenancy agreement.[48] A tenant wishing to make use of the statutory scheme must submit a claim on the prescribed Tenant's Repair Claim Form. The landlord then has 21 days in which to accept or to refuse it. The grounds for refusing a claim are limited[49] and where the landlord fails to respond, and the estimated cost is less than £200, a default notice can be served. If the landlord fails to respond within a further seven days, the tenant is entitled to carry out the repairs and claim their cost from the landlord.

2.3.9 'THE RIGHT TO BUY'

A 'right to buy' was introduced for tenants in the public sector by the HA 1980. The provisions are now to be found in Part V of the HA 1985, as amended by the HPA 1986. This right applies to all secure tenants, (other than those expressly excluded by the Act), who have occupied the dwelling for two or more years.[50] The right is preserved upon the disposal of the dwelling by a public landlord authority to a private sector landlord.[51] The Housing (Extension of Right to Buy) Order 1987 also confers a right to buy the freehold of a house upon secure tenants who have an intermediate public sector landlord and a public sector freeholder. In other words, the secure tenant's landlord has a lease and the freeholder and each intermediate landlord (should there be any) is an authority or body which would be subject to the right to buy were it the secure tenant's immediate landlord.[52]

2.3.10 Where tenancies are expressly excluded from the provisions of the HA 1985, the statutory right to buy will not arise. Those expressly excluded are tenancies granted by charitable housing trusts, charitable housing associations, housing co-operatives (that is, housing associations registered or deemed to be registered under the Industrial and Provident Society Act 1965 (IPSA 1965)), and housing associations which have never received public housing funds.[53]

Certain types of dwellings, listed in Sched. 5 of the HA 1985, are automatically excluded. They include specially designed dwellings for the physically disabled (paras. 6-8), group dwellings for persons who are mentally disordered (para. 9), group sheltered housing for persons of pensionable age where social service or special facilities are provided (para. 10). Dwelling houses which are particularly suitable for occupation by persons of pensionable age, having regard to their location, size, design, or heating system, can also become excluded from the provisions governing the right to buy. In determining whether a dwelling is 'particularly suitable', it is necessary to consider whether it is easily accessible on foot; is on one level; is accessible by lift if located above the ground floor; has no more than two bedrooms; or has a heating system serving the living room and at least one bedroom.[54] Dwelling houses which are particularly suitable in this way are not automatically excluded from the right to buy. In order to exclude them, the public authority must apply to the Secretary of State who, if satisfied that the dwelling house falls within the definition and that it has been the practice of the landlord to let it only to those of pensionable age, or to those who are physically disabled, must confirm the authority's decision. Single dwellings can also be excluded under paras. 6-8 of the Schedule. Para. 8 applies where one or more of three specific alterations have been carried out by the landlord. These are the provision of not less than 7.5 square metres of additional floor space; the provision of an additional bathroom or shower room; and the installation of a vertical lift.

Where there is a right to buy, three kinds of entitlement arise. First, a secure tenant may purchase the freehold from the landlord authority at a notional market value.[55] In effect, the purchase price is calculated on the basis of what the dwelling would fetch if sold by a willing vendor. The market value is set by the landlord authority but an appeal against it can be made to the district valuer.[56]

Secondly, the secure tenant is entitled to a discount which will vary according to the length of time he/she has occupied the dwelling as a public sector tenant. The minimum discount, where the dwelling is a house, is 32 per cent, plus one per cent for every complete year by which the qualifying period exceeds two years. At present, the maximum discount entitlement for a house is 60 per cent. The maximum discount for a flat, however, is 70 per cent. The way in which the discount is calculated also differs. In the case of a flat the minimum discount is 44 per cent plus a two per cent addition for each complete year by which the period of the qualifying tenancy exceeds two years.[57] On divorce from a secure tenant, or upon his/her death, the ex-spouse or widow/er may be able to take the time spent occupying the property with the secure tenant into account.[58]

Thirdly, a secure tenant has a right, provided he/she is not a bankrupt, to a mortgage to cover the purchase price and costs.[59] A tenant who is entitled to the right to buy but is not eligible for a full mortgage, has a right to a shared ownership lease at a premium.[60] This is a lease whereby the purchaser pays a premium for a share in the dwelling. The purchaser is thereafter able to purchase further shares until he/she has acquired a 100 per cent share. The rent paid during the period of acquisition is reduced in accordance with the percentage share that the purchaser has already acquired.

Alternatively, private financial arrangements can be made, for example, with a bank or a building society. Many building societies are prepared to consider giving elderly people interest-only mortgages with the capital being repaid when the property is eventually sold. Some societies apparently require applicants for interest-only schemes to be at least 60 years of age. Others are more flexible, especially where the applicant is already retired.[61]

A purchaser may nominate up to a maximum of three family members to share the right to buy. To qualify automatically, an individual must either have been living with the secure tenant as his/her spouse, or must have been living in the dwelling for at least twelve months before the right to buy is exercised. In all other circumstances, the right to nominate additional joint purchasers can be exercised only with the landlord's consent. If the power to nominate 'deemed joint tenants' is exercised, however, but the parties are subsequently in dispute, the additional purchasers may be unable to demand that the property be sold.[62]

2.3.11 The 'right to buy' option has already been exercised by many elderly people. It may also be extended to those living in accommodation purpose-built for disabled people. The social and financial implications of taking this step should, however, be carefully considered. Those contemplating it should be advised that becoming a home owner is likely to lessen their chance of being accepted on to waiting lists for public sector rented accommodation in the future.[63] Any housing benefit (HB) received by the purchaser would be unlikely to cover all housing costs. Help may still be available with rates, in spite of changes to the social security provisions, but even those on income support (IS) will have to contribute 20 per cent towards their rates bill. A notional figure of £1.30 towards rates payments has been added to IS provisions in the form of a personal allowance. Under the new social security scheme, water rates and residual housing costs, such as maintenance and insurance, will have to be met from personal allowances. The new income support rules are more specific than the previous ones in relation to housing costs which are deemed 'excessive'. Restrictions apply where a dwelling is 'larger than is required .... having regard in particular to suitable alternative accommodation occupied by a household of the same size'.[64] The restrictions may, therefore, be applied more vigorously in future.[65] Assistance with mortgage interest payments and certain service charges are among the items deemed eligible as housing costs under the new scheme.(see Chapter 1 at 1.24.15) Those not entitled to IS should establish whether service charges will be payable after purchase. In a recent case[66] it was decided that landlords have a right to levy service charges (which include elements for both improvement and repair) where the purchaser has been expressly notified that such expenditure would be necessary.

Any discount received by the purchaser is not repayable on his/her death. A subsequent disposal by his/her dependants could, however, bring the repayment provisions into operation, since a discount is normally repayable in whole or in part if the property is sold within three years of the purchase.[67]

Tying up savings in property can lead to financial hardship. Several schemes have been devised to assist owner-occupiers with cash flow problems which are most likely to arise where maintenance costs are high. It should be noted that some 84 per cent of local authority housing stock needs renovation, at an average cost of £4,900 per dwelling.[68]

2.4.1 *SHELTERED HOUSING*

Sheltered housing units provide special facilities for elderly or disabled people which may include the services of a resident warden. In some areas, other support services are provided such as care officers, special home-helps, or a meal service.[69] It is estimated that about 700,000 residents in England and Wales are accommodated in public sector housing (that is, local authority or housing association property) specially designed for elderly people. This is approximately seven per cent of the pensioner population. Only about half the sheltered housing units also have a resident warden attached to them.[70] Research sponsored by the House Builders Federation in 1983 concluded that, had sheltered housing been available, about twelve per cent of elderly owner-occupiers would choose to buy such accommodation.[71] Indeed, the sheltered housing market has recently been assuming the characteristics of a mixed economy. Conferences on housing for the elderly are frequently sponsored by private developers. A working party set up by Age Concern concluded that the private sector may well become 'the third arm' of sheltered housing provision.[72] According to a study by the National Institute of Social Work up to approximately one-third of residents currently in residential homes could be successfully re-accommodated in specially adapted sheltered housing.[73] But the number of elderly persons accommodated in sheltered housing, although increasing, remains well below estimated need.[74] Many of the elderly from ethnic minorities, for example, apparently receive poor and inappropriate services. At least two housing associations, ASRA and CARIB, have been established to provide for the respective needs of elderly people from Asian and West Indian backgrounds.[75]

2.4.2 As indicated in para. 2.3.2, those living in sheltered accommodation provided by housing authorities or housing associations are likely to be secure tenants and so will enjoy all those benefits with the possible exception of the right to buy.(see para. 2.3.10 above) Local housing authorities may make such reasonable charges as they may determine. They have considerable freedom, therefore, in setting rent levels as long as they act reasonably.[76] On the other hand, housing associations are currently subject to the 'fair rent' procedure.(see para. 2.6.1 below) Excess payment of rent may be recovered by the tenant up to two years after it was paid.[77]

2.4.3 Sheltered housing in the voluntary or private sectors fall outside the full protection of the RA 1977 (see para. 2.6.1 below) if a substantial part of the rent is payable for 'attendance'.[78] 'Attendance' is not defined in the Act, but has been interpreted by the courts to mean provision for the tenant of personal services which benefit his/her enjoyment of the premises.[79] The emphasis has been on services being personal rather than communal, for example, the cleaning of parts of the premises which are used in common. The statutory exception will apply where the provision of personal services, which might include the services of a warden, constitutes a substantial proportion of the total rent. From decided cases, it would appear that this is legally satisfied if the cost of attendance amounts to 14 per cent of the rent.[80] Since the 'attendance' element is calculated from the commencement of the tenancy, Rent Act protection may be available to many whose dependence upon personal services is initially small. Should the cost of providing personal services subsequently rise substantially, the court might decide that the tenancy should then be brought within the statutory exception.[81]

2.4.4 SERVICE CHARGES

Service charges levied as a result of the provision by the landlord of common services to all residential lettings or flats in a particular area, are often a source of complaint since tenants may feel they have little control over the level of charges which are made. Tenants of flats other than those owned by a local authority, or by the Development Board for Rural Wales are, however, provided with some protection by the Landlord and Tenant Act 1985 (LTA 1985).[82] Section 19 of the LTA 1985 provides that 'reasonably incurred' amounts only are payable for services, and that work carried out must be of reasonable standard. Tenants also have a statutory right, either individually or collectively,[83] to ask the landlord for a written summary of the relevant costs. They are also entitled to inspect the accounts, receipts, and other supporting documents relating to the summary of expenditure. Failure on the part of a landlord to comply with the above provisions is an offence which, on conviction, can lead to a maximum fine of £1000.

Similar restrictions on levying service charges where houses have been disposed of by public sector authorities are contained in the HA 1985.[84] Public sector authorities include registered housing associations as well as local authorities and other public bodies. For this purpose, 'disposal' includes the conveyance of the freehold. Thus, the restrictions would apply, for example, where services are provided to an estate of houses, some of which have been purchased under the statutory provisions relating to 'the right to buy'.(see para. 2.3.9 above)

2.4.5 A growth in the market for private sheltered housing for sale has led to a variety of schemes devised to assist purchasers with the capital cost. The available options include shared ownership schemes; special leasehold schemes; loan stock and investment schemes; and purchase at a discount.[85] Full discussion of the various schemes is beyond the scope of this book and prospective purchasers, particularly those with insufficient means to make outright purchases, are advised, before they commit themselves, to refer to the booklet 'Housing Options for Older People' published by Age Concern.[86]

2.5.1   PRIVATELY RENTED ACCOMMODATION

Approximately ten per cent of elderly couples and 14 per cent of the single elderly live in rented accommodation in the private sector.   The rights of such tenants are of particular importance since private tenants, generally, and private elderly tenants, in particular, live in accommodation of a poorer standard than any other housing group.[87]   Three issues, in particular, require examination.

2.5.2   SECURITY OF TENURE

The tenant of a house let as a separate dwelling, who neither shares accommodation with the landlord nor pays for board and attendance[88] is normally protected under the RA 1977.   There are some exceptions, however, including tenancies at low rents, holiday lettings and shorthold tenancies (that is, tenancies for fixed periods of twelve months or more).   Licences (see para. 2.3.6 above) are excluded from full Rent Act protection but the use of this statutory loop-hole so as to avoid Rent Act protection, has been largely closed by the courts and few agreements are now treated as licences.[89]

Under the RA 1977, security of tenure is provided in two ways.   First, the Act restricts the grounds upon which a landlord can obtain possession.   Secondly, through the creation of a statutory tenancy, it provides the tenant, or a person entitled to succeed to the tenancy, with a personal right to remain in possession at the end of the contractual tenancy.

2.5.3   The statutory grounds upon which possession can be obtained are listed in Sched. 15 to the RA 1977.   In some cases, the court has discretion whether or not to grant possession whereas, in other circumstances, it is mandatory.   The discretionary grounds (cases 1-10) closely resemble grounds 1-8 under the HA 1985 (see para. 2.3.3 above) though differences also exist.   The existence of alternative suitable accommodation, for example, effectively amounts to an additional discretionary ground.[90] Another difference is that case 9 has no parallel with provisions under the HA 1985. This allows a landlord to recover possession under the RA 1977 where the dwelling is reasonably required for occupation by him/herself, or by a parent or a parent-in-law. It must be shown that the need is genuine. It would not be sufficient, for instance, for it to be needed simply as temporary accommodation while repairs are being carried out at the home of the landlord or a relative.[91] It is not possible either to rely on case 9 if the landlord 'purchased' the dwelling after the protected tenant had come into possession of it. This restriction does not apply where the landlord 'inherited' the dwelling or acquired it through a family settlement.[92] A tenant has a complete defence to possession proceedings brought under case 9 if it can be shown that he/she would suffer greater hardship if a possession order were granted, than would be caused to the landlord if it were refused. One of the factors which a court can take into account in assessing the extent of hardship is the health of the parties and their physical proximity to relatives.[93]

The grounds for mandatory possession in the RA 1977 may be more relevant to elderly people as landlords than as tenants. Case 11, as amended by the Rent (Amendment) Act 1985 (R(A)A 1985)[94] provides for possession by owner-occupiers who have let their property during a period of absence. It also provides, *inter alia,* for possession where the owner has died, and a member of the family residing with him/her at the time of death, requires the house as a residence. Case 12 may have even greater relevance since it allows possession to be granted to an owner who requires the premises as a retirement home. It is not necessary for the landlord to have resided in the dwelling. Case 19 applies where a dwelling was let as a protected shorthold tenancy. Such tenancies must be for a fixed period of not less than one year and for not more than five. If the tenancy includes a 'break clause' which permits the landlord to bring it to an end before the expiry of the fixed period for any reason other than non-payment of rent, or breach of any of the obligations of the tenancy, it will not be valid as a shorthold tenancy.[95]

A landlord must give a tenant written notice that possession is recoverable on one of the mandatory grounds. Sched. 15, however, provides that this requirement can be dispensed with if the court thinks it just and equitable to grant a possession order. Where one of the grounds for mandatory possession exists, it may be held sufficient, in some circumstances, for oral notice only to be given.[96]

2.5.4 A court may suspend or postpone the coming into operation of a possession order based upon one of the discretionary cases.[97] Even where valid grounds for possession exist, a tenancy can normally be terminated only by service of a notice to quit in the prescribed form.[98] The Protection from Eviction Act 1977 (PfEA 1977) requires at least four weeks notice to be given.[99] Where a tenancy has become a statutory tenancy, however, a landlord is not obliged to provide notice to quit before possession proceedings are brought. A statutory tenant will, nevertheless, remain liable for rent until the statutory tenancy comes to an end. It can be terminated either by the granting of a possession order, or through a voluntary agreement between landlord and tenant, or by the tenant serving notice to quit.[100]

2.5.5 SUCCEEDING TO A TENANCY

When a protected tenant dies, a surviving spouse who was living with the tenant at the time of his/her death, or, if there is no such spouse, a member of the tenant's family who had lived with the tenant for two years immediately before his/her death, has a right to have the tenancy transmitted to him/her.[101] The spouse provision has been extended by the Housing Act 1988 (HA 1988) to include a person who was living with the original tenant as his/her wife or husband.

The surviving spouse, and other members of the tenant's family, must show they were 'residing with' the tenant at the time of death.[102] From the decision in *Foreman v. Beagley [1969]*,[103] it would seem, however, that the courts may be prepared to extend the definition of 'residing with' to include situations where family members were not in fact residing with one another at time of death, for example, where the tenant was in hospital when he/she died. In that case, a widow had succeeded to the tenancy of a flat upon the death of her husband. From 1965 until her own death in 1968 she was in hospital. In 1967, her son moved into the flat and lived there until his mother's death. Evidence was presented to show that he would have stayed there to look after his mother had she been able to return from hospital. The court held, however, that there had been no factual 'community of living', nor any agreement to establish such community during the relevant period. It took the view that, throughout, the son had been in the position of caretaker. A similar decision was reached in *Swanbrae Ltd v. Elliott [1986]*[104] where a daughter, who retained another residence, spent three or four nights a week with her mother during the latter's terminal illness. It was held that she was not residing with her mother.

Not all of those who are relatives of the tenant are to be treated as members of his/her family. The courts have applied the common-sense test of what an ordinary person would say when asked whether or not a particular individual was a member of the tenant's family. This is known as 'the family nexus test'.[105] The conduct of the parties can also be taken into account and the more remote the relationship the more important that is likely to be. In *Longdon v. Hoiton [1951]*,[106] the court held that two sisters who had gone to live with their widowed cousin and remained with her until she died 29 years later, did not qualify as members of her family. They had simply shared the flat with their cousin for their own convenience. But in *Jones v. Whitehill [1950]*,[107] it was held that a niece who had moved to look after her elderly aunt and uncle was a member of their family.

With one exception, a person not related to the tenant by blood or marriage cannot qualify under these provisions. It would not be sufficient, for example, for a person to refer to the tenant as 'aunt' or 'uncle'.[108] The exception applied to unmarried cohabitees but only where the relationship was permanent and had resulted in children. In such cases, the survivor would probably qualify.[109] The law, however, was amended and clarified by the HA 1988.

2.5.6 Where a qualifying relative existed, two transmissions of the statutory tenancy were possible until the HA 1988 came into force. From January 15, 1989, only one statutory succession will be possible, irrespective of whether or not there was a succession prior to the implementation of the Act.[110]

Where more than one member of the family is eligible to succeed and a dispute arises, the issue will need to be decided by the courts. The RA 1977 does not indicate the grounds upon which the court should reach its decision, but, in deciding relative merits, a claimant's age is relevant.[111]

2.5.7 RESTRICTED CONTRACTS

Tenants or licencees excluded from full Rent Act protection may be given a limited degree of security by means of a restricted contract which can arise in two situations. First, the contract for the occupation of the dwelling may provide for a sum to be paid for the use of furniture, or for the provision of services (see para. 2.4.3) and, secondly, the landlord may be resident.[112] Where a restricted contract exists, there will be limited security for up to three months only, or up to six months where the letting began before November 28, 1980.[113]

Purpose-built blocks of flats are expressly excluded, thus giving the tenants full protection. In this context, a 'purpose built block of flats' means no more than a building containing two or more flats.[114]

No restricted contract tenancies can be created after January 15, 1989. New tenants of residential landlords will be completely unprotected. Existing restricted contracts will continue to enjoy limited protection.

2.5.8 UNLAWFUL EVICTION AND HARASSMENT

Section 1 of the PfEA 1977 provides 'residential occupiers' with a degree of protection from unlawful eviction and harassment. Two separate offences are created by this provision:

(1) attempting to evict without getting a court order; and
(2) harassing a residential occupier.

Section 1(3) of the PfEA 1977, as amended by the HA 1988, provides that:

> If any person with intent to cause the residential occupier of any premises

a) to give up the occupation of the premises or any part thereof; or
b) to refrain from exercising any right or pursuing any remedy in respect of the premises or part thereof;

does acts *likely* to interfere with the peace or comfort of the residential occupier or members of his household, or persistently withdraws or withhold services reasonably required for the occupation of the premises as a residence, he shall be guilty of an offence. (*our emphasis*).

The term 'residential occupier' covers most licensees although protection under the PfEA 1977 does not extend to restricted contract licensees if the licence was created before November 28, 1980.[115] Restricted contract licensees of longer standing are not totally unprotected, however, since anyone who, without lawful authority, uses or threatens to use violence (against the person or against the property) to secure entry against the will of the lawful occupier will be liable to prosecution under the Criminal Law Act 1977 (CLA 1977).[116] The offence of harassment under the PfEA 1977 can be committed by 'any person' and not simply by the landlord, and can extend to any 'member of the household'. Harrassment could be committed against friends of the tenant and might even extend to acts against pets.[117] The HA 1988 will make it easier to establish the offence since it is now only necessary to prove that the landlord *knows or has reasonable cause to believe* that the conduct is likely to cause the occupier to cease occupation. Previously it had been necessary to show specific intent. It must be shown that the act is likely to interfere with the peace and comfort of the residential occupier. Failure by a landlord to pay a gas or electricity bill which resulted in disconnection on one occasion, for example, may not be sufficient to establish the offence.[118] In such cases, the tenant's remedy is to sue for breach of the right to quiet enjoyment.[119] Penalties for the offence are a fine or imprisonment, or both.

It will also be possible under the HA 1988 to bring an action for damages. The sum involved could be substantial. The amount is to be calculated by subtracting the value of the premises, if the tenant had remained in occupation, from the value of the premises with vacant possession.

Every local housing authority must employ a harassment officer, part of whose job is to investigate allegations of harassment and to prosecute if that is deemed appropriate.

2.6.1 RENT CONTROL

The rent of privately rented accommodation is normally what is specified in the agreement to let. A rent book must be provided for weekly tenancies. This duty applies both to tenants and to contractual licensees.[120] Those whose rent includes payment in respect of board are denied this protection, however.[121] A landlord's failure to provide a rent book does not excuse the tenant from paying rent.[122]

On application by either the tenant or the landlord, tenancies covered by the RA 1977 may be subject to the 'fair rent' procedure. A Rent Officer, who can be contacted via the local authority, has a right to impose a fair rent, which on registration, replaces the one which had been contractually agreed. The landlord may not, for a subsequent period of two years, charge rent in excess of the fair rent. There is a right of appeal from the decision of the Rent Officer to a rent assessment committee.[123] In determining a fair rent, the type, location and condition of the premises must be taken into account but not any improvements which have been carried out, nor any disrepair caused by the tenant, nor the personal circumstances of the parties. In the case of a restricted contract, a procedure exists for registering a 'reasonable' rent. The limited security of the restricted contractee may, however, make it less likely that the matter will be referred to a Rent Officer.

Prior to the HA 1980, certain lettings at a low rent, and of a low rateable value, were known as controlled tenancies. The rent of such premises was strictly limited at law. Since November 1980, this category of letting has been abolished and is now subject to the fair rent review. Those affected may be eligible for help under the housing benefit scheme.

2.6.2 A recent development in this field is the erosion of protection previously provided by protected shorthold tenancies and assured tenancies. Protected shorthold tenancies were initially subject to the 'fair rent' procedure but, since May 4,

1987, there have been no prescribed rent levels for such tenancies.[124] Assured tenancies are of two types. The first, little used,[125] arose under the HA 1980 when an 'approved landlord' constructed or carried out works on a dwelling involving expenditure of a prescribed amount.[126] The prescribed amount in London was £7,000 and £5,000 elsewhere. No statutory rent levels apply to assured tenancies.[127] The second type, created under the HA 1988, bears no similarity to the above. After January 15, 1988, it will be impossible to create the old type. Existing assured tenancies will be automatically converted into the new form of assured tenancy. (see below at para. 2.13.1) The term is somewhat of a misnomer for the Act provides for minimal rent control and minimal security. The lettings will be at market rents. Rent officers will have no jurisdiction over the initial rents charged. The only control will be where landlords wish to increase the rent. Even this limited control can be excluded by an express provision in the tenancy agreement. Where objection is possible, the matter will be determined by a rent assessment committee (RAC). An application to a RAC must be made within three months of service of the notice proposing new terms. If the time limit is passed, the proposed new terms take effect automatically.

2.6.3 No rent control as such exists in the public sector. Local authorities can charge whatever rent they wish in accordance with their housing policy, subject only to review by the courts of what is reasonable.

2.7.1 REPAIRS AND IMPROVEMENTS

A number of important statutory provisions ensure that privately rented houses and flats are put into, and kept in, reasonable repair, and that certain basic facilities are provided. Many of these provisions also apply to publicly rented accommodation and owner-occupied property. Where there is overlap, this is noted below. In many cases, however, secure tenants will not need to use these remedies since they are able to take advantage of the statutory repair scheme. (see para. 2.3.8)

The landlord of property rented after 1961 must keep the structure, exterior, services and installations in repair and in working order.[128] This duty is independent of, and in addition to, any repairing obligations set out in the tenancy agreement itself. These provisions apply in both the public and private sectors. A landlord must maintain premises let at a low rent in a condition fit for human habitation.[129] Should the state of disrepair or lack of facilities cause a statutory nuisance prejudicial to health or safety, the environmental health department of the local authority or, ultimately, the magistrates' court, can order the nuisance to be eradicated.[130] Statutory remedies are also available to tenants to compel a landlord to meet his/her obligations.[131] These appear to be little used.

Local authorities have a duty to investigate any complaint that property is unfit for habitation, or in a state of substantial disrepair. Notice can be served under the HA 1985 to compel repairs to be carried out, or to order the closure or demolition of the property.[132] A tenant or occupier displaced in this way is entitled to be rehoused.[133] The courts have held that where a local authority is itself responsible for the disrepair, it cannot be forced to serve notice on itself under the Act.[134]

2.7.2 Given the apparent extent of disrepair and lack of facilities in many premises (particularly in the privately rented sector), a more effective method may be needed to oversee complaints about the condition of rented property. Currently, neither the County Court nor the High Court appear to provide the necessary remedies.

In some circumstances, it is legally possible for tenants themselves to carry out repairs. First, where landlords are in breach of their contractual obligation to repair, a right exists at common law to do what is necessary, and recover the costs out of the rent.[135] This right provides a tenant, sued for unpaid rent, with a complete defence. Tenants need to show, however, that they have followed certain procedures. They must inform the landlord what action they intend to take and then allow a reasonable time for the work to be carried out. They should then submit copies to the landlord of estimates for carrying out the work, together with a final warning. They may engage a contractor at the lowest tender and submit a copy of the invoice to the landlord. If the landlord makes no payment, tenants may then recoup the amount which has been spent through deductions from rent.

Where a tenant is in receipt of HB, the paying authority will need to be informed of the tenant's intention to use this procedure, otherwise payment of HB may be withheld. In order that direct action can be taken, benefit should be paid in cash rather than by means of credit.[136] The right to use rent for repairs may not always be available, however. It is uncertain at present whether the right can be excluded by an express term in the tenancy agreement.

The equitable remedy of set-off provides a similar remedy. This allows a tenant to claim not only the cost of repairs but also the cost of any damage that may have resulted from lack of repair, for example, the replacement of furniture or carpets. The set-off can be raised as a defence to any claim for rent by the landlord. It would need to be shown that it would be inequitable to allow the landlord to recover the amount claimed in view of the counter-claim made by the tenant. It will be in the most serious cases only that a tenant will succeed in establishing a counter-claim sufficient to amount to a complete defence to the landlord's claim. Nevertheless, the procedure can be usefully employed to hold off, for a considerable period of time, proceedings for arrears or possession.[137]

These remedies have to be distinguished from a rent strike. Tenants have no right in law to withhold rent in protest where landlords have failed to carry out repairs. Tenants in the private sector can, however, apply to the court for the appointment of a receiver where disrepair arises from the landlord's neglect. The Landlord and Tenant Act 1987 (LTA 1987) simplifies the procedure. It provides a tenant with the right to apply to a County Court for an order appointing a manager to take over management of the premises. The court will need to be satisfied, *inter alia*, that the appointment of a manager is the appropriate remedy.[138]

2.8.1 IMPROVEMENTS TO PROPERTY

On the whole, elderly people live in housing which is older, which is in the worst state of repair, and which is least likely to contain standard amenities. According to information from the 1981 Population Census, 6.8 per cent of the elderly aged 75 living alone, live in houses with no inside toilet, compared to 2.5 per cent of all non-elderly households. Almost half the households headed by a person who is 65 years old, or over, lack at least one basic amenity, for example, an inside WC or a bath. Fifty-five per cent of accommodation with no indoor WC is owned by people of retirement age.[139] Substantial financial assistance is available to help owners and tenants improve their homes. The legal provisions are to be found in the HA 1985. Intermediate grants, which are mandatory, are available for the installation of standard amenities, including a bath or shower, hot and cold running water, an inside WC and access facilities for the disabled. Normally, applicants receive 75 per cent of the cost of the work. In cases of hardship, the local authority can increase the grant to 90 per cent of the cost. Circular 21/80 suggests that very sympathetic consideration should be given to an applicant whose main source of income is a state retirement pension.[140] Moreover, if houses lack these basic amenities, housing authorities are entitled to enforce improvements against a private landlord. Where other improvements are needed, however, these cannot be enforced against the wishes of the private landlord. The landlord's consent is usually necessary. Landlords are entitled to apply for grants themselves but, from January 15, 1989, will only be entitled to 20 per cent of the cost of the work

Improvement grants are discretionary but are available for a wider range of improvements. They can be used to bring property up to the required standard and can cover installation of a damp proof course as well as structural alterations. Eligibility depends upon the rateable value of the premises. The Secretary of State has expressed the hope that authorities will give maximum help for improvements to premises occupied by disabled people.[141] The rules concerning the amount of grant available are similar to those which apply to intermediate grants, but since local authorities have discretion in this matter, the amount awarded may be less than the maximum possible.

Repair grants are available for pre-1919 houses to cover the repair of existing structures or fixtures, such as roofs, windows and walls. Over 40 per cent of those who are 75 years old or over live in property dating from this period.[142] These grants are also discretionary, unless the work has been ordered under the 'unfit' procedures described above. (see para. 2.7.1) The same rules apply to grants available to improve houses in multiple occupation.

In certain circumstances, local authorities can give more

than the specified statutory amounts for work carried out under the HA 1985. They may even lend an applicant the balance of the cost not covered by the grant.[143]

2.8.2 Grants made by local authorities range in amount from £400 to £13,000 depending on the type of grant, the area, the maximum percentage grant and so on.[144] It should be noted that work carried out for disabled people or to secure basic amenities are not subject to rateable value limits. The government has indicated, however, that major changes are to be made to the way financial aid is given to owner-occupiers wishing to improve or repair their properties. A new form of mandatory grant will be available to bring a property to a new standard of fitness. Additional grant aid will also be available at the discretion of local authorities. Eligibility for grants will no longer be based on a property's rateable value but will be means-tested and linked to IS and HB.[145]

2.8.3 Where an applicant is an owner-occupier, or the tenant of a local authority, or a housing association, he/she may be eligble for a grant towards the cost of insulating the property if the landlord agrees. Grants are available for those in receipt of IS or HB. A 90 per cent grant is available, subject to a maximum amount of £137. Local authorities have been asked to give priority to applications by elderly people but are free to determine their own priorities.[146]

2.9.1 PURCHASING THE FREEHOLD

Owner-occupiers in leasehold property can, in certain circumstances, purchase the reversionary interest and become owners of the freehold. To do so could well be in the interest of an individual whose lease has a relatively short time to run. Under the Leasehold Reform Act 1967 (LRA 1967), a lessee of at least three years standing may compel the lessor (landlord) to sell the freehold or extend the lease by 50 years, if the lease is of a house (not a flat) below a certain rateable value and the original lease was for at least 21 years. Where there is dispute, the price can be settled by a valuation tribunal and is normally a multiple of the existing ground rent. The LTA 1987 gives tenants of privately owned blocks of flats a right of pre-emption on the sale by their landlord of his interest in the property.[147] On receipt of notice from the landlord of his/her intention to sell and the proposed price, the tenant has two months in which to accept, reject or make a counter-offer. An acceptance will be valid if it is agreed by a bare majority of tenants. A rejection allows a landlord a year in which to dispose of his/her interest, provided that it is not for less than the offer made to the tenants.

2.10.1 ADAPTATIONS FOR THE DISABLED

There are statutory provisions which allow accommodation to be adapted to suit the needs of some disabled and many elderly people. These duties apply both to owner/occupied and rented accommodation. The Chronically Sick and Disabled Persons Act 1970 (CSDPA 1970) (as amended) sets out the rules in general terms. (see Chapter 3 at paras. 3.8.2; 3.10.1) A duty is also imposed on local housing authorities under the 1970 Act and the HA 1985 to consider the housing needs of their district and to have particular regard for the special needs of chronically sick and disabled people. There is no need for a person to be registered as disabled in order to benefit from these provisions.

Social service authorities may levy charges so as to recover all or part of any sum spent on an adaptation. It is always advisable, therefore, to make maximum use of the grants discussed above.(see para. 2.8.1) The only assistance which is available, however, may be that provided under s.2 of the 1970 Act, since improvement grants, as indicated above, are discretionary and may not be available at all in some areas. Social service assistance could also be used to top-up any grant received under the HA 1985 provisions. It would, however, be necessary to satisfy the local authority that need, as defined under s.1 of the CSDPA 1970, existed. (see Chapter 3 at paras. 3.8.1-3.8.4)

2.10.2 Special grants from the Housing Corporation are available for housing associations engaged in providing housing for handicapped people. Information about these grants and their availability does not seem to be widespread. As a consequence, government spending in this area has been below target.[148]

It should also be noted that goods and services supplied in connection with the provision of services to disabled people are zero-rated for the purpose of VAT.[149]

2.11.1 RENT REBATES FOR PERSONS WITH DISABILITIES

The Rating (Disabled Persons) Act 1978 (R(DP)A 1978) requires rating authorities to grant rebates on premises where certain facilities are required to meet the needs of a disabled resident.[150] The amount of the rebate will vary according to the nature of the facility. Those which give rise to a rebate are: a room used predominantly by a disabled person; an additional bathroom or WC; heating in two or more rooms; floor space for a wheelchair; and a garage, car port or land for a vehicle. An applicant who is refused a rebate can appeal to the County Court. Legal Aid is available. Rating authorities and the court can backdate the rebate in appropriate cases.[151]

2.12.1 DISPOSING OF OWNER-OCCUPIED PROPERTY

Owner-occupiers may decide, for a variety of reasons, that they are no longer able, or no longer wish to remain in their own homes. The disposal of a substantial asset such as a house or flat can affect benefit entitlement and the amount to be paid for residential accommodation, (see Chapter 1 at para. 1.24.9 and Chapter 4 at paras. 4.5.9-4.5.16) Elderly persons may be caught in a dilemma whether or not to dispose of property. The house they live in may be too large for their needs, but they may hesitate to dispose of it for fear of depriving family members of a valuable asset. They may, however, need to convert a capital asset into realisable income.

What choices are available? Capital could be realised by the sale of the property and the purchase of something smaller or more suitable. This trade-down may result in considerable outlay on legal and related fees. Or property could be mortgaged to realise an income and the money used to purchase an annuity. The Chancellor is currently considering proposals that would give tax relief to elderly home owners who raise a mortgage on their property so as to buy an annuity. The loan itself is then repaid out of the person's estate when he/she dies. Such schemes are usually referred to as home income plans. Expert advice should usually be sought because some may be unsuitable. The loan interest may be fixed at the outset and does not change, but in other schemes the interest rate fluctuates with the market, which means the level of income also fluctuates. The latter type would be unsuitable for individuals who want to know exactly how much they are to receive each week.[152] A third alternative, which might be considered by those with large houses, is to donate the property to a charity which in return for the transfer, maintains it and allows the donor to live there rent free. While this could be made into a legally enforceable agreement, in practice, arrangements for the maintenance of the property are often informal, once the property has been transferred to the charity. It has been suggested elsewhere that arrangements of this kind are frequently unsatisfactory.[153]

Many people with a house too large for their needs may choose to let part of it. It has been noted already that a tenant with a resident landlord will have no security of tenure under the HA 1988, although possession proceedings would have to be brought should the tenant not leave on being served with the requisite notice. Possession under the HA 1988 will be a much simpler and less complex process since only limited security is available. (see para. 2.6.1 above) One of the most commonly used options, however, is for elderly people to live with their families. At first sight, this may appear the most convenient and attractive arrangement. Where the elderly person continues to live in his/her own home, legal problems are unlikely to arise, except possibly where family members make a contribution towards the capital.(see Chapter 7 at para. 7.18.1) Difficulties can arise, however, where elderly people give up their own property and move to live with relatives or friends. Sharing a house may prove difficult, and the parties may have fundamental disagreements. At worst, this can lead to costly and distressing litigation. Unless an elderly person becomes a joint owner, he/she may have no security of tenure and, ultimately, may have to move into residential accommodation. Expert advice should be sought so as to avoid complications arising later.(see Chapter 7 at paras. 7.17.1-7.17.2)

2.13.1 THE HOUSING ACT 1988

When fully enacted, the Housing Act will introduce important changes to the rights of tenants in both the private and the public sectors. In relation to the private sector, new lettings by non-resident landlords will be classified as 'assured' or 'assured shorthold' tenancies. Such tenancies will give less security of tenure than is currently enjoyed under the RA 1977. The Act provides no less than 16 grounds for possession, including the landlord's wish to redevelop the property, and the tenant's persistent delay in paying rent. This would mean that possession could be granted on the latter ground even where the tenant has paid all the arrears by the time of the proceedings. This ground may not be available, however, where late payment is not the fault of the tenant (because, for example, of delay in paying HB). Tenancies of this kind will not be subject to the fair rent provisions.(see para. 2.6.1 above) Assured shorthold tenancies will arise where the letting is for at least six months, and the landlord has given the tenant proper notice of the nature of the tenancy before the tenancy began.

In the public sector, a highly controversial provision is for most tenants to be given an option to choose approved landlords other than the local authority. The new landlords could be commercial enterprises as well as housing associations and co-operatives. Companies are already being formed in the hope that they might at some date in the future be able to take advantage of this provision.

Notes

1. For a detailed analysis of accommodation occupied by the elderly see Rossiter, C. and Wicks, M. (1982) *Crisis or Challenge?* (Study Commission on the Family), London, pp. 27-34 and 58-9.
2. Housing Act 1985, s.59.
3. Department of Environment (1983) Code of Guidance para. 2.12. *R. v. Lambeth London Borough Council, ex parte Carroll,* the *Independent,* October 8, 1987.
4. *19 HLR, 51.*
5. Housing Act 1985, s.69(2).

6. The Code of Guidance sets out the Secretary of State's interpretation of how the Housing Act 1985, Part III should be implemented. It is not legally binding.

7. Luba, J. (1988) 'Recent Development in Housing Law' *Legal Action* March 1988 at p.17.

8. *Cocks v. Thanet DC [1982] 3 All ER 1135.*

9. Housing Act 1985, s.80.

10. s.79(2), Sched 1.

11. Housing Act 1985. Full security is gained after twelve months. Sched 1, para. 5.

12. It may also be possible to resist possession proceedings temporarily by showing that the notice to quit is defective. See Luba, J. et al. (1987) *Defending Possession Proceedings* (Legal Action Group) at p.41.

13. Housing Act 1985, Sched 2, Parts 1-3.

14. Luba, J. et al. (1987), op.cit., at pp.15-36.

15. added by Housing and Planning Act 1986, s.9.

16. Housing Act 1985, Sched 2, Part IV, paras. 1 and 2.

17. *Enfield LBC v. Fresh (1984) 17 HLR 211, CA.*

18. Luba, J. et al. (1987) op.cit., at p.29.

19. *10 HLR 54, CA.*

20. Ground 14 applies to dwellings provided by housing associations or housing trusts for persons whose circumstances make it especially difficult for them to satisfy their housing needs.

21. Housing Act 1985, s.85(2).

22. s.113. The cohabitee must be of a different sex.

23. s.87.

24. *3 All ER 831.*

25. Housing Act 1985, s.87, s.89(2)(a).

26. s.91.

27. *3 All ER 122.*

28. Housing Act 1985, s.92. The grounds for refusing consent are listed in Sched 3.

29. *Peabody Donation Fund (Governors) v. Higgins [1983] 3 All ER 122.*

30. Housing Act 1985, s.93(1)(b).

31. i.e. 'any obligation of the tenancy has been broken or not performed'.

32. Mitchell, B. (1987) *Landlord and Tenant Law* (BSP Professional Books), at p.61.

33. *2 All ER 809* at p.813.

34. Housing Act 1985, s.94.

35. s.93(2).

36. Luba, J. et al. (1987) op.cit., at p.14.

37. Housing Act 1985, ss. 81 and 84.

38. ss. 102 and 103.

39. s.103(3).

40. Mitchell, B. (1987) op.cit., at p.318.

41. Housing Act 1985, s.105.

42. s.104.

43. s.97(1).

44. s.97(2).

45. s.101(10).

46. s.100.

47. Secure Tenancies (Right to Repair Scheme) Regulations 1985 S.I. 1985 No.1493.

48. para. 1(2).

49. ibid., Annex A.

50. Housing Act 1985, s.119.

51. s.171A, inserted by Housing and Planning Act 1986, s.8.

52. S.I. 1987 No.1732.

53. Housing Act 1985, Sched 5.

54. Sched 5, para. 11(2) as amended by Housing and Planning Act 1986, s.1.

55. Housing Act 1985, s.127.

56. s.128.

57. Housing Act 1985, s.129; Sched 4, as amended by Housing and Planning Act 1986, s.2.

58. Housing Act 1985, Sched 4.

59. s.132.

60. s.143(1).

61. Bookbinder, D. (1987) 'Housing Options For The Elderly' *Roof* Sept-Oct 1987 at para. 39. See also 'Loans for the Retired' the *Sunday Times* May 15, 1988 at D.14.

62. Housing Act 1985, s.123. See also: *Current Law Statutes Annotated* (1985) vol. 4, chapter 68 (Sweet and Maxwell) at p.177.

63. Bookbinder, D. (1987) op.cit., *Roof* July-Aug 1987 at para. 38.

64. Social Security Act, 1986, Sched 3, para. 10.

65. Allbeson, J. (1988) 'The April 1988 Changes: Income Support' *Legal Action* March 1988.

66. *Sutton (Hastoe) Housing Association v. Williams (1988)* the *Independent* February 1, 1988 (CA).

67. Housing Act 1985, s.155(2) as amended by Housing and Planning Act 1986, s.2(3).

68. CSO (1988) *Social Trends* at p.133.

69. Leigh, A. (1987) 'A Better Way of Life' *Community Care* June 4, 1987 at pp. 14-16.

70. Chase, B. (1985) 'Private Sheltered Housing - Setting Standards for the Future' *Housing Review* vol.34, no.2 at p.66.

71. Baker, S. and Parry, M. (1983) *Housing For Sale to the Elderly* (Housing Research Foundation).

72. Age Concern (1984) *Sheltered Housing for Older People* at p.41. The other 'arms' would be public sector and housing association provisions.

73. Leigh, A. (1987) op.cit., at p.15.

74. Edgar, W. M. and Bochel, D., 'Sheltered Housing in Scotland: Estimating Need and the Impact of the Private Sector' *Housing Review* (1987) vol.36, no.5 at pp.151-5. Fox, D. (1985) 'Housing Especially Designed for the Elderly' *Housing Review* vol.34 at p.3.

75. Smith, P. (1988) 'Meeting the Housing Needs of Elderly Asian People' *Social Work Today* February 4 at p.9.

76. Housing Act 1985, s.24(2).

77. Rent Act 1977, s.94(1).

78. s.7.

79. *Palser v. Grinling [1948] 1 All ER 1.*

80. Mitchell, B. (1987) op.cit., at p.281.

81. *Seabrook v. Merfyn [1947] 1 All ER 295.*

82. Landlord and Tenant Act 1985, s.26. These public authorities are excluded unless there is a long tenancy, i.e., a term exceeding 21 years.

83. i.e., if a Tenants Association exists.

84. Housing Act 1985, s.45.

85. Bookbinder, D. (1987) op.cit., September-October 1987.

86. See also: Age Concern (1987) *A Buyer's Guide to Sheltered Housing* (Age Concern England).

87. Rossiter, C. and Wicks, M. (1983) op.cit., at p.32.

88. See above at para. 2.4.3. For meaning of 'board' see *Otter v. Norman (1988)* the *Independent* July 8, 1988.

89. *Street v. Mountford [1985] 2 All ER 289.*

90. Luba, J. et al. (1987) op.cit., at p.74.

91. *Johnson-Snedden v. Harper (1977) LAG Bulletin 114.*

92. *Thomas v. Fryer [1970] 2 All ER 1.*
93. ibid.
94. Rent (Amendment) Act 1985, s.1.
95. Luba, J. et al. (1987) op.cit., at p.96.
96. *Fernandes v. Pervadin (1982) 264 EG 49.*
97. Rent Act 1977, s.100.
98. s.3(4).
99. Protection from Eviction Act 1977, s.5.
100. Luba, J. et al. (1987) op.cit., at p.53.
101. Rent Act 1977, s.2(1)b, Sched 1 Part 1 as amended by the HA 1988. The original qualifying period for other relatives was six months, although there are transitional provisions where a tenant dies within 18 months of the Act coming into force.
102. Rent Act 1977, Sched 1, paras. 2 and 7.
103. *3 All ER 838, CA.*
104. *The Times*, December 6, 1986, CA.
105. Mitchell, B. (1987) op.cit., at p.290.
106. *1 All ER 60, CA.*
107. *1 All ER 71.*
108. *Carega Properties v. Sharratt [1979] 2 All ER 1084*, see also, *Sefton Holdings Ltd v. Cairns (1987) The Times* November 3, 1987.
109. *Dyson Holdings Ltd v. Fox [1976] 3 All ER 1030, CA.*
110 See Madge, N. (1989) 'The Housing Act 1988. The Private Sector' *Legal Action* January, 1989, pp.14-20.
111. *Williams v. Williams [1970] 3 All ER 998, CA.*
112. Rent Act 1977, s.112.
113. s.102A; s.103(1).
114. Sched 2, para. 4.
115. Luba, J. et al. (1987) op.cit., at p.112.
116. Criminal Law Act 1977, s.6.
117. See Current Law Statutes Annotated (1977) (Sweet and Maxwell) at Chapter 43, p.1.
118. *R. v. Abrol (1972) Crim. L.R. 318, CA.*
119. Mitchell, B. (1987) op.cit., at p.75.
120. Landlord and Tenant Act 1985, s.4.
121. s.4(2).
122. *Shaw v. Groom [1970] 2 QB 104, CA.*
123. Rent Act 1977, Sched 11, para. 6.
124. Protected Shorthold Tenancies (Rent Registration) Order 1981 S.I. 1981 No.1578; S.I. 1987 No.265.

125. Assured Tenancies (Approved Bodies) (No.4) Order 1987 S.I. No.1525 adds another 35 approved bodies to the list of those capable of creating assured tenancies.
126. Housing Act 1980 s.56(1) as amended by Housing and Planning Act 1986, s.12.
127. There is no security of tenure either, but simply a procedure for renewal which restricts a landlord's right to possession.
128. Landlord and Tenant Act 1985, s.11.
129. s.8.
130. Public Health Act 1936, s.99.
131. Housing Act 1985, ss.189-204 and ss.264-279. See also Defective Premises Act 1972, s.4. A detailed discussion is to be found in Luba, J. (1986) *Repairs: Tenants Rights* (Legal Action Group) at pp.31-34.
132. Housing Act 1985, s.265.
133. Displaced tenants and other occupiers are entitled to be rehoused by the local housing authority either by virtue of the Land Compensation Act 1973 or under the Housing Act 1985, Part III. See Luba, J. (1986) op.cit., at p.99.
134. *R. v. Cardiff City Council ex p. Cross (1983) 6 HLR1, CA.*
135. *Lee Parker v. Izzet [1971] 1 WLR 1688.* See also Luba, J. (1986) op.cit., at p.38.
136. Luba, J. (1986) op.cit., at p.39.
137. ibid., at p.40.
138. Much of the Landlord and Tenant Act 1987 is now in force. See the Landlord and Tenant Act 1987 (Commencement No.2) Order 1988 S.I. 1988 No.480.
139. Casey, J. (1987) 'Providing Repairs, Improvements and Adaption Service for Elderly People at Home' *Housing Review* vol.36 no.3 May-June, at p.88.
140. Shelter (1987) *Care and Repair: A guide to setting up care and repair agency services for elderly people.* Note also that the grants are subject to an eligible expense limit.
141. Department of Environment Circular 36/81.
142. Casey, J. (1987) op.cit., at p.88.
143. See Arden, A. (1986) *Manual of Housing Law* (3rd ed.) (Sweet and Maxwell) at pp.216-217.
144. Shelter (1987) op.cit., at p.79.
145. Department of the Environment (1987) *Housing: The Government's Proposals* Cmnd 214, (HMSO).

146. Robertson, S. (1988) *Disability Rights Handbook* (Disability Alliance) at p.143.

147. Landlord and Tenant Act 1987, s.1. Brought into force on February 1, 1988.

148. See 'Disabled miss out on home adaptations' *Therapy Weekly* September 8, 1983.

149. Robertson, S. (1988), op.cit., at p.139.

150. Rating (Disabled Persons) Act 1978, s.1.

151. s.3(3)(b).

152. The *Guardian*, April 16, 1988. For a brief discussion of the problems connected with home income plans, see Irving, J. 'Pitfalls await elderly in search of income', the *Sunday Times*, August 7, 1988, p.D9.

153. The *Guardian*, March 23, 1984.

Chapter Three

CARE IN THE COMMUNITY

3.1.1 COMMUNITY CARE

Most elderly people needing some form of support, even those who are bed-ridden or severely disabled, remain in the community.[1] Yet community care is in many respects the least developed aspect of social policy, with standards consistently falling short of those set by departmental guidelines.[2] As a result, the current situation has been described as community care 'by default'. Considerable variation in the provision of services also exists from region to region, which cannot be explained by differences of need or demand.[3] The variation is so marked that a crude league table has been constructed to highlight these differences.[4] A shortfall in funding community care has been recognized by the Audit Commission in a report which also pointed to the lack of cooperation between the various agencies involved in the provision of community care. It concluded that there was a preference for 'horse trading' rather than for proper joint planning and the sharing of resources.[5] Little wonder that the Griffiths Report spoke of community care as 'a poor relation, everybody's distant relative, nobody's baby'.[6]

There is no one generally accepted definition of community care. Some definitions include residential care as a form of care in the community, as distinct from hospital care, but the term is more commonly used, as here, to indicate help given to individuals so that they can live at home or with relatives. Boarding-out schemes which, in effect, are intermediate between residential and community care are also included. It should be noted, however, that some of the statutory provisions, which apply mainly to those living in the community, can also apply to those living in residential settings. The Chronically Sick and Disabled Persons Act 1970 (CSDPA 1970), for example, though aimed primarily at assisting those living at home, or with relatives, applies equally to individuals receiving residential or hospital care.

3.1.2 Legislative provisions relating to community care can be divided into two distinct categories which, however, frequently overlap. In the first place, there are those provisions which relate specifically to the elderly as a group. In the second place, there are provisions which apply to those who are 'disabled' or 'handicapped'.[7] It seems that most people, including a surprising number of the disabled themselves, visualize the disabled as users of wheelchairs or as people on crutches. But many people suffer from disabilities such as heart disease, or diabetes, to say nothing of loss of sight and loss of hearing.[8] It should be pointed out in this context that provisions relating to disability are not limited to physical and sensory handicaps but also include mental disorder.

Since 1979, there has been a dramatic growth in community care provided by the private sector. No specific legal rules exist to control and regulate such services, in contrast to the position which exists in relation to residential care.[9] (see Chapter 4)

3.2.1 WELFARE PROVISIONS AND THE ELDERLY

Section 45 of the Health Services and Public Health Act 1968 (HSPHA 1968) provides that:

An authority may, with the approval of the Secretary of State, and, to such extent as he may direct, shall make arrangements for promoting the welfare of old people.

The purpose of this provision is to secure services for elderly people who are not yet 'substantially' and 'permanently handicapped' in order to prevent or postpone personal deterioration or breakdown as far as possible.[10] The Secretary of State has not, as yet, *directed* local authorities to make arrangements of this kind. This is somewhat surprising since the explanation originally given for not issuing directions was the absence of practical experience in this field. It is more than 15 years since the section came into effect, and it might be supposed that sufficient time had elapsed to make mandatory measures feasible.

3.2.2 By virtue of DHSS Circular 19/71, the Secretary of State has given approval to arrangements made for the welfare of the elderly for any of the following purposes: to provide meals and recreational facilities in an elderly person's home or elsewhere; to give elderly people information about the services which are available and for enabling schemes to be set up which identify elderly people in need; to assist with travel to local authority or similar services; to find suitable households for boarding-out; to provide practical assistance in the home, including adapting it or providing additional facilities designed to secure greater safety, comfort or convenience; to employ a warden for welfare functions in warden-assisted housing schemes; and to provide a warden service for private accommodation.

The specific approval of the Secretary of State will be required before an authority can legally provide any other service which is not generally sanctioned by the provisions of the Circular. Although it anticipated that general approval would be extended to other kinds of arrangements, this has not yet happened.

The 1968 Act precludes authorities from making payments of money to elderly people, apart from remuneration relating to the provision of suitable work in accordance with the above arrangements.[11]

A local authority may recover the costs of providing approved services from those who use them.[12]

3.2.3 In carrying out their functions under s.45, local authorities can use any voluntary organization as their agent which has among its principal objects the promotion of the welfare of old people.[13] The Act defines a voluntary organization as a body carrying out its activities otherwise than for a profit. The criterion might be satisfied if an organization could show that making a profit was subsidiary to its main objects.[14]

3.3.1 MEALS AND RECREATION PROVIDED BY DISTRICT COUNCILS

Under the Health and Social Services and Social Security Adjudication Act 1983 (HSSSSAA 1983), district councils[15] have the power to provide meals and recreation for people in their homes or elsewhere.[16] The Act also empowers health authorities to make grants to assist district authorities in performing these functions. There is no statutory definition of 'recreation' in this context although it would seem from an earlier Circular that, in the DSS's view, recreation can include the provision of 'work centres' or 'occupation centres' where elderly people could earn small sums of money. Providing elderly people with an opportunity to earn money must be ancillary to the main purpose, however, which is to help them remain fit and active.[17]

Since August 1983, district councils can employ a voluntary organization to carry out its functions under the HSSSSAA 1983 so long as the organization's activities consist of, or include, the provision of meals or recreation for elderly people.[18] A district council can give support in various ways to enable voluntary organizations to act on its behalf. It can contribute directly to their funds; or permit them to use council premises on agreed terms; or make available furniture, vehicles or equipment for their use (whether by way of gift or loan or otherwise) plus assigning to them the services of relevant staff.[19]

The Secretary of State has power under the HSSSSAA 1983 to prepare regulations relating to powers of inspection and to the qualification of staff (including those working for voluntary organizations). No regulations have been issued to date.[20]

The above provisions overlap with those which assign certain functions to social service authorities. The extent to which district councils respond to these new statutory powers may have a bearing on how social services authorities make use of their powers under s.45 of the HSPHA 1968 (see para. 3.2.1). Such issues might be best addressed at the joint care planning meetings which the two authorities must hold from time to time.[21]

3.4.1 HOME HELP AND LAUNDRY FACILITIES

Social service authorities must provide or arrange for a home help service to be provided where there is need for such assistance for those who are aged. The scale of the service must be adequate for the needs of the social service area.[22] An identical duty exists in respect of a person suffering from illness, or handicapped as a result of congenital deformity or illness. Illness includes mental disorder, as well as any injury or illness requiring medical or dental treatment or nursing.[23]

The inclusion in this provision of the words 'where such help is required' gives local authorities considerable discretion in determining need. They must, however, act reasonably in coming to any decision.

This duty will be satisfied if local authorities simply make arrangements for a home help service to be made available rather than providing it directly. The importance of this distinction can be seen in a particularly imaginative example of home help use described elsewhere.[24] A daughter caring for her mother was finding it impossible to look after her own house as well. Instead of the home-help being sent to the mother, she went to the daughter's house, thus enabling the daughter to continue caring for her mother by being relieved of chores in her own home. There appears to be no statutory justification for an arrangement of this kind other than that the authority had 'arranged' indirect provision for an aged person.

Local authorities may recover from the user the cost of what has been provided by way of a home help service.

3.4.2 Local authorities also have power to provide or arrange for the provision of laundry facilities for those householders for whom a home-help is being, or might be, provided. There is no reference in the relevant literature to any use being made of this power by local authorities, despite evidence which shows that a service of this kind would be of value for carers.[25]

Where no laundry service exists, extra assistance may be made available through the home-help service. Since April 1988 there is no additional allowance available under the income support scheme (IS) for persons who need assistance to pay for extra laundry costs. Discretionary help may be available from the new Social Fund.(see Chapter 1, para.1.25.1) Transitional protection will be given to claimants previously on supplementary benefit who would otherwise suffer a drop in income. Community care grants (CCGs) are also available to purchase and connect, or repair, a washing machine where a person is incontinent. Eligibility for the grant is conditional on the claimant being able to show that no help is being received from another agency. (see Chapter 1 at para. 1.25.2)

3.5.1 BOARDING-OUT SCHEMES FOR THE ELDERLY

It has been legally possible for about 20 years to provide adult boarding-out schemes under s.45 of the HSPHA 1968, that is, schemes to assist individuals in finding suitable lodgings. Yet developments in this field are relatively recent. Boarding-out schemes, sometimes referred to as adult placement schemes, exist at present in only about half the authorities in England and Wales and tend to be fairly small scale.[26] About half of them make use of less than 20 carers, although there are notable exceptions. Some local authorities provide the service directly, while others (as they are entitled to do under s.45(3) of the HSPHA 1968) employ voluntary organizations as their agents. A number of the schemes provide short-term arrangements only. There is, therefore, no single or standard model, since the schemes have different origins, aims and practices. That is the reason, perhaps, why the legal issues have not been widely discussed. Two issues, in particular, warrant further attention here.

3.5.2 First, what type of tenure does an elderly person enjoy as a boarder? A boarding-out scheme has been described as 'a living situation involving less than four elderly people accommodated as paying tenants of a private householder who lives in the same premises. The householder provides care and attention and is responsible to the local authority which ensures "satisfactory standards"'.[27] To describe elderly people as 'tenants' is probably misleading since few boarders, if any, will be able to establish a right to the 'exclusive possession' of the premises, an essential pre-requisite for establishing a tenancy. Even if a boarder could establish that he/she has exclusive use of a particular part of the premises, this might not amount to 'exclusive possession' since the householder might retain overall control. For instance, the householder might reserve the right to move the occupier from room to room as the occasion demanded.[28] In other words, even those able to establish exclusive occupation of part of a property might still be regarded as having no more than a licence to occupy. The existence of a licence will give rise, however, to the right to reasonable notice to quit, unless it can be shown that the arrangement was for a fixed period only. In that case, no notice need be given since, in effect, it was given at the outset. Many short-term boarding-out placements probably fall into this category.

3.5.3 Secondly, the nature of the legal relationship between the local authority, the elderly person, and the carer is even more uncertain. Some authorities are more directly involved in the arrangements than others. In Leeds, for example, the local authority pays the householder a fixed weekly amount[29] and the boarded-out person pays the local authority a flat rate equivalent to the statutory minimum charge for local authority residential accommodation. (see Chapter 4 at para. 4.5.1) In other areas, no money is paid to the householder by the local authority. The authority simply acts as the intermediary between the householder and the elderly person. Such arrangements are often funded by means of a DSS Board and Lodging Allowance.[30] (see para.3.5.5 below) Local authorities invariably vet both the householder and the elderly person, however, so that in actions for negligence, for example, a court might hold that a duty of care existed between the authority and the boarded-out person, between the authority and the householder, or between the authority and both other parties. (see Chapter 6 at para. 6.4.2)

3.5.4 The nature and extent of any legal liability would depend upon whether the householder was regarded in law as acting as an agent for the local authority. An agency can arise without formal agreement in that anyone who gives the impression that another has authority to act on his/her behalf may later be unable to deny the existence of an agency. The principal, that is, the person on whose behalf the agent acts, is liable for the civil wrongs (the torts) of an agent acting within the limits of his/her authority. No cases involving the possible existence of an agency in relation to the boarding-out of the elderly have been reported. In a case involving the boarding-out of a child in local authority care, the Court of Appeal held the local authority not liable for the negligent acts of the foster-parents in relation to the foster child.[31] It was emphasized that the relationship between the child and the local authority, and between the child and the foster parents, was regulated by the provisions of a statutory scheme, that is, the Boarding-Out of Children Regulations 1955. Those provisions were held to be entirely inconsistent with the notion that foster-parents were agents of the local authority in carrying out their duties. The local authority had a duty to provide accommodation for a child; that duty was satisfied by boarding-out. The foster-parents were not fulfilling a duty to provide accommodation, but only providing a means whereby the local authority could carry out its duties.

This case might well be persuasive authority for the view that no action in negligence would be possible against a local authority in relation to an elderly person boarded-out under a scheme organized by a local authority. It might be distinguished, however, in that boarding-out arrangements for elderly people are not part of a 'statutory scheme'. The basic difference lies in the fact that no statutory regulations can be made to cover boarding-out schemes for elderly people. It might be argued that where local authorities are extensively involved in organizing and running a boarding-out scheme, an agency could arise. Under the Leeds scheme, for example, boarded-out persons pay the local authority. No money passes between the elderly persons and their carers. Indeed, this local authority, apparently at the request of householders in the scheme, has extended its public liability policy to include them within its insurance cover against claims for negligence by elderly persons or their relatives.[32] Other local authorities claim that, in relation to such schemes, they have no insurable interest to protect. It could be argued that DHSS Circular 19/71 supports this interpretation, since authorities are only allowed 'to assist' in finding suitable households for boarding-out elderly persons. In recruiting householders to take part in boarding-out schemes, local authorities should, perhaps, advise them to take out additional insurance cover, particularly since the occupiers of premises owe a separate duty of care for the safety of anyone who enters and remains there, even as a visitor.[33]

3.5.5 FINANCIAL SUPPORT

The extent of DSS financial support for boarding-out schemes will depend in part on the nature of the care being given. The Supplementary Benefit (Requirement and Resources) Amendment Regulations 1987 make it clear that unless the boarding-out scheme provides two experienced carers, with one being available throughout the day, and one on call at night, it will not attract residential care rates for those boarded-out there. (see Chapter 4, Table 4.1 at p.170). Less generous financial assistance is available from the DSS, however, under the board and lodgings rules. Under those provisions the basic charge can be met by the DSS, provided that the amount falls below the local limits. Existing local limits vary between £45 and £70.[34] Provision also exists for the local limits to be 'extended' by a maximum of £17.50 where the person is elderly, or mentally or physically disabled. Boarders will usually qualify for an attendance allowance as well. (see Chapter 1, para. 1.22.1) In addition, local authorities can make 'topping up' payments to claimants of *any age* to meet charges which are over and above the local limits, if the payment is designed to meet a part of the charge which the DSS will not pay.[35] Where a topping up payment is made, however, the DSS could, perhaps, refuse to pay an attendance allowance on the ground that the cost of the accommodation is being borne partly out of public funds.[36]

The rules relating to these allowances are to change in April 1989. Thereafter, boarders will receive the appropriate rate of IS plus premiums. No specific allowance will be available for board and lodging as such, and claimants will have to rely on housing benefit (HB) which makes no provision for extra costs such as meals, laundry, heating. Those already receiving board and lodgings allowance will be protected. New claimants will, however, lose out as a result of the revised arrangements.

3.6.1 TRAVEL CONCESSIONS FOR THE ELDERLY

A local authority, or two authorities acting jointly, may set up a travel concession scheme for use on public passenger transport services.[37] Those eligible for travel concessions include men over 65 and women over the age of 60.[38] A scheme can also include a companion travelling with an eligible person who is so severely handicapped as to require assistance in using public transport.

3.6.2 Authorities enjoy complete discretion whether or not to run travel concession schemes and what concessions to make. They might make provision for free travel, for example, or for a percentage reduction in fares (for example, half-fares), for a flat-rate reduction, or for the issue of tokens or travel vouchers. The services for which concessions can be made are not limited to local bus services but can include travel by rail, taxi, 'social care schemes', ferries and any service specially designed 'to meet the needs of elderly or disabled people'.[39] The Transport Act 1985 (TA 1985) adds to the powers of local authorities by enabling them to oblige operators of eligible transport schemes to make travel concessions.[40] Operators participating in such schemes must inform the local authority of any change in fares, either when it takes place, or not more than seven days later.[41]

3.6.3 The absence of a mandatory concessionary fares scheme on a nation-wide basis has led to considerable variation in the provision which is available. According to one DHSS survey, 25 per cent of expenditure on concessionary travel was concentrated on ten per cent of elderly people, and ten per cent of elderly people lived in areas where no concessions were made at all.[42] It should be noted that the power of social service authorities under s.29 of the National Assistance Act 1948 (NAA 1948) to provide free or subsidised travel for registered handicapped persons does not apply to elderly people since, as a group, they are included within the terms of the Transport Acts and are therefore ineligible for assistance under s.29.

3.7.1 DISABLED AND HANDICAPPED ELDERLY PEOPLE

Section 29(1) of the National Assistance Act 1948 (NAA 1948) provides that:

> A local social services authority may, with the approval of the Secretary of State, and to such extent as he may direct in relation to persons ordinarily resident in the area of the local authority, shall make arrangements for

promoting the welfare of persons . . . . who are blind, deaf or dumb, and other persons who are substantially and permanently handicapped by illness, injury or congenital deformity or other such disability as may be prescribed by the Secretary of State.

DHSS Circular 13/74 extends the phrase 'substantially and permanently handicapped' to include the partially-sighted and the hard-of-hearing and also confirms that, in this context, illness includes mental disorder.[43] Those who are not blind, deaf or dumb or do not suffer from one of the specified handicaps will need to show they are suffering from a handicap which is both substantial and permanent.

Local authorities must keep registers of all individuals in their area to whom s.29(1) applies, and must also provide them with a social work service and such advice and support as they may need. Arrangements must be made for the provision of facilities for social rehabilitation and adjustment to disability, including assistance in overcoming limitations with mobility and communication.[44] Local authorities must also make arrangements for social, cultural, and recreational activities and, where appropriate, for paying persons for any work undertaken by them.

3.7.2 Social services authorities have powers to make arrangements in relation to handicapped persons similar to those relating to the elderly under s.45 of the HSPHA 1968.(see paras. 3.2.1, 3.2.2 above) There is an important difference, however, in that the power to provide services for those who are handicapped is not restricted to provision by public bodies or voluntary organizations, but extends to provision by private sector enterprises acting as agents of the local authority.

3.8.1 EXTENDED DUTY TO PROMOTE WELFARE

The duty of social services authorities to make arrangements under s.29 of the NAA 1948 has been extended by the CSDPA 1970.

Section 1 of the 1970 Act requires local authorities to inform themselves of the number of handicapped persons in their area and the extent of their need for services; to publish information about the services available; and to inform any user of such services about any other services which may be relevant to his/her needs. Registration with the local authority as a handicapped person is not necessary in order to be eligible for assistance under this section. Should any person coming within the provisions of s.29 specifically indicate that he/she does not wish to have his/her name included on the local authority's register, assistance must not be withheld for that reason.[45]

3.8.2 Under s.2 of the 1970 Act, social services authorities must make arrangements for the provision of the following services to those to whom they owe a duty:

a) practical assistance in the home;
b) radio, television, library or similar recreational facilities;
c) recreational and educational facilities outside the home;
d) facilities for travelling and for the purpose of using such facilities;
e) assistance in carrying out adaptations to the home or the provision of additional facilities to secure an individual's greater safety, comfort or convenience;
f) holidays at holiday homes or elsewhere, whether provided under arrangements made by the authority or otherwise;
g) meals at home or elsewhere;
h) a telephone and other special equipment necessary for its use.

The services included in s.2 are similar, though not identical, to those which can be provided for the elderly under s.45 of the HSPHA 1968, except that the legal provisions under s.45 are in the form of powers and not duties. Under the CSPDA 1970, a local authority has a duty to assess the need for these services of any person with a substantial and permanent handicap. Once a local authority has accepted that a need exists, it must make arrangements for that need to be met.[46]

3.8.3 DHSS Circular 12/70 indicates that the process of assessment should lead to a consideration of all relevant needs, and not merely those to which s.2 refers. Section 1 of the Act requires the assessment to take account of the particular needs of each individual person. It seems, nevertheless, that local authorities increasingly use standardized criteria as guidelines for their staff. The following quotation, from a letter sent out by one local authority, is an example of such practice:

> . . . . you will no doubt be aware of the criteria for eligibility . . . Unfortunately at this time of cutbacks and recession, we are having to interpret the criteria very strictly and cannot regard Mr and Mrs F. as eligible.[47]

3.8.4 An assessment of need should not, in law, be conditional upon funds being available for the provision of appropriate care. Moreover, local authorities which make no provision in their budgets to enable them to provide those services specified in s.2 may be acting unlawfully. This was apparently recognized by one local authority when, under threat of legal action, it reversed an earlier decision and reinstated a budget for holidays.[48] Local authorities which use waiting lists as a method of rationing services for those they have acknowledged to be in need may also be acting in breach of their statutory duty.[49] A waiting list will be lawful only where it does not give rise to excessive delay in supplying the necessary service. Attempts at enforcing statutory duties through the courts have generally proved unsuccessful, however. (see 3.16.2 below)

Some of the services set out in s.2 may be available under the terms of other statutory provisions. For example, a person receiving home dialysis could have a telephone provided by a health authority.[50] Adaptations to premises which are directly related to the installation of dialysis equipment at the patient's home are also the responsibility of health authorities.[51] Usually, however, the responsibility for adapting premises falls upon either social service authorities or upon housing authorities. Arrangements for adaptations to be made are discussed below at para 3.10.1.

3.9.1 APPLIANCES

Social service authorities and health authorities can provide appliances free of charge to help an individual living in the community cope with a disability or handicap. Until recently appliances supplied by social service authorities were referred to as 'aids for daily living' whereas those supplied by health authorities were known as 'aids to home nursing'.[52] Where a disability is permanent, the statutory responsibility for providing any necessary appliances falls upon the social service authority because of the terms of s.29 of the NAA 1948 (as extended). (see para. 3.8.1 above) Where a condition is acute rather than chronic, responsibility falls upon the health authority. Arrangements can be made by social service authorities and by health authorities for appliances to be made available by voluntary organizations, such as the Red Cross or St John's Ambulance Society.[53]

3.9.2 On occasion, the medical prognosis in relation to a particular disability may be uncertain. There are reports of commodes and other appliances being removed by health authority staff after a period of about six weeks, without any prior arrangement for their replacement by a social services authority.[54] Most health authorities and social services authorities have jointly agreed procedures to determine which authority should supply an appliance in any particular circumstances. In spite of this and other procedures employed by both authorities, the value of the appliances which are supplied can vary from 'very useful' to 'completely useless'. In one study of persons aged 65 and over, about half the appliances which had been supplied were found not to have been 'fully useful'.[55]

3.9.3 Other appliances can be made available on prescription by a hospital consultant or a GP. General practitioners can prescribe only the aids and equipment included in the drug tariff. These include catheters, elastic hosiery, and trusses. Hospital consultants can provide a variety of appliances including surgical footwear, hearing aids and low vision aids. Wheelchairs (including powered wheelchairs) can be supplied by the special health authority known as the Disablement Services Authority (DSA) to a handicapped or disabled person who has permanent need of one.[56] Most health authorities, and some social service authorities have a supply of wheelchairs which can be made available for temporary use.

3.10.1 ADAPTATIONS

Adaptations are either appliances which need installing, or any structural work aimed specifically at helping a handicapped or disabled person live at home. Social service authorities and housing authorities have wide powers to assist with adaptations to premises in public or private ownership. Apparently, some local authorities prefer to rehouse disabled people rather than adapt their homes. This is a worrying development since, as the Royal Association for Disability and Rehabilitation (RADAR) suggests, the effects can be both disruptive and counter productive.[57] Disabled people, perhaps more than others, may become attached to a particular neighbourhood. Moving to an unfamiliar area could be more detrimental than remaining in unadapted premises. Pressure to move, exerted by a housing or social services authority, should be resisted since the duty placed on local authorities by s.2 of the CSPDA 1970 is to carry out adaptations at the person's home. The Act does not allow other arrangements to be made. Even where tenants in council property need the prior consent of their local authority landlord before proceeding with a proposed adaptation, that consent cannot be withheld without good reason.[58]

3.10.2 Both housing authorities and social service authorities can assist with adaptations to local authority housing. Housing authorities have an express duty under s.3 of the CSDPA 1970 to have regard for the special needs of disabled people when discharging their duty under s.91 of the Housing Act 1957 (HA 1957) to consider the housing conditions and needs of their districts. Their statutory powers extend, where necessary, to adapting existing accommodation.[59] As indicated above, s.2 of the CDSPA requires social services authorities to make arrangements for the adaptation of public sector housing, where necessary in the interests of the safety, comfort, or convenience of disabled people. Since housing authorities have been specifically requested by Department of Environment Circular 59/78 to accept responsibility for work involving the structural modification of dwellings owned and managed by them, there should be a minimum of conflict between housing and social services authorities over their respective responsibilities.[60] The duties of social service authorities, under s.2 of the CSDPA 1970, also extend to adapting premises which are privately owned. Grants for the improvement of property are discussed in Chapter 2 at para. 2.8.1.

3.11.1 THE ORANGE BADGE SCHEME

The orange badge scheme, introduced under s.21 of the CSDPA 1970, allows parking concessions to be made to assist individuals with mobility problems. Revised regulations governing the issue of orange badges have been in force since March 1983.[61] At present, the scheme covers only four categories of people, namely, recipients of a mobility allowance; persons using a government-supplied vehicle or receiving a grant towards the use of their own vehicle; registered blind people; and other people with a permanent and substantial disability which causes them inability, or very considerable difficulty in walking. Orange badge holders travelling abroad may also be able to take advantage of concessions offered by the host country.[62] The scheme applies to the whole of England and Wales, except central London. A vehicle displaying an orange badge may, but need not, be driven by the disabled person him/herself.

Authorities may charge a small fixed fee for issuing a badge.[63] Badges can be refused for non-payment; where evidence of need is inadequate; or where there is evidence that the badge-user has misused it at least three times, leading to a conviction or liability to prosecution. A right of appeal to the Secretary of State, against refusal or withdrawal of a badge, exists only where a badge is refused or withdrawn on grounds of misuse, and in no other circumstances. Wrongful use of a badge is an offence, giving rise on conviction to a maximum fine of £200.[64]

3.11.2 Although stricter criteria are being used in issuing orange badges, there has been a 17 per cent increase in the numbers issued since 1983. Widespread misuse by car owners persists. It has been suggested in a Department of Transport Discussion Paper that local authorities should be free to decide what to charge for issuing them.[65] It has further been suggested that the badge itself should be re-designed to include a photograph of the holder, and that blind people should no longer have automatic eligibility under the scheme. A non-controversial proposal is that persons in receipt of the war pensioners mobility supplement should automatically qualify for an orange badge.

3.12.1 ADDITIONAL ASSESSMENT DUTIES

Not all the provisions of the Disabled Persons (Services, Consultation and Representation) Act 1986 (DP(SCR)A 1986) are in force at time of writing. If and when this Act is fully implemented it will introduce new duties, rather than extend existing ones, since its provisions are not linked to other legislative measures.

3.12.2 The Act's primary intention is to improve services for the disabled through better assessment of their needs. A prerequisite for proper assessment will be that the views of disabled persons themselves are adequately heard. Section 1 of the Act (not yet in force) will allow a disabled person to appoint a representative or 'advocate'.[66] Under the same section, local authorities are authorized to appoint representatives for persons deemed incapable of making such appointments themselves by reason of physical or mental incapacity. The legal powers of representatives under this legislation must be distinguished from those of adult guardians appointed under the Mental Health Act 1983 (MHA 1983), (see Chapter 4 at para. 4.10.8) and persons having powers of attorney.(see Chapter 7 at paras. 7.20.7-7.20.14) Even when appointed by a local authority, representatives of disabled people will have no right, under the DP(SCR)A 1986, to take decisions on their behalf.

Section 3 (not yet in force) is probably the most crucial of the provisions. It requires a local authority, before making any assessment, to allow a disabled person, or his/her authorized representative, to make representations on the extent of his/her need for social services and support. The section also stipulates that a local authority must provide a written statement setting out the assessment of need. This statement must give reasons for the decision, and where the existence of a need has been recognized, it must refer to the services which the local authority is proposing to provide. Even when an authority decides that a disabled person has no need for 'statutory services', reasons for the refusal will have to be given. When the decision is negative, the disabled person, or the authorized representative, must be told of their statutory right to have the decision reviewed by the authority.

3.12.3 The s.3 procedure is limited to 'statutory services' under 'welfare enactments'.[67] Local authorities are not, therefore, obliged to make an assessment of other needs. Moreover, since 'statutory services' are those which local authorities are *required* to provide, it would seem that the procedure does not extend to services which they *may* provide under discretion vested in them by their statutory powers.[68]

3.12.4 This may not be the position in relation to s.8(1) of the Act. Section 8(1) provides for an assessment, in specific circumstances, of the needs of carers. The words used are '*any service*' rather than '*statutory services*'. The section covers any person (other than someone employed to do so) who is providing a substantial amount of care for a person living at home. The wording of the section does not restrict its application to carers living in the same household as the disabled person. It requires a local authority, in assessing a carer's needs, to take account of his/her ability to continue providing help on a regular basis. Under s.8(2) (when in force) local authorities will, where necessary, be obliged to provide services to help with any problems of communication arising between the carer and the authority as a result of the carer's disability. Section 8 does not, however, provide a right to a statutory review where the carer is dissatisfied with the level of support which has been offered.

3.12.5 Section 4 of the Act is also partly in force. It confirms that a local authority must assess the need of a disabled person for any of the services listed in s.2 of the CSDPA 1970.(see para. 3.8.1) The duty will arise if an assessment is requested by the disabled person, or a carer, as defined in s.8.

3.12.6 Section 9, which amends s.1 of the CSDPA 1970 has also been brought into force. The earlier Act required social service authorities to inform disabled people receiving services from them of other relevant services provided by the authority. Section 9 now requires local authorities to inform disabled people of services provided by *any other authority or organization*, if such particulars are in the authority's possession.

3.13.1 CHARGING FOR LOCAL AUTHORITY SERVICES

The basis upon which those receiving any of the domiciliary services discussed in this chapter can be charged has been re-defined by s.17 of the HSSSSAA 1983.[69] Section 17 stipulates that an authority which provides a service may recover whatever charges it considers reasonable. Local authorities are, therefore, not obliged to charge for the services which they provide. DHSS Circular LAC(84)7 suggests, however, that when they are deciding what charges are reasonable, local authorities need not have specific regard for a particular individual's ability to pay. Nor is the local authority required to inform the person receiving a service of the likely cost. In fact, authorities vary considerably in their policy on charges: a number provide free services; others impose flat rate charges; and some assess charges in relation to income.[70]

3.13.2 A degree of protection for persons of limited means is provided by s.17(3) of the Act. Where an authority is satisfied that the user of a service has insufficient means, then it cannot require him/her to pay more than appears reasonably practicable. The decision to charge a reduced amount is, therefore, at the discretion of the authority. Its decision can be challenged, however, on the grounds only that no reasonable authority would act in that way.[71] Research published before the enactment of this particular provision suggests that authorities are reluctant to reduce charges even when they have established procedures for doing so.[72] Indeed, some authorities apparently insist upon charging the full amount to persons who rely upon or qualify for means-tested benefits. Most complaints over the imposition of charges relate to difficulties in paying for a home help service.[73] In this context, local authorities may need reminding of the provisions of DHSS Circular 53/71, which advises against the imposition of charges on persons who qualify, or would qualify for supplementary benefit, now replaced by IS.

3.13.3 A local authority which refuses or withdraws a service because of an individual's unwillingness or inability to pay could be acting unlawfully.[74] Where an individual refuses to pay, and the authority is not satisfied of his/her inability to meet the imposed charge, the only course of action open to it will be recovery by means of a civil action in debt.[75]

3.14.1 CARERS

Those who care for elderly people at home have been described as the 'forgotten army'[76] and several reports testify to their neglect by government and welfare agencies. Carers are principally women, often looking after an elderly person alone, and receiving little or no support from other relatives, neighbours or organized services. Evidence also suggests that an increasing number and proportion of carers are themselves elderly.[77]

The social and financial costs of being the carer of an elderly person can be substantial.[78] The domestic assistance allowance (maximum £48.70 per week) once available to persons in need of help with ordinary household tasks, like cleaning and cooking, was discontinued in April 1988. Persons already receiving the allowance, however, will have their income protected under the transitional arrangements, providing they continue to qualify. Those receiving a domestic assistance allowance of more than £10 a week will have their allowance protected against inflation by means of a 'special transitional addition'. It has been estimated that only some 4,500 people will be protected in this way.[79] Those needing additional assistance in order to remain in the community, could possibly qualify for CCGs. These are available to assist individuals leaving institutional care; to prevent individuals from having to enter care; for travelling expenses in particular circumstances; and where such assistance would ease exceptional pressures on an individual and his/her family.(see Chapter 1, para. 1.25.2)

3.14.2 The rules relating to eligibility for Invalid Care Allowance (ICA), are discussed in detail elsewhere.(see Chapter 1, paras. 1.23.1 - 1.23.6) It should be noted, however, that in appropriate circumstances the allowance is now payable to married women and to cohabitees.[80]

3.15.1 PRIVATE DOMICILIARY CARE

It is not known how many arrangements for the provision of domiciliary services exist in the private sector. One estimate suggests that there may be between 200-300 registered employment agencies, employing between 2,500-4,000 staff, which currently provide services of this kind for elderly people in England and Wales.[81] Some agencies provide services such as gardening, house maintenance, pet and plant care, driving and catering, and financial advice, which fall outside the usual range of statutory services. Charges and method of payment vary from agency to agency. Users may be asked for an initial registration fee[82] as well as being charged an hourly, nightly, or weekly rate.

3.15.2 Under the Employment Agencies Act 1973 (EAA 1973), every person involved in setting up an employment agency must be licensed by the licensing authorities, as defined by s.13. The Secretary of State for Employment is empowered to make regulations relating to the conduct of such agencies. The Act specifically prohibits regulations to be made which control or restrict the amount such agencies can charge for their services.[83] A licence may be refused or revoked because of the unsuitability or misconduct of the person carrying on the agency, but it must be stressed that he/she will probably not be the individual actually delivering the domiciliary service to the elderly person. Under the Act, Registration Inspectors are empowered to ensure only that the agencies themselves comply with the statutory requirements. They have no statutory right to examine the suitability of those who are employed by them. It is the agency alone which is responsible for ensuring that suitable carers/helpers are recruited.

Registration Inspectors are not empowered either to examine services provided in private day-care centres, which also fall outside the provisions of the Registered Homes Act 1984 (RHA 1984). The absence of statutory regulation in this area must give cause for concern.[84]

3.16.1 LEGAL REMEDIES

Because of the absence of legislative control over private domiciliary services, those who are dissatisfied with the quality of the services they receive may find themselves without legal redress. One possibility, however, might be to sue (usually for damages) for breach of a contract for the supply of services. The Supply of Goods and Services Act 1982 (SGSA 1982) implies terms into a contract for services to the effect that reasonable care and skill must be exercised in the performance of any services provided under it. The express terms of the contract itself may provide additional safeguards which could also be relied upon in an action for breach of the agreement. A contract of this kind need not be in writing, but elderly customers would be well-advised to insist on that. A model agreement has been drafted by the Centre for Policy on Ageing.[85] Any agreement entered into should refer in detail to the services to be provided, the length of time for which the agreement is made, and the financial costs which will arise. It is also suggested that at least one month's written notice on either side should be required to bring the contract to an end.

3.16.2 The courts have so far declined to uphold claims against local authorities for breaches of statutory duty in relation to domiciliary care. In the leading case of *Wyatt v. Hillingdon London Borough Council (1978)*[86] a disabled woman claimed damages against a local authority for negligence and for breach of statutory duty under s.2 of the CSDPA 1970. The basis of the claim was that the authority had failed to meet her need for adequate home help services and for practical assistance in the home. In dismissing the claim, the Court of Appeal held that where a local authority fails to discharge its function under the CSDPA 1970, the proper procedure is to make use of the default powers of the Secretary of State under s.36 of the NAA 1948.

In a more recent case, *R. v. London Borough of Ealing, ex parte Leaman (1984)*,[87] the court again took the view that it had no power to award damages when an authority had refused to consider a request for assistance under s.2 of the CSDPA 1970 from an individual wishing to take a privately arranged holiday. The policy of the authority was to sponsor only those holidays which it had itself organized. Before the case came to court, the applicant had tried, unsuccessfully, to persuade the Secretary of State to make use of his default powers. Although the court declined to award damages for breach of statutory duty, it did issue a declaration that the local authority's decision to refuse to consider the application was an error in law. It is not clear from the reporting of the case whether or not the court would have been prepared to grant a declaration if the applicant had not first asked the Secretary of State to make use of his default powers. If this decision were to be followed in future cases, its significance is that a request to the Secretary of State to exercise his default powers under s.36 of the NAA 1948 may not necessarily be the sole remedy available in cases of breach of statutory duty.

The evidence upon which Ministers decide not to exercise their default powers often appears slim since those who lay a complaint are seldom, if ever, approached directly.[88] On the other hand, the procedure is cheap and does not place the disabled person under the same pressures as a court appearance. It seems, however, that successive Secretaries of State have been reluctant to make use of their default power. Only one case has been reported,[89] though the use of the default procedure might have been appropriate on a number of occasions. (For further discussion of breach of statutory duty and default powers see Chapter 6 at paras. 6.2.2, 6.2.4).

3.17.1 COMPLAINTS TO THE OMBUDSMAN

Where maladministration results in an injustice, a complaint can be made to a local Ombudsman (Local Government Commissioner). An Ombudsman cannot investigate in those circumstances in which recourse is available to a court or a Minister, unless satisfied that in the particular circumstances it is not reasonable to expect the aggrieved person to exercise that right. A local authority has been criticized by the Ombudsman for allowing a three-month delay in making an assessment of the need to adapt a son's home to provide a ground floor flat for his disabled father.[90] The delay had apparently occurred because an occupational therapist had gone to the wrong address on a number of occasions.

The Ombudsman may conclude that there was no maladministration; that there was maladministration but no injustice was suffered as a consequence; or that maladministration causing an injustice occurred. An *ex-gratia* payment by way of compensation from the authority can be ordered if a positive finding is made which has led to injustice. (see Chapter 4 at para. 4.12.7) In the case discussed above, the failure to make an assessment was held to amount to maladministration as no attempt had been made by the occupational therapist to check that she had called at the right address. The Ombudsman also said it was unfortunate that the authority did not have a leaflet to explain how grants to adapt the home of disabled people were determined. The individual concerned had missed the opportunity of obtaining an improvement grant because conversion work had been started before his application was set in motion. The Ombudsman concluded, however, that no injustice had been suffered as a consequence of the maladministration. He was, therefore, unable to recommend that compensation be paid to the complainant.

Notes

1. Walker, A. (1981) 'Community Care and the elderly in Great Britain: theory and practice' *International Journal of Health Services*, vol.11, no.4 at pp.541-557. OPCS Survey (1988) *The prevalence of disability among adults* (HMSO).
2. MOH (1963) *Health and Welfare: the Development of Community Care* Cmnd. 1973 (HMSO). See also DHSS (1972) *Local Authority Social Services 10 Year Development Plans 1973-83.* Circular 35/72.
3. i.e., lack of 'territorial justice'. See Goldberg, E.M. and Connelly, M. (1982) *The Effectiveness of Social Care in the Community* (Heinemann) at p.48.
4. Hilditch, C. (1981) 'The Disabled Person and the Local Authority' in Guthrie, D. (ed.) *Disability, Legislation and Practice* (Macmillan Press) at p.36.
5. The Audit Commission (1986) *Making a Reality out of Community Care* (HMSO).
6. Griffiths, R. (1988) *Community Care: Agenda for Action* (HMSO).
7. The words 'handicapped' and 'disabled' are both used in the legislation. To date, no attempt has been made to give the two terms a legal definition. See DHSS Circular 19/71.
8. Greaves, M. (1981) 'The Disabled Person Looks at the Legislation in Disability' in Guthrie, D. (1981) op.cit., at p.20.
9. The Employment Agencies Act 1973 may provide some protection but not all private domiciliary care is provided by

Care in the Community

agencies. In any event the protection offered is very limited. (see discussion at para. 3.15.2).

10. DHSS 19/71 and WO 47/71.

11. Health Services and Public Health Act 1968, s.45(4)(a).

12. s.45(2).

13. s.45(3).

14. *National Deposit Friendly Society Trustees v. Skegness Urban District Council [1959] A.C. 293* at p.319. See also *Victory (Ex Services) Association v. Paddington Borough Council [1960] 1 All ER 498* where Lord Denning's dictum in the Skegness case was disapproved.

15. i.e., local authorities which are not social services authorities.

16. Health and Social Services and Social Security Adjudication Act 1983, Sched 9, Part II.

17. MOH Circular 12/62.

18. Health and Social Services and Social Security Adjudications Act 1983, Sched 9, Part II at para. 1.

19. para. 2.

20. para. 3.

21. National Health Reorganisation Act 1973, s.10.

22. National Health Service Act 1977, Sched 8.

23. s.128.

24. Walker, A. (1982) *Community Care - the Family, the State and Social Policy* (Blackwell and Robertson) at p.193.

25. Sanford, J.R.A. (1978) 'Tolerance of debility in elderly dependants by supporters at home' in Carver, V. and Liddiard, P. (eds) *An Ageing Population* (Hodder and Stoughton/Open University Press) at p.140.

26. Association of Directors of Social Services (1983) *Report on Adult Homefinding Scheme.*

27. Ware, P. *Research Outline* sent to Social Services Authorities dated May 5, 1981. At the time of the project, the researcher was employed by the City of Bradford Metropolitan Council.

28. *Luganda v. Services Hotels Ltd. [1969] 2 All ER 692.*

29. Traynor, J. (1981) 'Home from Home' (1981) *Health and Social Services Journal* October 2, 1981 at pp.210-11.

30. Income Support (General) Regulations 1987 S.I. 1987 No.1967, reg 20(2).

31. *S. v. Walsall Metropolitan Borough Council (1985)* reported in *Adoption and Fostering* vol.19, no.4 at p.60.

32. Leeds City Council (1979) *A New Approach to Caring for the Elderly.*

33. Occupiers' Liability Act 1957, s.1(1).

34. Burgess, P. 'Changing the Rules and Rulings on the charges' *Community Care* June 2, 1988 at p.15.

35. Vaux, G. 'Attendance Allowances may be hit by top-up payments' *Community Care* June 30, 1988.

36. Social Security (Attendance Allowance) (No.2) Regulations 1975 S.I, 1975 No.598 (as amended). See reg 4(1)(b).

37. Transport Act 1985, s.92.

38. s.93(7).

39. Department of Transport *Explanatory Notes on the provisions of the Transport Act (1985).* Ref. P5V359.

40. Transport Act 1985, s.97(2).

41. Travel Concession Schemes Regulations 1986 S.I. 1986, No.77.

42. Department of Transport Circular No.2/78.

43. LAC 13/74 at para. 11(ii).

44. ibid. at para. 80. Speech therapists might usefully be employed by social service authorities.

45. Welsh Office (1974) *Notes on s.29 of the National Assistance Act 1948.*

46. See oral answer given by Mrs. Barbara Castle to a question in the House of Commons. Hansard, August 5, 1975 at col. 219. Local authorities, nevertheless, enjoy considerable discretion since they need only make arrangements when satisfied that need exists.

47. Royal Association for Disability and Rehabilitation (RADAR) (undated) *Putting Teeth into the Act* at p.22.

48. ibid., at p.26. The number of holidays provided by local authorities has declined of recent years. See CSO (1987) *Social Trends*, Table 7.42.

49. RADAR op.cit., at p.30. See also *The Times* December 15 and 30, 1981.

50. DHSS Circular, HSC (15) 11.

51. LAC Circular (78) 14.

52. The official terms probably remain unchanged but some social service departments now use the word 'appliances' rather than 'aids'.

53. For a detailed discussion, see Keeble, U. (1981) 'The Disabled Person's Aids and Adaptations', in Guthrie (1981) op.cit., at p.196.

54. ibid.

55. Barrow, S. and Derbyshire, M. E. (1975) *Survey of the usefulness of aids* (unpublished) Lancashire Social Services Department.

56. See Robertson, S. (1988) *Disability Rights Handbook* (Disability Alliance) at p.137.

57. RADAR op.cit., at p.24.

58. Department of Environment Guide (1983) *Home Improvement Grants* at p.6.

59. LAC (78) 14, (Appendix 3).

60. ibid., at para. 6.

61. Disabled Persons (Badges for Motor Vehicles) Regulations 1982. S.I. 1982 No.1740.

62. Details can be obtained from the Department of Transport.

63. Maximum £2 at present.

64. Road Traffic Regulation Act 1967, s.86(a).

65. Copies of the *Discussion Paper* are available from the Department of Transport.

66. The term 'advocate' is not used in the Act.

67. i.e., National Assistance Act 1948, Part III; Chronically Sick and Disabled Persons Act 1970, s.2; National Health Service Act 1977, Sched 8.

68. Carson, D. (1986) 'Recent Legislation' in the *Journal of Social Welfare Law* November 1986 at p.365.

69. The Acts covered are listed in Health and Social Services and Social Security Adjudication Act 1983, s.17(2).

70. Goldberg, E. M. and Connelly, M. (1982) op.cit., at p.76.

71. See the principle in *Associated Provincial Picture Houses v. Wednesbury Corporation [1947] 2 All ER 680.*

72. Hyman, M. (1981) *The Home Help Source : A case study in the London Borough of Redbridge* (Redbridge Social Services Department).

73. RADAR op.cit., at p.19.

74. ibid., at p.28.

75. Health and Social Services and Social Security Adjudication Act 1983, s.17(4) provides for recovery in the magistrates court. Other methods of recovery are also possible.

76. Family Policy Studies Centre (1984) *The Forgotten Army : Family Care and Elderly People.*

77. Levin, E. et al. (1983) *The Supporters of Confused Elderly Persons at Home* (National Institute of Social Work).

78. Nissel, M. and Bonnerjea, L. (1982) *Family Care of the Handicapped Elderly: Who Pays?* (Policy Studies Institute).

79. Useful advice can be obtained from the Association of Carers. See also, Social Security Consortium (1987) *Of Little Benefit - An Update: A Critical Guide to the Social Security Act 1986*, at p.11.

80. *Drake v. Chief Adjudication Officer [1986] CMLR 43*.

81. Midwinter, E. (1986) *Caring for Cash* (Centre for Policy on Ageing) at p.9.

82. ibid., at p.11.

83. Employment Agencies Act 1973, s.5(1).

84. Midwinter, E. (1986) op.cit., at p.41.

85. ibid., Appendix I.

86. *122 SJ 349*; *76 LGR 727*; *The Times*, May 10, 1978.

87. *The Times*, February 10, 1984.

88. RADAR op.cit., at p.26.

89. *R. v. Kent County Council (1986) The Times* February 8, 1986.

90. See 'News' in *Community Care* June 5, 1986 at p.3.

Chapter Four

RESIDENTIAL CARE

4.1.1 INTRODUCTION

About 233,000 people over 65 now live in residential establishments, as compared with 152,000 ten years ago. This is less than four per cent of the elderly population of England and Wales;[1] and it would seem that about one in ten only of the retired population is likely to enter residential care at some stage in their lives.[2] The ratio falls to about one in five, however, for those aged 85 and over.[3]

It is predicted that, on present population trends, the demand for residential care will grow steadily for the remainder of this century and beyond, even if more emphasis is placed upon community care as an alternative form of social support. This is because the number of vulnerable elderly people in Britain is likely to grow considerably during the next 20 to 40 years. By the end of the century, the number of those aged 85 and over is expected to have doubled to almost one million, and the age-group 75 and over is expected to grow by more than a third over the next 30 years.

4.1.2 Currently, increasing demand for residential care is being met mainly by growth in the independent sector. The number of beds has increased dramatically since 1977, with an almost four-fold increase in the private sector between 1979 and 1985.[4] Privately owned homes now substantially out-number those run by charities and religious bodies, a reversal of the situation of 20 years ago.[5] A similar shift in the balance between public and private provision will be the probable consequence of continuing with current policies. In some counties, provision in the private sector has already out-stripped that in the public sector. In Devon, for instance, the number of those being financially supported by the DSS in private establishments exceeds, by 50 per cent, the number of residents in local authority care. This growth is undoubtedly related to the present government's indirect sponsorship of the private sector by means of the social security system. There is some evidence to suggest, however, that the rate of growth is slowing down. The setting of national limits in April 1985 to the amount of DSS benefit payable to particular categories of people in residential care in the independent sector may prove a disincentive to those contemplating entry into this market. Nevertheless, even opponents of privatization concede that it would be difficult to return to the pre-1979 situation when local authority provision was virtually regarded as synonymous with residential care.[6]

4.1.3 The Firth Committee, a joint central and local government working party, proposed that responsiblity for financing residents in care should rest entirely with local authorities.[7] The Griffiths Report came to a similar conclusion. It recommended that social services authorities should establish a system for enabling it to decide whether residential care was the most appropriate way of meeting an individual's need for care, in the light of the other available options. The social security system should contribute an assessment of the applicants' financial means as part of the overall assessment of need so as to decide whether or not there was entitlement to an income-related social security benefit. The Griffiths Report also suggests that social security benefit payments for residential accommodation should be limited to a fixed sum substantially lower than the current rate, with the balance being paid by the social services authority should it conclude that residential care was the most appropriate way of meeting the individual's care needs. The report suggests that implementation of its proposals would help ensure that individuals were not placed in residential accommo-dation when that was not in their best interests.[8] The recent report of the independent review of residential care (the Wagner Committee) similarly suggests that the feasibility of intro-ducing community care allowances should be studied. Allowances could be used either to recruit help in the home, or to procure admission to a particular residential establishment or, if preferred, to secure a package of care resources.[9]

4.2.1 INSTITUTIONAL LIVING

The problems associated with institutional living are well documented.[10] As a result, entry into residential care is often perceived as a last resort rather than a preferred option. A large-scale study of some 7,000 residents in local authority homes concluded that 'minimal routines' - that is, policies and practices designed to leave as much freedom of action open to residents as possible - are not found in the majority of homes.[11]

Yet residential life need not be institutional. A large-scale study of local authority, voluntary, and private homes in the London area concluded that around 18 per cent of those studied could be described as 'homely' while 15 per cent were categorized as 'institutional', 'rigid', 'unrelaxed', and 'tense'.[12] This and other research suggests that very few homes are uniformly good or bad. They are mostly a confused mixture of sensitive practice and unhelpful and unnecessary rules, with the balance between the two varying from home to home.[13] A significant improvement in standards can probably be achieved only when those concerned with the management and provision of residential care become more concerned over particularizing the rights of residents as consumers. Some steps in that direction have already been taken in both the public and independent sectors, but the end products in the form of so-called 'contracts' or 'charters' often show lack of proper understanding of the complicated legal issues involved. In general, the legal profession has taken little interest in this area of the law, its failure to do so being compounded by the lethargy, indifference, or, possibly, the antipathy of those who plan and provide residential care.[14] The Wagner Committee recommended that a panel of advocates/personal representatives should be made available to residents. An advocate would need to be someone entirely independent of those providing the service, and one or more of the panel members would need to be legally trained.[15]

4.2.2 VARIATIONS IN STANDARDS

It has been suggested that residential establishments in the independent sector offer the best quality of care.[16] There are disturbing reports, however, of poor conditions in some private homes. A study of private establishments in the West Midlands revealed that in several homes, residents were often forced to wear what was put out for them, which sometimes included communal clothing. Apparently, residents were occasionally denied even that limited dignity.

> I noticed that residents who stayed in their rooms were seated in chairs. These residents needed assistance when going to the toilet. To help staff in cutting down on their work, none of the residents wore underwear. This enabled them to just be lifted onto a commode. I also noticed that they were dressed over their night clothes.[17]

4.2.3 Standards vary considerably in the public sector, too. Some authorities have made a significant effort to enhance the individual freedom of elderly residents.[18] Others, however, have not managed to ensure satisfactory standards of care. For instance, after receiving complaints from a local medical officer, one London borough admitted that conditions in most of its residential homes were 'unacceptably poor'.[19] Following a second report, the authority acknowledged a lack of flexibility and choice in matters of daily living; too little consultation with residents; and too little regard for their dignity as individuals. It concluded that only three of the authority's ten homes met the standards of good practice which ought to prevail in the private sector in order to accord with the provisions of the Registered Homes Act 1984 (RHA 1984).[20] More serious were the allegations of actual cruelty at one of the residential homes in another London borough. The appalling conditions and bad treatment which existed there are said to have led to the death of at least one resident. Evidence considered by a three-member inquiry panel included allegations of sexual and physical abuse, financial irregularities, dirty conditions, male and female residents forced to queue naked for a bath, care workers stealing residents' cash, and care workers using the home's bar for drinking sessions.[21]

As the words of one residential worker indicate, there can be considerable risk in entering certain kinds of residential care:

It's surprising how quickly you can take away dignity and self-respect. One place I worked in they used to greet new residents with a bath - like it or not. In six months, they weren't the same people.[22]

4.3.1 ADMISSION

Substantial overlap exists between the clientele of local authority homes, of private and voluntary homes, and of nursing homes. Admission into one kind of establishment and not another is often a matter of chance.[23] The trend, however, is for local authority homes to become increasingly like nursing homes.[24]
For the individual, choice over what kind of establishment to enter may be a minor part of the process of entering residential care.[25] Although less than one per cent of those going into residential establishments are admitted compulsorily, it seems that many of the remainder may not have given their consent freely.[26] It appears that all too frequently individuals are given insufficient information for making a rational choice. This situation was highlighted by a survey which concluded that about half the residents admitted to local authority homes possessed no information about them beforehand.[27] Some were 'taken for a ride' to a place where they had never been before.[28] An example of the kind of collusion which can occur between professional workers and carers is for admission forms, and other particulars, to be completed by relatives in the absence of the elderly person, whose signature had been obtained after being given only a cursory explanation.[29] If this is common practice, then it is worrying that a survey of admission to both public and private sector homes showed that two out of every three applications had been instigated by relatives.[30] Other evidence suggests that four out of five applications to private homes are also processed in this way.[31]

4.3.2 A person's entry into residential care is often an easy solution to other people's problems. A possible way forward might be to encourage elderly people to become more assertive, particularly since it seems that as many as one in three elderly people in residential care could cope in the community without much difficulty if they were to receive the services they require.[32] Given proper assessment procedures, it would have been possible for them to remain in the community.

4.4.1 THE DUTY TO PROVIDE RESIDENTIAL ACCOMMODATION

Section 21 of the National Assistance Act 1948 (NAA 1948) provides that a social services authority

> *may* with the approval of the Secretary of State, *and to such extent as he may direct, shall* make arrangements for providing residential accommodation for persons who by reasons of age, infirmity or any other circumstances are in need of care and attention which is not otherwise available to them. *(our emphasis)*

DHSS Circular 13/74 sets out current Ministerial directions made under s.21. A duty is placed upon local authorities to provide residential accommodation, plus the following incidental services. First, authorities must make arrangements for supervising the hygiene of the accommodation which is provided. Second, authorities must enable residents to obtain medical and nursing attention during illnesses of the kind which would ordinarily be nursed at home, as well as enabling them to benefit from any other NHS service which they may need from time to time. Third, authorities must make provision for such other services, amenities and requisites as the authority considers necessary in connection with the accommodation. Finally, authorities must regularly review provision made under the foregoing arrangements and make such improvements as are considered necessary.[33] Although local authorities possess a degree of discretion in these matters, that discretion is not unfettered since they must regularly review their provision and give proper consideration to matters which are specified in the section. A complaint against an authority for failing to perform duties under the Act might initially be put in the form of an enquiry whether or not a statutory review had been carried out.

4.4.2 THE STATUTORY CRITERIA

Although these Ministerial directions confer a duty upon local authorities in relation to any individuals satisfying the criteria set out in s.21, s.24 of the Act also requires that the person is either in urgent need of residential accommodation, or else ordinarily resident within the local authority's area.

The meaning of the phrase 'ordinary residence' was considered in *R. v. Waltham Forest, ex parte Vale (1985)*. An application was made to quash a local authority's refusal to provide residential accommodation for a 28 year old woman with a mental handicap. The applicant had been living in the Republic of Ireland but claimed to be ordinarily resident in the area of the local authority as she had been living in the area with her parents for a month. Reference was made to an earlier decision in which Lord Denning had held that the 'ordinary residence' of a child of tender years was his/her parental home. It was held that since the applicant herself was not capable of forming a 'settled intention' where to live, her application should succeed.[34] A similar argument might be put in circumstances where a mentally infirm elderly person had moved in temporarily with a younger relative and then applied for residential care in that district.[35]

4.4.3 The NAA 1948 contains specific provisions for determining the residential status of patients discharged from hospital. As might be expected, they are deemed to be residents of the area in which they were 'ordinarily resident' prior to admission.[36] Where no previous ordinary 'residence' can be established, it must be shown that urgent need exists in order for a duty to be placed upon the local authority of the area in which the hospital is situated. (s.24(3)(b)) Any question relating to ordinary residence must be referred for determination by the Secretary of State. (s.32(3)) He acts as referee, therefore, where two or more local authorities are in conflict.

The other criteria set out in s.21 relate to 'age, infirmity or any other circumstances' coupled with a need for care and attention not otherwise available. The fundamental test is therefore *need*. The relevant guidelines suggest that admission should be for 'those who are found, after careful assessment of their medical and social needs, to be unable to maintain themselves in their own homes, even with full support from outside,

but are not in need of continuous care by nursing staff'.[37]
Hasty emergency admissions abound, however;[38] medical assessments are often inadequate or non-existent;[39] and residential
staff complain that they sometimes have to cope with individuals
who need hospital or nursing care.[40]

4.4.4 THE DUTY TOWARDS MENTALLY DISORDERED PERSONS

A duty to provide residential care for those suffering from
mental disorder was originally created by s.12(1) of the Health
Services and Public Health Act 1968 (HSPHA 1968) which had
similar provisions to those discussed above.[41] This duty, too,
is dependent upon a residential criterion being satisfied but
here the test is either that the person is ordinarily resident
in the area or has 'no settled residence'. The distinction
between having 'no settled residence' and being in 'urgent
need' (the phrase used in s.24 of the NAA 1948) is probably
academic, since it seems inconceivable that a mentally
disordered elderly person without an established ordinary
residence would not be regarded as in 'urgent need' and
therefore covered by both provisions.

4.4.5 POWERS TO PROVIDE ACCOMMODATION AND OTHER SERVICES

Where a person is neither ordinarily resident in the area of a
local authority nor in urgent need, there is no duty upon the
authority to provide residential accommodation, although it
possesses statutory *powers* to do so. An authority may also
arrange for an individual to be accommodated in a home run by
another local authority or in a home run by a voluntary
organization or by a registered person.[42] The terms of such
arrangements are a matter of agreement between the supporting
authority and the other party involved. Indeed, local authorities have wide powers to contribute to the funds of any
voluntary organization providing, or proposing to provide,
accommodation for like purposes as that provided by an
authority. (s.26(6)) All such arrangements are subject to the
approval of the Secretary of State.

General approval has been given under s.29 of the NAA 1948 for the provision of certain hostels and holiday homes.(see Chapter 3, para. 3.8.2) The NAA 1948 also enables local authorities to provide for the conveyance of persons to and from the premises in which residential accommodation is provided.(s.21(7)(a)) The words used are clearly permissive since provision is to be made in 'such cases as they [local authorities] consider appropriate'. Discretion is not absolute, however. In the unlikely event of an authority refusing to provide a service it would need to show that it had given the matter proper consideration before reaching a decision.

4.5.1 CHARGING FOR RESIDENTIAL CARE

Section 22 of the HSPHA 1968 requires charges to be made for residential accommodation. Each local authority is required to set a 'standard charge' which is the *maximum* weekly amount a resident can be required to pay. A lesser sum is payable where a resident elects not to pay the standard charge and his/her resources are assessed as inadequate to meet the charge. This assessed charge which, with one exception, must not fall below a ministerially prescribed minimum, will depend upon the amount of the resident's capital and income.(see para. 4.5.3) From April 1988, the minimum weekly charge for accommodation provided under the NAA 1948 is £32.90.

The same procedure applies, in essence, where the individual is being sponsored by a local authority at a voluntary or private home registered under the RHA 1984. Although a local authority is obliged to pay the agreed fee direct to the organization providing the service, it should also assess the resident's ability to pay, and collect as much of the fee as the resident is able to afford. The requirement to charge a prescribed minimum also applies.(NAA 1948, s.26(3))

The legislation contains no set formula for calculating the standard charge but government guidelines stipulate that it should reflect, as closely as possible, the true economic cost of providing the accommodation.[43] In practice, most if not all authorities calculate their standard charges on the basis of guidelines prepared by the Association of County Councils.[44] The amount charged varies from authority to authority. A telephone poll of the eight Welsh local authorities in April 1986 revealed that charges ranged between £107 and £149. The average charge was £117.

Whatever procedure is adopted in fixing the rate, an authority must act reasonably otherwise its action will be unlawful. The courts have been reluctant to interfere, however, and will do so in exceptional circumstances only. This reluctance might be overcome if it could be shown that a social service authority had set the standard charge simply by comparison with other authorities.[45] In fact, the Association of County Councils Guidelines include notional elements calculated on a national basis, though some scope for local discretion is also allowed.

4.5.2 Section 22(5)(A) of the NAA 1948 (inserted by s.20 of the Health and Social Services and Social Security Adjudication Act 1983 (HSSSSAA 1983)) enables authorities to levy the prescribed minimum charge for the first eight weeks only of each and every period in residence, whatever the resident's means. Some authorities, possibly the more enlightened, have taken full advantage of this provision. Where a person is in residence for less than a week charges must be levied on a pro rata rate. (s.22(6)). Only about one resident in 20 pays the standard charge even after the first eight weeks, whereas some seven out of ten pay the prescribed minimum charge.[46] Some residents find it difficult to accept that the quality of service they receive is not dependent upon their ability to pay the full standard charge.[47]

4.5.3 THE PERSONAL ALLOWANCE

Section 22(4) of the NAA 1948 permits a resident to retain a prescribed sum to meet his/her personal requirements, or such sum as, in special circumstances, the authority considers appropriate. From April 1988, the minimum weekly sum which local authorities are to assume that persons provided with residential accommodation will need for their personal requirements is £8.25. The prescribed personal allowance has been set by regulation at about one-fifth of the basic single retirement pension. The minimum charge, referred to above, is thus set at approximately four-fifths of that amount. Where the income of the resident is less than the total of the minimum charge plus the prescribed sum, as will be the case where the resident is one of a couple in receipt of income support (IS), the DSS must make up the balance to the stipulated amount.

In special circumstances, s.22(4) of the NAA 1948 enables a local authority to allow an individual more or less than the prescribed amount, as appropriate. Authorities tend to interpret this power in a negative way. Indeed, it is not uncommon to find a personal allowance has been reduced. The relevant guidelines suggest that usually a reduction should be made only after consulting the resident's GP. The balance should then be deposited in a special account and spent on the personal needs of the resident. Any sums accumulated in this way must not be taken into account as part of the resident's capital resources for assessment purposes.[48] Increasing the personal allowance above the prescribed amount might be appropriate where a resident continues to lead an active life. This is possible, apparently, only where a resident is paying more than the minimum charge since s.22(3) provides that liability to pay the minimum charge cannot normally be reduced. The only statutory exception is where charges are waived for persons who assist in the running of premises.(s.23(3)) The DSS acknowledges that this could have the effect of reducing a resident's charge below the prescribed minimum. The power to waive charges does not apply to residents sponsored by local authorities in voluntary or privately run homes.[49]

4.5.4 The prescribed personal allowance is lower than the parallel DSS allowance for those who have entered voluntary or private residential homes under private arrangements. This is because it is assumed that a local authority will supply residents at its homes with basic requirements, including toiletries and clothing. This obligation has been acknowledged indirectly by government, although it has also been stressed that a resident should be free to choose and buy his/her own clothing, even if these are paid for by the local authority.[50]

4.5.5 THE ASSESSMENT

Section 22(5) of the HSPHA 1968 (as amended by the Social Security Act 1980 (SSA 1980) (not yet in force) provides for regulations to be made specifically in relation to assessing a

resident's ability to pay.[51] Until such regulations are made,
local authorities must continue to apply paras. 17 to 20 of Part
III of Sched. I of the Supplementary Benefit Act 1976 (SBA 1976)
when making assessments.

The link between local authority assessment and the social
security system has led to an apparent misunderstanding of the
legal position. The assessment unit for IS purposes can include
more than one person, whereas, as the DSS has re-emphasized, the
NAA 1948 provides that the resident's ability to pay for
accommodation relates only to his/her own resources. As a
result, there is no statutory provision under which local
authorities themselves can require the husband or wife of a
resident to disclose his/her resources. Circular LAC (85)(2)
requests all authorities to review their procedures to ensure
compliance with the statutory provisions. The Income Support
Regulations also reflect this position.[52] The regulations
relating to people temporarily staying in local authority
residential accommodation have now been amended. If one of a
couple is temporarily staying in residential accommodation, the
couple's benefit will consist of £32.90 for the cost of the
residential accommodation and £8.25 for personal expenses for
the member in that accommodation, and the other member's IS will
be calculated as if he/she was a single person. If both members
of a couple are temporarily staying in residential
accommodation, they will receive two lots of £32.90 and of £8.25
plus their housing costs for their normal home, if appropriate.
If a single person is temporarily staying in residential
accommodation, he/she will be paid benefit under the normal
rules.

4.5.6 Confusion over assessment procedures is understandable
given the provisions of s.42 of the NAA 1948 under which spouses
are liable to maintain each other. The only method by which a
local authority can enforce a contribution against a liable
spouse is by way of a complaint to a magistrates' court under
s.43 of the NAA 1948, against a spouse's refusal to contribute.
Only the court has the right to decide whether or not it is
reasonable for the spouse to contribute, and if so, what that
amount should be. DHSS Guidelines point out that a contribution
to the weekly charge should not be pressed to the point where
the resources of the spouse living at home become inadequate.[53]
No liability can arise until such time as the court directs,

although it could order payment to be made in respect of care provided before the making of the order (s.43(5)). If made, the court order is enforceable as an affiliation order.[54] Costs can be awarded to either party.[55] If the resident's spouse has deserted him/her, a complaint under s.43 will be unsuccessful, although the existence of a separation order (even if maintenance between the spouses has been agreed) does not in itself bar the local authority from applying for an order under this section.

4.5.7 As an alternative to bringing a complaint under s.43, an authority can enter into a voluntary agreement with the spouse. Where such an agreement is contemplated it is in the local authority's interest to ensure that the spouse has been advised to seek independent advice, otherwise an inference of undue influence might arise.(see Chapter 7 at para. 7.8.6)

4.5.8 RELEVANT RESOURCES

The combined effect of the various provisions in Sched. I of the SBA 1976 is to ensure that both income and capital are taken into account when calculating a resident's resources for the purposes of assessment. Some resources are disregarded in full, some in part, and others may be disregarded, wholly or partly, as is reasonable in the circumstances. For instance, up to £4 of weekly income over and above the basic state pension,[56] and capital below £1,200, together with income from such capital, must be wholly disregarded.[57]

It also seems clear from the decision in the *Chief Supplementary Benefit Officer v. Leary [1985]*[58] that capital amounts above the specified figure may be disregarded. An action was brought by a Supplementary Benefit Officer against the personal representatives of the deceased person on discovery that the capital sum was more than had previously been disclosed. It was held by the Court of Appeal that para. 20, which relates to capital disregards, and para. 27, which provides for discretion in the treatment of any resources not specified in the foregoing provisions, were not mutually exclusive. The Supplementary Benefit Officer's claim failed, and the court concluded that the provisions of para. 27 should not be restricted to casual receipts, such as birthday presents, or windfalls such as winnings made at gambling. In the light of this decision, authorities should, perhaps, abandon the practice of automatically taking into full account all capital amounts above the specified sum. The circumstances of individual residents should be considered on their merits.

4.5.9 THE FORMER DWELLING HOUSE

Assessment procedures relating to the treatment of a resident's former dwelling house should be examined carefully, since authorities may be acting unlawfully at times. Some local authorities, for example, give the impression that they are bound to take a dwelling into account in deciding a resident's liability to pay charges, whereas there is no compulsion upon them to do so.[59] A local authority which operated a rigid policy in this respect might be deemed to be fettering its discretion and thereby acting beyond its powers.[60] In other words, a court might hold the policy to be *ultra vires*. It is also clear from the wording of para. 17 of Sched.1 of the SBA 1976 that only a dwelling which is not the person's residence can be included for assessment purposes. Local authorities must decide, in the circumstances of each case, whether the resident has effectively given up residence of his/her former home. In fact, local authority residential homes are increasingly being used for short-term care. Whereas in 1967, less than a third of admissions were for short periods of time, two-thirds currently fall into this category.[61] It is only in a minority of cases, therefore, that a property should fall for assessment.

4.5.10 Some authorities distinguish on the application form between a short-term and long-term admission. At least one authority, in fact, operates on the basis that all new admissions will be short-term until a detailed assessment has been completed.[62] Some authorities, however, require residents to agree to a valuation of their home when they enter care. The authors were told of one individual who was visited some weeks after her return home from short-term care by a valuer intent on valuing her property. This example, although exceptional, perhaps, highlights the need for authorities to look at each case individually. A local authority which automatically assumes that residence is permanent after a designated trial period -

for example, six months - will have failed to do so. A rule of this kind could be challenged in the courts on the grounds that its use was a fetter on the local authority's discretion and upon the need to consider each case individually.

4.5.11 Even where long-term residence can be established, it may remain inappropriate for an authority to take the value of the resident's dwelling into account. Since s.42 of the NAA 1948 imposes a liability on spouses to maintain each other and children of the family, where a spouse or child remains in the dwelling, it should not be included in making the assessment. These are not the only circumstances, however, in which it might be appropriate to disregard or reduce the value of a person's dwelling for the purposes of assessment.[63] It might, for example, be reasonable for an authority to exercise its discretion in circumstances in which a person who has been caring for the resident remains in the dwelling.

4.5.12 CHARGES ON PROPERTY

Even when it might seem appropriate for a former dwelling to be taken into account in assessing liability to pay, local authorities cannot compel a resident to sell.[64] Where he/she declines to do so, the assessment should be based on a professional estimate of the property's current selling price, less ten per cent in recognition of the expenses which would be incurred were the property to be sold, and minus any mortgage or loan secured against the property.[65] Should the resident be unable to meet the assessment from available funds, the authority must agree a lower rate and defer levying the assessed amount, plus interest, until such time as the house is eventually sold. Invariably, an authority will want to protect its interest by securing a legal charge on the property and so protect its right to payment from the proceeds of a sale at any time.

A legal charge can be imposed by the court as the result of a civil action for debt. The more usual method will be an attempt at getting the resident to agree a voluntary charge. A charge created in this way might, however, be set aside by a court unless it could be shown that the resident exercised his/her free will in executing it.[66] Evidence that the resident had received independent legal advice in the matter would probably be sufficient.

The need to show that a voluntary charge resulted from a resident's independent and informed judgment may shortly become unnecessary. Under s.22 of the HSSSSAA 1983, local authorities will be empowered to create charges whenever residents have an interest in land and have failed to pay the assessed charge for accommodation.

4.5.13 Where a resident owns property as joint tenant,[67] his/her financial interest arising from the sale of the land may be subject to a charge. This cannot exceed the value of the interest the resident would have enjoyed had the property been split. The creation of a charge does not, however, sever a joint tenancy. Although the vast majority of married couples hold property as joint tenants, (that is, on the death of one spouse, the other is entitled to the whole of the equity) it is not envisaged that these particular provisions will have a marked impact since, as suggested above, only a minority of properties can properly fall into charge. The major impact of s.22, therefore, will be to remove the need to obtain consent to charges. The section will enable a local authority to create a charge by a declaration in writing, and places no duty upon authorities in England and Wales to notify the resident of its existence either before or after it is made.[68]

4.5.14 When in force, s.24 of the HSSSSAA 1983 will provide that no interest on a charge should accrue to the local authority until after the death of the resident. The section also provides for the rate of interest to be such reasonable amount as the local authority may determine. At present, no legal right to any interest exists in the absence of a court order unless the right arose from an agreement.[69] Residents and affected relatives would be well-advised to scrutinize assessments as well as questioning the existence of any alleged debts so as to ensure that they reflect true liability, whether the claims relate to property subject to a charge or not. The existence of a charge does not excuse the chargee, that is, the local authority, from an initial responsibility to prove that the debt exists.

4.5.15 ABANDONMENT OR DISPOSAL
OF RESOURCES

Another important section of the HSSSSAA 1983 is s.21 which, when in force, will provide local authorities with additional powers to control the deliberate disposal of assets so as to avoid or to reduce charges for residential accommodation. It will impose liability upon any third party to whom a resident in local authority accommodation has transferred assets with the intention of avoiding charges for accommodation.

The extent of liability created by s.21 will be the difference between the amount owing and the amount that the local authority has received in accommodation charges. The section applies to any cash or other assets which are to be taken into account for the purposes of assessment under s.22 of the NAA 1948.[70] The section clearly applies to real property, that is, to transfers of land as well as to personal property, such as shares, saving certificates and the like. The section only applies, however, to the transfer of any asset which took place during the period of six months prior to admission or during residence. It must have been made for no consideration, (that is, it must have been a gift), or for consideration less than the value of the asset. Nevertheless, the fundamental test is whether or not the resident deliberately gave away the asset with the intention of avoiding any charges. Where such intention can be shown, any person receiving such assets would be liable to pay the charge, even if unaware of the resident's motive. Liability must not, however, exceed the amount of benefit accruing to him/her from the transfer.[71]

4.5.16 The HSSSSAA 1983 is silent on the question of transfers made with the aim of avoiding liability prior to the six months period immediately before admission. It is, therefore, assumed that in such cases, local authorities would have to rely on the remedies available under the SBA 1976. The Memorandum of Guidance suggests unequivocally that any assets of which a resident can be shown to have deprived him/herself at any time with the intention of reducing the amount payable, can be included in the resident's resources for the purpose of assessment.[72] This arises from the interpretation placed by the Department upon para. 28 of Sched. 1 of the SBA 1976 by the DHSS. Para. 28 reads:

If a person has deprived himself of any resources for the purpose of securing *supplementary benefit*, those resources may be taken into account as if they were still his. *(our emphasis)*.

The DHSS (now the DSS) has accepted that the paragraph in question seems to refer to claims for supplementary benefit (IS) only,[73] but argues that since the 1976 Act was a consolidating enactment, the courts can have recourse to an earlier statutory provision which referred to 'benefit' rather than 'supplementary benefit'. The difference is said to consist of a 'slight change of wording' only. It is also claimed that the anomaly would fall within a dictum of the House of Lords which decided that a consolidation statute is assumed to reproduce pre-existing statute law without correction or minor improvements.

The dictum being relied upon is not referred to in the Memorandum. In fact, two years earlier than publication of the Memorandum, the House of Lords had departed from the tradition of interpreting consolidation statutes in the way suggested by the DSS.[74] The new approach - that if words are clear and unambiguous it is not permissible to have recourse to the earlier statute - has been confirmed by the House of Lords in subsequent cases.[75] It would, therefore, seem that the important question legally is whether the wording of para. 28 can be regarded as ambiguous, and so permit reference to be made to the earlier provision. It is suggested that no ambiguity exists in this context and that DSS guidance is open to question.

A local authority would in any case need to satisfy a court that the resources in question had been abandoned for the purpose of securing benefit or increasing its amount. There are no reported cases on the construction of para. 28, although the meaning of 'purpose' has been discussed in the courts, mainly in the context of revenue cases. Little is to be gained from a review of such cases, however, since they are hard to reconcile. Nevertheless, it seems that where the purpose of an arrangement is to deal with ordinary business or with family matters, the courts are unlikely to impute an ulterior purpose.[76] If an ulterior purpose could be established, a local authority might face the additional problem, where the resident has insufficient assets to meet the assessed charge from available resources, of having the disposal in question set aside.

4.5.17 Although no cases involving residents in local authority
accommodation have been reported, it has been suggested that a
disposal could in some circumstances be defeated by initiating
either bankruptcy proceedings under s.42 of the Bankruptcy Act
1914 (BA 1914) or, alternatively, by applying under s.172 of the
Law of Property Act 1925 (LPA 1925) for the transfer of property
to be set aside as being intended to defraud creditors.[77] Local
authorities contemplating bankruptcy procedures face several
obstacles. Unless legal action is taken within two years of the
settlement, it will fail if it can be shown that, at the time of
the settlement, the settlor was able to pay all his/her debts
without using the settlement property.[78] Proceedings might also
be defeated if it could be shown that the settlement had been
made in good faith and for valuable consideration. The consideration given need not be adequate although it must be more
than a nominal amount. Section 172 of the LPA 1925 is in similar
terms to s.42 with the additional proviso that an action for
recovery can always be defeated if it was made for *good*
consideration. The giving of natural love and affection can
amount to good consideration. Section 21 of the HSSSSAA 1983,
which is not yet in force, avoids such legal niceties by
stipulating that transfers for less than market value will give
rise to liability. In the meantime, local authorities can
probably do little. At most, they can rely only on highly technical procedures which may be threatened but are rarely used in
practice.

4.6.1 THE CONDUCT OF HOMES

Under s.23 of the NAA 1948, a local authority may make rules as
to the conduct of residential establishments under its management and for the preservation of order within them. The validity
of rules made under s.23 could possibly be challenged on the
grounds that they had not been properly sanctioned by the local
authority.[79] Evidence suggests that only a minority of local
authorities prepare detailed rules in relation to the management
of residential premises. The question which then arises is what
precisely can be defined as a 'rule' in this context? There is
no relevant case-law and predicting the probable outcome of
litigation is difficult since the courts have not always
insisted that publication of a rule should be a precondition for

compliance. Clearer judicial guidance might help in establishing practices which, for example, better protect the privacy of residents. Although authorities often pay lip-service to the need for privacy, there is clear evidence that, in practice, this is often ignored.

Residents may suffer false imprisonment in certain homes since some local authorities sanction the locking of residents' rooms particularly at night.[80] This practice has not been challenged directly in the courts but judicial disapproval was expressed in one Crown Court case relating to private residential care. There the judge stated categorically that to secure doors by latching them was unacceptable practice and that the way to deal with a wandering, confused elderly person was to have night staff awake and about, with somebody else on hand to give further help if necessary.[81] Many residents, it seems, would like locks on their doors but there is no excuse for the continued existence of rooms which can be locked from the outside only.[82]

4.6.2 Rules relating to the conduct of a home may also set out the circumstances in which a person can be required to leave, although that can only happen where there has been a change in the resident's circumstances, or where he/she has otherwise become unsuitable. The NAA 1948 makes no specific provision for removal for non-payment of an assessed charge, and it has been suggested that such action would be inappropriate, since local authorities have recourse to less draconian methods for protecting their interests.[83] The fact that a local authority can make rules relating to the conduct of homes implies that residents are licensees rather than tenants. To be a 'licensee' means that the person has no more than permission to stay, which can be withdrawn at any time. Even so, the law implies into a licence a condition that it will not be brought to an end without reasonable notice being given. What is 'reasonable' will depend upon the circumstances, although the courts have rarely stipulated a period of more than four weeks.[84] A decision to remove an elderly person from a home could also be challenged on principles established in administrative law. Public authorities are not only required to exercise their powers reasonably but also in accordance with the general aims of the relevant legislation. In this context, the purpose is clearly to ensure that people falling within the statutory definition are provided with the care which they need. For these reasons, judicial interpretation of s.23 of the NAA 1948 may be long overdue.

4.7.1 PUBLIC NURSING HOMES

Three experimental, centrally funded, nursing homes for the elderly have been opened at Sheffield, Fleetwood and Portsmouth. Each provides for between 25-30 residents. The major objective is to provide total care in a homely, supportive environment for elderly people who are heavily dependent on nursing care. Individuals who require psychiatric care are not admitted although those who deteriorate mentally after admission will not be transferred unless they require active treatment or become severely disruptive.[85] The classification of the residents at these establishments is not discussed in literature issued by the DHSS, and the only clues are that the beds are classed as NHS hospital beds, and that pension entitlement resembles that of hospital patients.[86] Hopefully, the issues which arise from their ambiguous legal status will be considered before any decision is taken whether or not to continue or to extend the existing scheme. (This experiment is being evaluated by the University of Newcastle Health Care Research Unit.) It should be noted, however, that premises of this kind, maintained or controlled by a government department, are not included within the statutory definition of nursing homes as set out in the RHA 1984.[87]

4.8.1 REGISTRATION CATEGORIES IN THE INDEPENDENT SECTOR

A range of establishments in the independent sector fall within the compass of the RHA 1984, from small proprietor-run residential care homes at one end of the spectrum, to nursing homes, often with sophisticated medical equipment, at the other. The primary legal concern is not what an establishment calls itself, whether a 'rest home', 'guest house', or 'hotel', but whether or not the establishment provides either board and personal services to persons in need of personal care, or nursing services for persons suffering from any sickness, injury, or infirmity.[88] A person who deceitfully describes or holds out premises as a Nursing Home or as a Mental Nursing Home within the meaning of the Act will be guilty of an offence unless properly registered.[89] This provision is primarily intended to dissuade proprietors of residential establishments from offering a level of service which they are unable or unqualified to deliver. In an attempt to regulate standards, the RHA 1984 provides different, though similar, regulations in respect to Residential Care Homes, on the one hand, and Nursing Homes, on the other. In effect, the Act creates no less than six different categories of private establishment relevant to the care of the elderly, namely: Residential Care Homes; Unregistered Residential Care Homes; Nursing Homes; Mental Nursing Homes; Dually Registered Homes; and Exempt Residential Care Homes and Exempt Nursing Homes.

4.8.2 THE CODES OF PRACTICE

Guidelines for the registration and inspection of Residential Care Homes and Nursing Homes are to be found in *Home Life: a Code of Practice for Residential Care* and *Registration and Inspection of Nursing Homes - A Handbook for Health Authorities*. Local authorities have been asked by the Secretary of State to regard *Home Life* in the same light as any other general guidance issued from time to time under ministerial powers contained in s.7 of the Local Authority Social Services Act 1970 (LASSA 1970). Nevertheless, neither the Code nor the Handbook has any legal force. Before the RHA 1984 was passed, the Secretary of State had indicated that there would be 'a legally binding obligation on homes to conduct their affairs in a way that complied with a Code of Practice'[90] but no legal obligation has as yet been imposed. It has been suggested that problems of enforcement could be overcome if registration authorities insisted on compliance with the Codes as a condition of registration under the Act.[91] The Department, however, regards it as futile for registration authorities to insist on making such conditions on the grounds that the Codes are too general to be used in this way.[92] The authors of the Nursing Homes Handbook suggest that the guidelines set out in it need not be followed *in toto* by District Health Authorities (DHAs) when carrying out their registration functions. Similar advice is given to local authorities in a DHSS Circular LAC (86) in relation to standards of accommodation in Residential Care Homes. The contents of the Circular in effect water down the building standards previously advocated in *Home Life*. The Circular concludes that 'existing guidelines' should be interpreted flexibly when used in connection with the registration of premises under the RHA 1984. Nevertheless, to ignore the Code and the Handbook would be unwise since, as some had predicted, they seem to be used as rule-of-thumb reference points by Registered Homes Tribunals when hearing appeals which turn on the quality of care being provided.[93] Indeed it has been suggested that Tribunals should refer to the relevant provisions of the Code and record in their decisions how they were applied in each case.[94]

4.8.3 RESIDENTIAL CARE HOMES

Section 1 of the RHA 1984 defines a Residential Care Home as an establishment which provides, or intends to provide, whether for reward or not, residential accommodation with both board and personal care for persons in need of personal care by reason of old age, disablement, past or present dependence on alcohol or drugs, or past or present mental disorder. 'Old age' is not defined in the statute. It seems from remarks made during the Committee stage of the Bill, that the government felt it unnecessary and imprudent to do so.[95]

Carrying on a home which comes within the definition of a Residential Care Home without being properly registered is an offence under the Act which, on conviction, could lead to a fine of up to level 5 on the standard scale.[96] Authorized persons may at all times enter and inspect any premises which are used or which are reasonably believed to be used as a Residential Care Home.[97]

4.8.4 The distinguishing feature of a Residential Care Home is that it provides both 'board' and 'personal care'. The requirement to register depends on whether or not such services are being provided for a minimum of four persons falling within any one or more of the categories of dependency referred to above.[98] If so, it is of no consequence that the majority of the residents are receiving neither board nor personal care. The Department acknowledges that it would be impracticable to register every hotel or guest-house accommodating an occasional group of residents falling within the categories specified above. Establishments which accommodate such people for holidays regularly (if only for a week or a fortnight) will, however, need to be registered. The Guidance Notes suggest registration will be necessary where accommodation is made available for more than a month in the year. Some seaside establishments may fall well within the requirement for registration under the Act.

4.8.5 The term 'board' is not defined in the RHA 1984. It has been suggested that supplying, as well as preparing food, would be sufficient to bring an establishment within the Act.[99] Residents must, in any case, be supplied with 'suitably varied' and properly prepared wholesome and nutritious food in *adequate* quantities. Adequate facilities must also be provided, as far as is reasonable, for residents to prepare their own food and refreshment.[100] The Nursing Home Regulations are, in comparison, more specific in this respect since there is a duty to supply food adequate *for every patient*. This may imply that Nursing Homes are obliged to cater for individual palates.[101]

4.8.6 The term 'personal care' is not further defined in the Act (other than that it can include assistance with bodily functions where such assistance is required).(s.20(1)) The term seems broad enough, therefore, to embrace social work support from residential staff. The term 'bodily functions' is not further defined. It has been discussed, however, in a case focusing on eligibility for Attendance Allowance where 'bodily functions' were held to relate to 'those functions which the fit man normally performs for himself'.[102]

The Guidance Notes suggest that personal care is 'broadly equivalent to what might be provided by a competent and caring relative' and includes help with washing, bathing, dressing, assistance with toilet needs, the administration of medicines, and, when a resident feels sick, the kind of attention a person would receive from a caring relative under the guidance of a GP or nurse-member of the primary health care team. It has been suggested that such care can be dubbed 'household nursing' to contrast it with 'professional nursing'. Personal care might include taking temperatures, changing simple dressings, and the management of incontinence, whereas 'professional nursing' would encompass more technical procedures such as giving injections and using specialist equipment.[103] The distinction, although helpful, does not appear to be clear-cut. Given that it determines how premises are to be registered, it may only be a matter of time before interpretation of the term is raised in the courts.

4.8.7 If neither board nor personal care are being provided it may still be possible for a local authority to intervene by other means in order to safeguard the interests of elderly people, that is, where it appears that the house in which they are living is in multiple occupation, or is a common lodging house. A house is in multiple occupation if it is occupied by persons not forming part of a single household. Elderly people are among the most common occupants of such premises.[104] Some of the worst instances of disrepair are to be found in properties subject to more than one occupancy.[105] Local authority environmental health officers have wide powers of control. For instance, where the conditions represent a danger to the health, safety, or welfare of the occupants, a local authority has the right to assume management of the property.[106] A common lodging house is one which provides accommodation for poor people, not being members of the same family, who are allowed to occupy one common room for the purpose of sleeping or eating. No one is allowed to keep a common lodging house unless it is registered under the Public Health Act 1936 (PHA 1936). Local authorities are empowered to make bye-laws governing the way in which they are run.[107]

4.8.8 UNREGISTERED RESIDENTIAL CARE HOMES

An Unregistered Residential Care Home is an establishment where board and personal care are being provided for less than four people. According to one estimate, there could be as many as 20,000 elderly people living in unregistered, unsupervised homes existing under the guise of a small hotel or guest house.[108] It has also been suggested that since the implementation of the RHA 1984, the number of Unregistered Homes caring for two or three people has increased.[109] Most sheltered housing schemes need not be registered, although a number, catering for 'frail elderly' people, have been.[110]

For the purposes of registration, the number of residents

does not include those carrying on, or intending to carry on the home, nor any persons employed or intended to be employed there, nor their relatives.[111]   A parent of the proprietor/trix, or of a member of staff living on the premises and needing personal care, would not count for this purpose.

Where the number of residents is fewer than four, registration is optional.   It is unlikely, however, that such premises will be registered, given that fees have to be paid, and particularly since there is no legal prohibition on describing an establishment as a Residential Care Home, whether or not it has been registered.   Even more surprising, perhaps, is the fact that refusal or cancellation of registration as a Residential Care Home is no bar to running a home with less than four residents.[112]   The Wagner Committee was offered advice suggesting that such houses should be brought within the scope of some measure of regular inspection and control. The Committee concurred with this advice but stressed that it did not wish the full mechanism of registration and inspection to be brought to bear on such establishments unless a number of them were being operated by one proprietor.   In such circumstances, the Committee felt that the full requirements of the Act should apply.[113]

4.8.9 NURSING HOMES

The term 'Nursing Home', as defined in the Act, embraces a wide variety of establishments ranging from small Nursing Homes catering for a few patients only, to sizeable private hospitals. Three types of premises fall within the legal definition set out in s.21 of the Act, two of which are relevant in this context. First, premises used, or intended to be used, for the reception of, and the provision of nursing for, persons suffering from any sickness, injury, or infirmity; and secondly, premises used for the provision of specified medical services such as endoscopy or haemodialysis.   Premises falling into this last category must be registered even if they provide day care only.[114]

4.8.10 There is no statutory definition of the phrase 'provision of nursing' in s.21 of the RHA 1984.   The NAHA Handbook suggests the following as an unofficial guide to conditions needing nursing care:

    i) where a resident's general health [has] deteriorated to a level that needs constant nursing care;

    ii) where a resident's health is such that one or more of the following procedures (the list is not exhaustive) is required periodically over twenty-four hours:

       a) administration of medication by injection
       b) dressing to an open or closed wound
       c) artificial feeding requiring nursing skills
       d) basic nursing care of the type given to bedfast or predominantly bedfast persons
       e) frequent attention as a result of double or single incontinence
       f) intensive rehabilitative measures following surgery or debilitating disease which is likely to continue for more than a short period
       g) management of complex prosthesia or appliances.[115]

Guideline (i) above, gives a broad description of the situation where nursing care is needed whereas (ii) endorses the essential distinction between household and professional nursing discussed above. (see para. 4.8.6) The Handbook states that premises, usually known as hospices, providing care for the terminally ill must be registered as Nursing Homes, although such establishments are not referred to in the Act. The Handbook also acknowledges that the health of residents in a Residential Care Home may fluctuate so that, at times, they may require extra nursing care. A flexible approach is advocated, however, since alternative registration as a Nursing Home may not always be appropriate. According to the Handbook, the 'distinction between a resident and a patient may in the end be a subjective decision' and the question whether or not an establishment ought to be registered as a Nursing Home should be settled on the basis of advice from the designated senior nurse of the Registering Health Authority.[116] This statement may be somewhat misleading in that the distinction between a Residential Care Home, on the one hand, and a Nursing Home, on the other, is a question of law in every case.

It seems unlikely that the issue will be left unresolved for long since the effect of s.21 is to require registration as a Nursing Home even where *one* person only is being provided with nursing care. The Secretary of State has made use of a power as to the exercise of functions, contained in s.17 of the National Health Service Act 1977 (NHSA 1977), to instruct health authorities to inspect and take appropriate action whenever they have reason to believe that premises should be registered as a Nursing or Mental Nursing Home. A DHSS Circular suggests that an inspection should be carried out even though the grounds for concern arose only from hearsay.[117]

4.8.11 MENTAL NURSING HOMES

Mental Nursing Homes, as defined by s.22 of the RHA 1984, are:

any premises used, or intended to be used, for the reception of, and the provision of nursing or other medical treatment (including care, habilitation and rehabilitation under medical supervision) for one or more mentally disordered patient whether exclusively or in common with other patients.

Care, habilitation, and rehabilitation under medical supervision are included within this definition as well as the provision of nursing and other medical treatment. It has been suggested that the distinction between habilitation and rehabilitation is that the former relates to acquiring social skills for the first time, whereas the latter relates to the re-acquisition of skills which have been lost or forgotten.[118]

'Mental disorder' has the same meaning here as under the Mental Health Act 1983 (MHA 1983).[119] The NAHA Handbook repeats advice contained in a DHSS Circular suggesting that establishments catering for persons who are mentally confused do not always need to be registered as Mental Nursing Homes.[120] The Circular and Handbook advise registration authorities to keep under consideration the number of mentally confused patients in an establishment, and the seriousness of their condition. It is difficult to reconcile this advice with the wording of s.22 since it seems clear that the issue is not one of numbers but whether or not a mentally confused patient's condition falls within the definition of mental disorder as defined in the MHA 1983. It could be that the nature and degree of a particular resident's 'mental confusion' brings him/her within the residual category of mental disorder in s.1 of the

MHA 1983, that is, 'any other disorder or disability of mind'. The Circular suggests a distinction can be drawn between temporary confusional states caused by infection, on the one hand, and organic dementia leading to intellectual deterioration or memory impairment, on the other, and that only premises catering for the latter need be registered.[121]

4.8.12 Where a Mental Nursing Home receives patients liable to be detained under the Mental Health Act 1983, that fact must be specified in the certificate of registration and recorded in a separate part of the register maintained by the health authority. Not all Mental Nursing Homes are, therefore, legally entitled to receive detained patients. According to the First Biennial Report of the Mental Health Act Commission 1983-5 only 24 homes in England and Wales fell within this category.[122] Premises providing day-care services only do not fall within the statutory definition.

4.8.13 DUALLY REGISTERED HOMES

This term does not appear in the RHA 1984, but Circulars subsequent to the Act refer to the provision for registering premises both as a Residential Care Home and as a Nursing Home as one of the main features of the new legislation. In spite of predictions that most care for the elderly in the independent sector was likely to be located in homes of this kind,[123] the number of dually registered homes has been small. Dual registration was introduced because it was recognized that the boundary between nursing and personal care is often difficult to draw. It was also hoped to avoid the need to transfer a resident or patient from one type of home to another when his/her condition changed.[124]

4.8.14 For the purposes of dual registration the number of residents in each registration system must be stated in both registers. For example, a home catering for 15 may have been approved for ten patients and five residents. The home could then be advertised as a Nursing Home without having to specify whether or not all the beds were registered for nursing purposes. There is no statutory requirement that advertisements must specify the number of patients or residents for which the premises are registered. Registration Certificates will, however, indicate the numbers for which approval has been given and the Act requires these to be affixed in a conspicuous place.[125] Further admissions into nursing beds must not exceed the approved number, since staffing arrangements will have been sanctioned by the registering authority on the basis of the approved registration figure only. Both Guidance Notes and a DHSS Circular stress the need for flexibility in this context; small and temporary changes in the condition of patients or residents are allowed. It is suggested that the situation should be reviewed annually at the end of each registration period and that registration conditions should be varied, where necessary, to take account of any permanent changes. Only where substantial change has taken place during the course of a year should immediate action to revise the registration conditions become necessary. This advice may be legally correct because of the probable application of the *de minimis* principle[126] but would not apply where it was proposed to admit a person needing nursing care when all the nursing beds were already occupied.

4.8.15 All Residential Care Homes providing or offering nursing care must be dually registered. Should a resident's condition deteriorate to such an extent that nursing provision is required, dual registration will become necessary to avoid that person's transfer elsewhere. On the other hand, where four or more of the occupants of a Registered Nursing Home are in need of personal, rather than nursing care, the home will have to be registered with a social services authority as well as with a district health authority. Where the number in need of personal care is fewer than four, registration with a social services authority will be optional. It is unlikely that this option will be exercised in practice, however, since, if registration as a Residential Care Home was refused, the possible effect of s.4(2) would be to make it unlawful for the home to offer 'board' and 'personal care'.[127] An alternative, and preferred, interpretation of s.4(2) is that where dual registration occurs, all the provisions in respect to Residential Care Homes contained in Part I of the Act will apply.

4.8.16 CANCELLATION OF RESIDENTIAL CARE HOME AND NURSING HOME REGISTRATION

Registration of a Residential Care Home and a Nursing Home (including Mental Nursing Homes) can be cancelled in certain circumstances such as that a person concerned with the running of the home is not 'a fit person'. 'Ordinary' and 'urgent' procedures for cancelling registration are provided in relation both to Residential Care Homes and Nursing Homes. Where the 'urgent' procedure is used, the social services authority or the health authority must also show that, on a balance of probabilities, the life, health, or well-being of the residents or patients is at serious risk.[128] Under the 'urgent' procedure, the registered person need not be informed. Cancellation could, therefore, occur *ex parte*. Authorities contemplating the use of the 'urgent' procedure, however, would be well advised to intiate 'ordinary' proceedings at the same time. Otherwise, as in *Lyons v. East Sussex County Council [1987]*, it would be incumbent on the authority to show that the risk to life, health, or well-being continued after the initial crisis had passed.[129]

4.8.17 HOMES EXEMPT FROM REGISTRATION

The RHA 1984 exempts several types of establishment from the requirement to register as Residential Care Homes, as Nursing Homes, or as Mental Nursing Homes. Only those exemptions which are relevant to the care of elderly people are discussed here.

All NHS hospitals, establishments managed by government departments, and by local authorities are exempt from registration,[130] as are Residential Care Homes and Nursing Homes managed by bodies established by Act of Parliament or incorporated by Royal Charter. Mental Nursing Homes do not fall within these exemptions, however. Bodies which claim royal patronage are not necessarily incorporated by Royal Charter.[131]

The Wagner Committee regarded the Royal Charter exemption as an anomaly and recommended that it should be ended as soon as possible.

Some exemptions apply only to registration as a Nursing Home. Premises used or intended to be used wholly or mainly as a private dwelling are exempt, as are premises used mainly by doctors for consultations, or by dentists or chiropodists for treatment. Premises used for the provision of occupational health facilities are also exempt, unless specific types of laser treatment are being provided there. The Secretary of State is empowered to make regulations exempting any premises which would otherwise fall within the definition of a Nursing Home.[132]

The Secretary of State has separate authority, under statute, to exempt Christian Scientist Nursing and Mental Nursing Homes.[133] Such an exemption has existed for some 60 years and arises from the practice in these establishments of relying upon prayer rather than upon medical techniques.[134] The legal difference between the exemptions discussed above and the one referred to here is that the former are absolute, whereas this is discretionary. An exemption can be withdrawn if it appears to the Secretary of State that the home is not being run in accordance with Christian Science principles. An establishment of this kind must use the name 'Christian Science House'.

4.9.1 SOCIAL SECURITY BENEFITS AND THE INDEPENDENT SECTOR

More than half the elderly residents in private and voluntary residential homes are funded through income support (IS). Expenditure from supplementary benefit funding on residential and nursing homes increased from £10 million in 1979 to £460 million in 1986. About 70 per cent of this increase resulted from inflation. The remainder resulted from the greater number of people claiming benefit, and a 200 per cent increase in the average amount of the payments made.[135] It is claimed, even so, that the level of government support remains inadequate.

A recurring complaint is that the national limits to supplementary benefit payments imposed in April 1985 led to hardship, and discrimination against elderly people.[136] The 'hardship' charge arose from the fact that the new system failed to take account of regional variation in costs. Before April 1985, limits were negotiated locally and were often significantly higher than the national limits which were then imposed.[137] The accusation of 'discrimination' stems from the fact that the national limits were based largely on registration categories contained in the Residential Care Homes (Assessment) Regulations 1986.[138] The financial limits in relation to the 'old age' category are lower than for other categories. The introduction, in July 1986, of higher financial limits in relation to the very dependent elderly may have diluted some of this criticism. National maximum limits for blind people over pensionable age have also risen substantially, possibly in response to reports that some voluntary homes which were making provision for blind elderly people had suffered financial short-falls as a result of the revised arrangements.[139]

The revised rates provide for higher limits in Greater London.[140] At present, the maximum limits in Greater London are £17.50 higher across the board than the other limits. (see Table 4.1 at p.170)

4.9.2 The introduction of a physical disability category within the benefit system was intended to avoid difficulty in distinguishing between those suffering from substantial and permanent disability, and those who have simply become frail in old age.[141] Claimants already on the higher rate of benefit can continue to receive it on reaching pensionable age. First-time claimants of pensionable age will qualify for the higher rate of IS if it can be shown that disability pre-dates pensionable age. A person wishing to claim the higher rate, however, would need to show that the Residential Care Home in which he/she is resident is registered to provide care for the physically disabled. Such homes are few and far between. Where a home is registered for more than one category of resident, it will be the responsibility of the DSS Adjudication Officer to decide upon the category in which the claimant should be placed.

4.9.3 This rule does not apply where the applicant is a patient in a Nursing Home. The appropriate rate in such cases will depend upon the type of care the patient is actually receiving. In *CSB 1085/86*, for instance, the patient who was terminally ill was resident in an ordinary nursing home. The Social Security Commissioner decided, therefore, that her entitlement could be raised from the lowest to the highest limit, an increase, in her case, of £60 per week. The Tribunal of Commissioners came to a similar conclusion in *CSB 1162/85* where the patient was again in a nursing home for general 'medical care'. The claimant was held to be entitled to the rate payable for patients with physical disablement. Many patients are likely to have been improperly assessed, and advisers should request a review or an appeal out of time where a different (and less generous) approach has been used.

4.9.4 It appears from the decision of the Tribunal of Social Security Commissioners in *CSB 842/85* that many wrong assessments were being made prior to the imposition of national limits in 1985. . As a consequence, some individuals who were living in Residential Care Homes or in Nursing Homes between 1983-5, may be entitled to substantial arrears. It appears that many adjudication officers had set the local limit at the lowest fee charged by a local home or had taken an 'average' figure. The Commissioners confirmed that the local limit should have been set high enough to embrace the maximum being charged at a home providing a suitable standard of care for the occupants, leaving out of account only those homes with an 'exceptional degree of luxury', or whose charges were so far out of line as to be unreasonable.

4.9.5 Increases in local limits will give some retrospective protection against the stringent national limits imposed in 1985. Transitional measures exist to protect those in residence before the imposition of national limits.[142] The income of claimants receiving supplementary benefit payments prior to 1985 in respect of fees for residential care is protected at the level which was being paid before the change was introduced. If the national limits become more generous than these protected payments at some time in the future, the claimants' entitlement will be re-assessed. The regulations introduced in July 1986 also allowed for a weekly supplement of £10 for protected claimants where any short-fall was due to increases in fees made since April 1985. Additional assistance may also be available for those resident at the time of these changes, but not claiming supplementary benefit. Some long-term residents may have become eligible to claim IS only recently. If so, they can claim sums equivalent to those paid before the national limits were introduced. Protective payments of this kind are at the discretion of the Secretary of State and will be payable only where it can be shown that exceptional hardship would result were the fees not paid.

Table 4.1
Residential Care Homes

	1988 Rates per week	Max. London Additions per week
Old age	£130	£17.50
Very dependent elderly	£155	"
Mental disorder (not handicap)	£130	"
Drugs/Alcohol dependence	£130	"
Mental handicap	£130	"

Physical disablement

- under pension age	£190	"
- over pension age	£130	"
- others	£130	"

Table 4.2
Nursing Homes

	1988 Rates per week	Max. London Additions per week
Elderly (together with others who do not fall into the categories below)	£185	£17.50
Mental disorder (not handicap)	£185	"
Drugs/Alcohol dependence	£185	"
Mental handicap	£200	"
Terminal illness	£230	"

Physical disablement

- under pension age	£230	"
- over pension age	£185	"

4.9.6 Eligibility for IS is dependent on the claimant having no more than £6,000 in the form of savings and capital, including property. Income on savings below £3,000 is disregarded in full. In comparison, local authorities are required to disregard only the first £1,200 of a resident's capital and to assume that each £50 in excess of that sum produces a weekly income of 25p which can be taken fully into account. Not surprisingly, it was suggested by the Wagner Committee, amongst others, that the rules on capital disregard for local authority homes should be brought into line with the rules on IS but the DSS has so far resisted the logic of equalization.[143]

The rules relating to the treatment of a dwelling house are essentially the same as in the public sector, but individuals entering residential care in the independent sector are more likely to have to realize this asset since the proprietors of a home are not required to defer the levying of charges. A person dependent on IS (whether resident in the public or independent sector) may have no option but to sell his/her home since only 52 weeks grace is normally given before a dwelling is treated as an asset to be taken into account in determining eligibility for IS.(see Chapter 1 at para. 1.24.9) The rules relating to income disregards are similar but not identical in both sectors. Any charitable grant or any family contribution made specifically towards the payment of the fees of an independent home must be disregarded in full by the DSS.[144] Since the claim will be specifically for IS, the rules relating to the abandonment of assets will undoubtedly apply unless the claim was originally for supplementary benefit.(see paras. 4.5.14 - 4.5.16 above) In that case, it may be that the rules which relate to notional capital under the IS scheme do not apply.[145]

4.9.7 SMALL UNREGISTERED RESIDENTIAL CARE HOMES

The regulations relating to those living in Small Unregistered Residential Care Homes, that is, homes with less than four residents who are in need of personal care, were amended by the Supplementary Benefit (Requirement and Resources) Amended Regulations 1987 S.I. 1987 No.1325 which came into effect on July 27, 1987. The major effect of this change is to ensure that IS is available for residents of Small Unregistered Homes only where adequate staff cover is provided. There must be:

  (i)   at least two responsible carers (with at least one year's experience of caring for the relevant client group) engaged predominantly on care duties
  (ii) at least one responsible person on duty throughout the day to care for residents
  (iii) at least one responsible person on call at night.

Residents must also have an unrestricted right of access to the home at all times.

Where a claimant is living in a home which an Adjudication Officer had decided, prior to July 27, 1987, was a Residential Care Home but which does not fall within the new definition, residents will continue to be fully entitled to residential care payments as long as they remain at that address. Temporary absences from the home do not amount to a change in circumstances.

Elderly persons who moved into a Small Unregistered Home after July 1987 which does not meet the criteria relating to staff cover will qualify for standard board and lodging payments only.

4.10.1 COMPULSORY ADMISSION TO RESIDENTIAL CARE

There are three ways in which an elderly person can be compulsorily admitted into residential care. The first arises under s.47 of the NAA 1948. The second is by means of temporary detention in a 'place of safety' under the MHA 1983; and the third is in relation to guardianship under the MHA 1983.

4.10.2 NATIONAL ASSISTANCE ACT 1948, SECTION 47

Section 47 provides for the removal to suitable premises of persons in need of care and attention

  a) who are suffering from grave chronic disease or, being aged, infirm or physically incapacitated, are living in insanitary conditions, and
  b) who are unable to devote to themselves, and are not

receiving from other persons, proper care and attention.

Those who become subject to the provisions of s.47 need not be suffering from mental disorder as statutorily defined.

The wording of s.47 provides for the compulsory admission into care of a range of vulnerable people but seems to be used mainly in relation to the elderly.[146] Although s.47 is not much used, since only about 200 orders are made every year, its continued presence on the statute book has led to pressure for its abolition.[147]

4.10.3 A s.47 application is made to a magistrates' court by an 'appropriate' authority which, in this context, means a District Council or a London Borough. It is the District Community Physician (DCP), employed by the DHA, who initiates this process, however. The DCP must decide, after thorough inquiry and consideration, whether a person's removal is necessary, either in his/her interests or in order to prevent injury to health or a serious nuisance to others. Under the accelerated procedure set out in the National Assistance (Amendment) Act 1951, (NA(A)A 1951) the DCP him/herself may make the application to the court if authorized to act in this way by the appropriate authority. In these circumstances, however, a second medical certificate will be required, although not necessarily from the individual's GP.

The main use of the accelerated procedure is to enable proceedings to be expedited where it is felt that a person should be removed *without delay*. According to one study, it seems that the accelerated procedure is used in no less than 94 per cent of cases.[148] This evidence has increased concern that the procedure is not subject to effective judicial control. Under it, an *ex parte* application is made to a single magistrate. It would seem that magistrates are given little or no guidance on their responsibilities under the Act.[149]

In this context, 'suitable premises' include hospitals and 'other places' such as residential homes. In some areas, the normal practice is to admit the individual into a local authority home but the phrase 'other places' makes it possible for a registered or unregistered private establishment to be used. In such circumstances, financial responsibility will fall initially upon the 'appropriate' local authority. The authority may subsequently recover the amount spent from the individual who was compulsorily admitted.[150]

4.10.4 NOTICE TO BE GIVEN

When the accelerated procedure under the NA(A)A 1951 is used, no notice need be given to the person to whom the application relates. The full procedure under s.47, however, requires seven days clear notice to be given. Alternatively, notice may be given to the person who is in charge of him/her. Notice must normally be given to the person 'managing' the premises to which the person is to be removed. Such notice can be dispensed with, however, if the manager is heard during the court proceedings although he/she cannot veto the order. The term 'manager' is not defined.

The provision that notice of the hearing must be given to the person 'in charge of' the individual suggests that being 'in charge of' another person does not necessarily imply the existence of a caring relationship since only when proper *care* is absent can the application be made.[151] The phrase 'in charge of' has been defined neither by Parliament nor by the courts. It may, however, imply a degree of legal control over the person who is the subject of the application.

4.10.5 DETENTION

The maximum period of detention under s.47 is three months, whereas under the NA(A)A 1951, the period is three weeks. In theory, indefinite extensions to the period of detention are possible under s.47. A right to apply for revocation of the order arises only six weeks after it was made. The DCP must be given seven days clear notice of the intention to make an application and of the time and place where it is to be made.[152] An application can be made by someone acting on behalf of the removed person as well as by that individual him/herself.

Legal Aid is not available for proceedings taken under s.47. An appeal to the High Court against the decision of a magistrates' court is possible on a point of law only.

4.10.6 There are several inconsistencies in the current legislation. An aged, infirm or physically incapacitated person in
need of proper care and attention under s.47, must also be
living in insanitary conditions. This proviso probably excludes
many who are at risk. There is no statutory provision either
for entry to be made onto land or into premises. If the
individual concerned is the occupier of the property, he/she
would be entitled to refuse entry to would-be medical examiners.
Neither the NAA 1948 nor the NA(A)A 1951 make specific provision
for the medical treatment of the person, once detained. It is
open to question whether or not treatment can be given without
the consent of the individual, except in those circumstances
which fall within the remit of the common law rules.[153]

4.10.7 REMOVAL TO A PLACE OF SAFETY

Section 135 of the MHA 1983 empowers a magistrate to issue a
warrant authorizing a policeman to enter premises, if necessary
by force, and remove a person to a place of safety. This is the
only statutory power allowing entry to be made onto premises.
It is rare, apparently, for a warrant of this kind to be
issued.[154] Application to a magistrate is made by an Approved
Social Worker who must lay information on oath to the effect
that there is reasonable cause to suspect that a person believed
to be suffering from a mental disorder

(i)   has been or is being, ill-treated, neglected of kept
       otherwise than under proper control; or
(ii)   being unable to care for himself, is living alone.

The maximum period of detention is 72 hours. A 'place of safety'
is defined as a hospital, police station, residential establishment and any other 'suitable' place, the occupier of which is
willing temporarily to receive the patient.

A similar provision exists under s.136 of the Act which is
more widely used.[155] Section 136 empowers a police officer to
remove from a public place a person who appears to him/her to be
suffering from mental disorder, and to be in immediate need of
care and control. The Home Office encourages the police to take
such persons, where practicable, direct to hospital[156] but there
is no legal obligation on hospitals to admit those detained in

this way. As a result, in some parts of the country, greater use is made of residential establishments. Neither s.135 nor s.136 permits medical treatment to be given without a person's consent, except under the rules of common law. (see Chapter 5 at paras. 5.10.1-5.10.4)

4.10.8 GUARDIANSHIP AND RESIDENTIAL CARE

At present, little use is made of guardianship as defined in the MHA 1983 and fewer than 200 orders are made every year.[157] It has been suggested that guardianship could be used more frequently, where appropriate, so as to protect mentally disordered elderly people in the community or to avoid the necessity for long-term hospital care.

The relevance of guardianship to residential care lies in the power of the guardian (that is, a social services authority, or a person approved by such an authority) to require the individual to reside at a place specified by the guardian, which could be a residential establishment. If the person subject to guardianship were to leave such premises without the guardian's consent, he/she can be taken into custody and returned within 28 days of any absence without leave.[158]

A guardian can require a patient's attendance at any place so as to receive medical treatment but cannot give consent to treatment on behalf of that person. A person subject to guardianship may, therefore, refuse treatment except where the common law rules apply. In effect, no statutory sanction exists against those who refuse to co-operate with the guardian. As a result, some social workers consider guardianship 'a waste of time'.[159]

An application for guardianship can be made only with respect to a person alleged to be suffering from one of the four forms of mental disorder specified in s.3 of the MHA 1983. There is no requirement that the mental disorder should be 'treatable', as is necessary where the application is for admission to hospital for treatment under s.3 of the Act.[160] The application for guardianship cannot proceed if the patient's nearest relative objects to it being made. If, on application, the County Court regards the objection as unreasonable[161] it has power to direct the functions of nearest relative should be exercised by another person.

4.10.9 PROTECTION OF PROPERTY

Should there be danger of loss or damage to any moveable property of a person who has entered residential accommodation provided under the NAA 1948, or who has been admitted to hospital, or been compulsorily removed to any other place of safety, a duty is placed upon the local authority under s.48 of the NAA 1948. This duty will be discharged by taking such steps as are reasonable to protect property or to mitigate any loss or damage to it. The local authority may enter the property at all reasonable times in order to deal with any moveable property in any way which is reasonably necessary in order to prevent or mitigate loss or damage to it. The local authority may recover from the person concerned any reasonable expenses arising from such arrangements, irrespective of whether admission was voluntary or not.[162] The duty under s.48 does not arise where residential care is being provided in the independent sector.

A problem which often faces a local authority is to arrange for the care of pets. The wording of the s.48 apparently precludes a local authority from having an animal destroyed without the owner's consent.

4.11.1 RACIAL DISCRIMINATION

The Race Relations Act 1976 (RRA 1976) makes it unlawful for anyone providing accommodation for the public, or any section of the public, at an hotel, boarding house, or other similar establishment to discriminate on the grounds of race.[163] Residential homes would seem to be sufficiently similar to an hotel or boarding house to be covered by the provisions of the Act. Some residential establishments may be exempt on the grounds that the proprietor/trix, or a near relative, lives on the premises and shares accommodation with others who are not members of the same household. This exemption applies only to establishments which do not normally provide accommodation for more than six persons. The average number of registered places in private residential homes is currently 15.[164] Local authority homes tend to be even larger.

The evidence suggests that neither local authority homes nor private homes are always free from racial tension.[165]

4.12.1 PUBLIC AND PRIVATE REMEDIES

Should a grievance arise in relation to residential care in the public or in the independent sector, the person affected may wish to seek legal redress. There are four main possibilities: to sue for breach of statutory duty; to attempt to make use of default powers; to sue for negligence at common law; to complain to the Ombudsman. The general issues arising in relation to these procedures are discussed more fully in Chapter 6. For that reason, discussion here is confined to listing the available remedies, highlighting any significant differences and commenting on areas of the law which are being developed.

4.12.2 BREACH OF STATUTORY DUTY

Where a complaint is over gaps, deficiencies and delays in the provision of residential care in the public sector, similar remedies are available to those which exist in the field of health care. (see Chapter 6 at paras. 6.2.1-6.2.4) Given the specific wording of s.21 of the NAA 1948, it might be easier in this context, than in the field of health care, to establish that an elderly person had *locus standi* to bring an action for breach of statutory duty. It would seem, however, that judicial opinion leans towards making the Secretary of State's default powers the exclusive remedy.[166] In a case focusing upon a local authority's duty to provide temporary accommodation for homeless individuals under the NAA 1948, Lord Denning said:

> It cannot have been intended by Parliament that every person in need . . . should be able to sue the local authority for [temporary accommodation].[167]

4.12.3 DEFAULT POWERS

Default procedures are contained in s.36 of the NAA 1948. These allow the Secretary of State to make an order transferring to him/herself such functions of a local authority as he/she thinks fit. When asked to intervene, the Minister cannot use his/her discretion to frustrate the policy of the Act and is bound to give proper consideration to the complaint.[168]

The courts will not allow default powers to be used as a substitute for ordinary remedies for breach of a statutory duty if what has been done is expressly forbidden by the Act, or is *ultra vires*.[169] As a result, other remedies may be available where, for example, a local authority failed to make arrangements for a resident to obtain medical attention, or where it has treated a dwelling as a capital resource when it had remained the elderly person's permanent residence, or where it acts in an *ultra vires* manner by refusing accommodation merely because of a refusal to pay charges.[170]

4.12.4 ACTIONS IN NEGLIGENCE AND TRESPASS TO PERSON

Similar considerations to those discussed in relation to health care apply to actions in negligence and trespass to person. No cases are reported of any action in the tort of negligence or alleging false imprisonment or assault in relation to providers of residential care.[171] The absence of reported cases is surprising given the existence of evidence of apparent failures to take adequate care. The following allegation was made in a letter sent to the Wagner Committee:

> There must be up to 30 residents and always at least 4 staff there. However, after their dinner at about 12.00 the staff are not seen until afternoon tea... Then the staff aren't seen again until the evening meal at 6.00... Anyone could have fallen, died, haemorraged, wet themselves and the staff wouldn't know.

Situations such as these are likely to occur given the low levels of staff training and the increased demands being made upon them. Local authorities complain that their homes are increasingly accommodating very frail and very old people needing regular or medical attention.[172] Yet the Barclay Committee found that 80 per cent of residential staff had received little training. In spite of this, it is in the public sector that the highest proportion of trained practitioners are found.[173] A survey of private establishments in the West Midlands revealed a preponderance of YTS recruits among the employees. Apparently, they were shown what to do, and then left to get on with it.[174]

Injuries to residents can be the result of inappropriate
handling by staff. The courts have already established that
public authorities have a legal responsibility to ensure that
their staff are trained in safe methods of lifting.[175] Although
not a precedent here, since that case related to the liability
of employers towards their employees, it would be surprising if
a court were to refuse to recognize the existence of a duty of
care where the injured party was a resident rather than a member
of staff.

4.12.5 It has been suggested that professional advice-givers in
the social services field may be liable to their clients and,
possibly, to third parties for negligent mis-statements which
cause loss.[176] If that were so, a social worker who negligently
advised a family about the cost of arranging public or private
residential care might be liable if a court were satisfied both
that loss had been incurred, and that a special relationship
existed between the plaintiff and the defendant of the kind
referred to in the leading case of *Hedley Byrne v. Heller &
Partners [1964]*.[177] A special relationship will arise if the
plaintiff reasonably relies on the statement made by the
defendant because of the professional position which he/she
holds.

A number of decisions have imposed liability on local
authorities for negligence in giving information or advice in
other circumstances.[178] The courts might, however, refuse to
recognize such a duty in social workers on the grounds that it
would be against public policy to do so.[179]

4.12.6 Under the Unfair Contract Terms Act 1977 (UCTA
1977) the proprietor/trix of a home in the independent sector
wishing to limit his/her liability by insertion of an exclusion
clause in a contractual agreement would need to show the clause
was reasonable in the circumstances. Section 2 of the Act also
stipulates that no one acting in the course of a business can
exclude his/her liability in contract or tort for death or
bodily injury arising from negligence, either by contractual
terms or by any notice given or displayed. Liability for other
loss arising from negligence can be excluded, but only if the
exemption is shown to be reasonable.[180] Where a supplier,
acting in the course of business, performs a contract for the

supply of services, a term that the services will be carried out with reasonable care and skill is implied by statute.[181]

Increasingly, it seems that private establishments are attempting to use contractual-type documents to regulate consumer rights. According to one survey of homes in Southern England, some 40 per cent of Nursing Homes in the study used such documents. One home, for instance, required patients 'to adhere to any instruction given by a trained nurse'.[182] It is suggested that the courts might be reluctant to give legal force to such a provision on the grounds of ambiguity or on grounds of public policy.[183] Other homes described in the study required residents to meet the full cost of any damage caused by incontinence. Such clauses might conceivably be resisted as 'unreasonable' on the basis of the UCTA 1977. Some private homes claim to be contractually entitled to two or even four weeks payment in lieu of notice after the death of a resident and have turned to relatives for settlement of the alleged debt.[184] Only assets available from the deceased's estate should be used to settle any outstanding debts. Further liability could probably arise only if the relatives had given a separate undertaking to the proprietor of the home that they would pay such sums.[185] In a recent County Court case, the judge dismissed as 'nonsense' a claim by proprietors of a residential home of a month's rent from the family of a deceased resident in lieu of notice in advance. The contract required 'one month minimum notice of departure to be given by either side'.[186] Many so-called contractual terms may therefore be legally ineffective. They are likely to be complied with, however, unless and until they are successfully challenged in the courts.

4.12.7 THE OMBUDSMAN

Complaints over maladministration in the provision of residential care in the public sector can be taken to a Commissioner for Local Administration (or Ombudsman). Complaints must normally be made in writing within twelve months of the cause of the complaint. They should, in the first instance, be referred to a member of the relevant local authority (that is, a councillor). If the member should fail to refer the complaint to the Obmudsman, this requirement can be waived and a direct complaint can be accepted by the Ombudsman. A Local Goverment Ombudsman can recommend *ex gratia* compensation from a local authority which the authority could not itself make had the recommendation arisen as the result of an internal investigation.

4.13.1 THE FUTURE - A POSITIVE CHOICE?

Those who enter residential care should do so out of positive choice, and life at residential establishments should be a positive experience. For this to be achieved, it would seem that greater attention must be paid to ensuring that the wishes of residents are respected. A first step in this direction would be to implement the Wagner Committee's recommendation for an advocacy scheme in residential establishments. If significant progress is to be made in protecting elderly people from unwarranted interference, however, it is surely necessary to include this aspect of the law in the training of lawyers. Given the issues involved, it is regrettable that so many lawyers remain, for the most part, ignorant of the law relating to residential care.

Notes

1. CSO (1988) *Social Trends* at p.128.
2. Rossiter, C. and Wicks, M. (1982) *Crisis or Challenge?* (Study Commission on the Family) at p.14.
3. OPCS Report (1985) *Census Guide 1. Britain's Elderly Population* at p.8.
4. See NALGO (1985) *A few (private) home truths.*
5. Davidson, N. (1983) 'Desirable residences?' *Health and Social Services Journal,* July 28, 1983, pp.904-5 at p.905.
6. See *Health and Social Services Journal,* December 20-27, 1984 at p.1485.
7. A similar recommendation is to found in the recently published Wagner Report (see footnote (9)).
8. Griffiths, R. (1988) *Community Care: Agenda for Action* (HMSO).
9. National Institute for Social Work (1988) *Residential Care: A Positive Choice* (HMSO).

10. Barton, R. (1959) *Institutional Neurosis* (J. Wright & Sons, Bristol). Most studies of institutionalization have been based on Goffman's concept of the 'total institution'. For a review of such studies, see Davies, B. and Knapp, B. (1981) *Old People's Homes and the Production of Welfare* (Routledge & Kegan Paul), pp.110-46.

11. Booth, T. (1985) *Home Truths* (Gower).

12. See DHSS (1979) *Residential Care for the Elderly in London* referred to by Norman, A.J.(1980) *Rights and Risk* (NCCOP) at p.39.

13. Booth, T. et al. (1982) 'A Confused Mixture' *Community Care* December 2, 1982 at p.14. One study concluded that only about six per cent of private homes for the elderly were 'bad'. See Klein, R. and O'Higgins, M. (1985) *The Future of Welfare* (Blackwell) at p.136.

14. For example, no lawyer was appointed to the panel entrusted by the government with the task of preparing a Code of Practice for residential care. This anomaly was first highlighted by Carson, D. (1985) in 'Registered Homes: Another Fine Mess?' *Journal of Social Welfare Law* March 1985 pp.67-85, at p.68.

15. National Institute for Social Work (1988) op.cit., at p.32.

16. Johnson, M. (1983) 'Private Lives' *Health and Social Services Journal* July 28, pp.901-3. Also see *New Age* Summer 1984, at p.1.

17. NUPE and West Midlands County Council (1986) *The Realities of Home Life.*

18. Pope, P. (1982) 'A New Approach?' *Community Care* December 2, 1982, at p.18.

19. See *Social Work Today* November 25, 1985, at p.3.

20. See *Community Care* February 26, 1987, at p.16.

21. See *Community Care* July 23, 1987, at p.1.

22. Whitehouse,A.,Crine,A.,andMurray,M.(1982)'Thereby hangs a tale' *Community Care* December 2, 1982, at p.18.

23. Wade, B., Sawyer, L., and Bell, J. (1981) *Different Care Provision for the Elderly* Report to the DHSS by Department of Social Administration, London School of Economics (unpublished). Referred to in Laing, W. (1985) *Private Health Care*, OHE.

24. Klein, R. and O'Higgins, M. (1985) op.cit.

25. Wilding, K. (1979) 'Choosing Part III' *Community Care* August 16, 1979, pp.20-21.

26. It is estimated that not more than about 400 people are subject to compulsory procedures under s.47 of the National Assistance Act 1948 or guardianship orders under the Mental Health Act 1983. See later discussion at paras. 4.10.1-4.10.8.

27. Shaw, I. and Walton, R. (1979) 'Transition to residence in Homes for the Elderly' in Harris, D. and Hyland, J. (eds) *Rights in Residence* (Residential Care Association) pp.19-31.

28. Brearley, P. (1982) 'Old people in care' in Carver, V. and Liddiard, P. (eds) *An Ageing Population* (Hodder and Stoughton/Open University Press), p.386.

29. ibid., at p.385.

30. Bowling, A. and Savage, A. (1986) 'With a little help?' *Community Care* March 13, 1986, pp.24-7.

31. Johnson, M. (1983) op.cit., at p.903. See also Bartlett, H. and Challis, L. (1985) *Private Nursing Homes for the Elderly - a survey conducted in the South of England Working Paper No.3* (Centre for the Analysis of Social Policy, University of Bath), at p.20.

32. Bowling, A. and Savage, A. (1986) op.cit., at p.27. Also see report by Social Work Service Group of the Scottish Office (1987) *The use of residential care by the elderly.*

33. See also discussion of DHSS guidelines on payment of retainer to a particular GP to accept all residents of a home as patients, in Chapter 5 at para. 5.4.1.

34. *(1985) TLR February 25, 1985 QBD.*

35. The Tenants' Rights Etc. (Scotland) Act 1980 provides that where a person is over 60 years of age and wishes to move into the area of a local authority in order to be near a younger relative, admission to the housing list does not depend on whether the applicant is resident in the area. See s.26(3)(d).

36. National Assistance Act 1948, s.24(6).

37. Ministry of Health Circular 10/65 *A memorandum on the care of the elderly in hospitals and residential homes.*

38. Brearley, P., Hall, F., Gutridge, P., Jones, G., and Roberts, G. (1980) *Admission to Residential Care* (Tavistock) at p.152.

39. There is evidence that some local authorities are not asking for medical assessments in order to avoid paying fees. See Age Concern (1986) *The Law and Vulnerable Elderly People* (Age Concern England). It should be noted also that Professor

Brocklehurst, a leading geriatrician, has advocated compulsory medical examination before Part III admission (in a letter to Age Concern England, September 14, 1982).

40. Hobman, D. (1983) 'New Strategy for Old Problem' (1983) *Health and Social Services Journal* July 21, 1983, pp.868-9.

41. See LAC 19/74 Appendix I at paras. 1a and 4. Although s.12 has now been repealed and Sched 8 of the National Health Service Act 1977 substituted for it, arrangements already made under the 1968 Act and Circulars in existence then continue to have effect (NHSA 1977, s.129(1)).

42. National Assistance Act 1948, s.26, as amended.

43. DHSS (1978) *Residential Homes under Part III of the National Assistance Act: Charging and Assessment Procedures. A Memorandum of Guidance,* para.3.

44. Association of County Councils (1955) *National Assistance Act 1948.* Standard Charges for Accommodation. See, in particular, Appendix (a) at p.101.

45. *R. v. Secretary of State for Education and Science, ex parte Inner London Education Authority (1984)* TLR June 20, 1985.

46. DHSS (1984) *Charges for Residential Accommodation under Part III of the National Assistance Act 1948 Consultative Document* at p.1.

47. Grey, J.A.M. and Wilcock, G.A. (1981) *Our Elders* (Oxford University Press) at p.36: 'They see other residents, whom they know to be making no direct contribution from savings, receive exactly the same food . . . they may even share a room with them'. See also Personal Social Services Council (1977) *Daily Living: Questions for Staff,* at para. 31.

48. See DHSS (1978) op.cit., at paras. 54 and 55.

49. ibid., paras. 8 and 60.

50. DHSS (1979) *A Happier Old Age* (HMSO) at para. 5:12.

51. Social Security Act 1980, Sched 4.

52. See DHSS LAC (85)(2) at para. 2; Income Support (General) Regulations 1987 S.I. 1987 No.1967 as amended by Income Support (General) Amendment Regulations 1988 S.I. 1988 No.663, Sched.7 at paras. 10A and 10B(1) and (3).

53. DHSS (1978) op.cit., at para.46.

54. National Assistance Act 1948 s.43(6). For the general provisions relating to the enforcement of an order, see Magistrates' Courts Act 1980, ss.93-5.

55. See Magistrates' Court Act 1980, s.64.

56. Supplementary Benefit Act 1976. Sched I, Part III at para. 23.

57. ibid., paras. 18 and 20.

58. *[1985] 1 All ER 1061.*

59. One authority directs its employees to obtain permission to value freehold property at the time of admission. (Information gained from studying admission documents of Welsh Local Authorities.)

60. See *Attorney General ex rel Tilley v. London Borough of Wandsworth [1981] 1 All ER 1162.*

61. Allen, I. (1985) 'A short, sharp stay' *New Society* May 2, 1985, at p.165.

62. See Research and Information Unit (1984) *Ready for Care* Nottinghamshire Social Services Department.

63. LAC (85)2 at para. 6.

64. DHSS (1978) op.cit., at para. 20.

65. ibid., at para. 19.

66. *Inche Noriah v. Shaik Allie Bin Omar (1929) AC 127, 136.*

67. i.e., ownership of land by two or more persons who have identical interests in the whole of the land. Under a joint tenancy the right of survivorship applies so that ownership passes automatically to the survivor on the death of one joint tenant.

68. The situation is different in Scotland - 'where the local authority shall intimate to the debtor in writing'.(s.23(3))

69. DHSS (1978) op.cit., at para. 20.

70. Health and Social Services and Social Security Adjudication Act 1983, s.21(2).

71. s.21(4).

72. DHSS (1978) op.cit., at para. 20.

73. ibid., at para. 27.

74. In *Commissioner for Metropolitan Police v. Curran [1976] 1 All ER 162*, the House of Lords held that where 'the actual words are clear and unambiguous it is not permissible to have recourse to the corresponding provisions in the earlier statute repealed by the Consolidation Act and to treat any difference in their wording as capable of casting doubt upon what is clear and unambiguous in the Consolidation Act itself.'

75. *Farrell v. Alexander [1976] 2 All ER 721.*

76. Aldous, G. (1982) *Housing Law for the Elderly* at pp.16-19. In particular, see *Mangin v. IRC [1975] 1 WLR 1615* at p.1622.

77. Terrell, R. (1979) 'Part III Accommodation: Problems in the Recovery of Charges' *Local Government Review* December 1979, pp.15-22.

78. Bankruptcy Act 1914, s.42.

79. Cross, C. (1981) 'What can be delegated to officers' *Local Government Chronicle* June 26, 1981, pp.659-60.

80. Brearley, P. and Roberts, G. (1982) *Safety in Residential Care* (unpublished) at p.4. For discussion of false imprisonment, see Chapter 7 at para. 7.19.3.

81. *Bradbury and Bradbury v. Stockport Metropolitan Borough Council (1983)* April 20, Manchester Crown Court.

82. Booth, T. (1985) op.cit., at p.155.

83. Aldous, G. (1982) op.cit., at p.7.

84. Arden, A. (1983) *Manual of Housing Law* 2nd ed. (Sweet and Maxwell) at p.11.

85. Hooper, J. (1983) 'An NHS home of their own' *Health and Social Services Journal* July 21, 1983, pp.870-1.

86. See DHSS Booklet (1983) *The Experimental NHS Nursing Homes for Elderly People - an example* (HMSO).

87. Registered Homes Act 1984, s.21(3).

88. DHSS *Guidance Notes on Registration System for Residential Homes*, at para.A6

89. Registered Homes Act 1984, s.24.

90. Address by Norman Fowler to HSSSSAA Committee, Stage C Standing Committee B, March 29, 1983.

91. Carson, D. (1985) The suggestion may be invalid since s.5 of the Registered Homes Act 1984 requires a more restrictive interpretation of the word 'conditions'.

92. DHSS Guidance Notes, at para. A35.

93. Harman, H. (1986) *No Place like Home.* Copies available from House of Commons. See also Brooke-Ross, R. (1987) 'Registered Homes and Residents Well-being' *Social Work Today* November 23, 1987, at p.12.

94. Harman, H. (1986) ibid., at p.48.

95. Jones, R. (1984) *The Registered Homes Act 1984* (annotated) (Sweet and Maxwell) at p.9.

96. Registered Homes Act 1984, s.2.

97. s.17(1).

98. s.1(4).

99. Carson, D. (1985) op.cit., at p.70.

100. Residential Care Homes Regulations 1984 S.I. 1984 No.1345, reg 10.

101. Carson, D. (1985) op.cit., at p.79.

102. *Woodling v. Secretary of State for Social Services [1984] 1 All ER 593-598* at p.598.

103. Jones R. (1984) op.cit., at p.23-8.

104. CSO (1988) *Social Trends* (HMSO) at p.142.

105. Luba, J. (1986) *Repairs: Tenants Rights* (LAG) at p.92.

106. 'Management Orders and their Effects' *LAG Bulletin*, February 1978.

107. Arden, A. (1983) op.cit., Chapter 14.

108. Davidson, N. (1983) op.cit.

109. British Association of Social Workers (1986) *The Impact of the 1984 Residential Homes Act*, (BASW Publications) at p.40.

110. Peaker, C. (1986) *The Crisis in Residential Care* (NCVO) at p.29.

111. Registered Homes Act 1984, s.1(4).

112. Shaw, W. (1985) 'Off Target' *Community Care* April 23, 1985.

113. National Institute of Social Work (1988), op.cit., at pp.57-8.

114. Maximum fine for non-registration £2,000.

115. NAHA (1985) *Registration and Inspection of Nursing Homes* (National Association of Health Authorities in England and Wales) at p.20.

116. ibid.

117. See H.C.(84)21 at para. 5.

118. Jones, R. (1984) op.cit., at p.23.

119. Registered Homes Act 1984, s.55.

120. See para. 18(2).

121. See H.C. (81)8 at para.47.

122. p.14. The Second Biennial Report 1985-7 contains no information on the number of such establishments.

123. See, for example, the remarks of the former Secretary of the Registered Nursing Home Association. *Health and Social Services Journal* July 28, 1983, at p.905.

124. H.C. 84(21) at para.3.

125. Registered Homes Act 1984, s.47.

126. i.e. the law does not take account of trifles.

127. Jones, R. (1984) op.cit., at p.11.

128. Registered Homes Act 1984, s.11, s.30.

129. *Law Society Gazette* March 2, 1988.

130. See s.1(5), s.21(3) and s.22(2).

131. Jones, R.(1984) op.cit., at p.10.

132. Registered Homes Act 1984, s.21(3).

133. s.37.

134. Explanation from a Church Official.

135. Harman, H. (1986) op.cit., at p.2.

136. Peaker, C. (1986) op.cit. (NCVO).

137. ibid., at p.24.

138. ibid., at p.68.

139. ibid., at pp.29-30.

140. According to Laing (1986) op.cit., high property prices have virtually excluded homes from being opened in inner London. The percentage of residential home residents accommodated by the private sector was 14 per cent as compared with 48 per cent in the South West.

141. DHSS Circular 58/87.

142. i.e. from April 29, 1985.

143. See DHSS (1984) *Charges for Residential Accommodation provided by Local Authorities* Consultative Document, at p.4.

144. Rawlins, R. (1986) 'Benefits' *Care Concern* July/August at p.17.

145. Mesher, J. (1988) *CPAG's Income Support, the Social Fund and Family Credit: The Legislation* (Sweet and Maxwell) at p.99.

146. Norman, A. J. (1980) *Rights and Risks* (NCCPP); see also Age Concern (1986) *The Law and Vulnerable Elderly People* (Age Concern England).

147. Grey, M. (1980) 'S.47 Life or Liberty', *New Age*, Summer, at pp.22-25.

148. Norman, A. J. (1980) op.cit., at p.35.

149. ibid.

150. National Assistance Act 1948, s.47(8)(9).

151. Hoggett, B. (1984) *Mental Health Law* (2nd ed.) (Sweet and Maxwell) at p.130.

152. See National Assistance Act 1948, s.47(7).

153. Hoggett, B. (1984) op.cit., at p.133.

154. See DHSS, Home Office, Welsh Office, Lord Chancellor's Department (1978) *Reform of Mental Health Legislation* Cmnd. 7320, at para. 2.202.

155. Hoggett, B. (1984) op.cit., at p.138.

156. Jones, R. (1988) *Mental Health Act Manual* (2nd ed.) (Sweet and Maxwell) at p.194.

157. Mental Health Commission Report, op.cit., at p.20. The Second Biennial Report, however, suggests that the power may be used more widely in the Southern Region but no statistical

information is provided.

158. Mental Health Act 1983, s.18.
159. Bedi, B. (1985) *Social Work Today* February 11, 1985.
160. cf. s.7 and s.3 Mental Health Act 1983. See also, Leckie, T. and Proctor, P. 'Guardianship and Senile Dementia' *Social Work Today* August 31, 1987, at p.8.
161. Mental Health Act 1983, s.29(3).
162. National Assistance Act 1948, s.48(3).
163. Race Relations Act 1976, s.20 and s.22(2)(b).
164. Laing, W. (1985) op.cit.
165. *Community Care* June 5, 1986, at p.1.
166. *Wyatt v. Hillingdon London Borough Council (1978) 122 SJ 349; 76 LGR 727, The Times,* May 10, 1978.
167. *Southwark London Borough Council v. Williams (1971) CL 734* at p.743.
168. *Padfield v. Minister of Agriculture Fisheries and Food [1968] (AC) 997.*
169. Wade, H. W. R. (1982) *Administrative Law* (Clarendon Press) at p.629.
170. The suggestion that such action may be *ultra vires* was first made by Aldous, G. (1982) op.cit., at p.8.
171. See earlier discussion at para. 4.6.1. It should also be noted that there is evidence to suggest that staff are more likely to assault residents than vice versa. See *Community Care* May 1, 1986, at p.7.
172. Association of County Councils (1979) Memorandum of evidence submitted to the Secretary of State in response to the Discussion Paper *A Happier Old Age.* See, in particular, para. 68.
173. Barclay Committee (1982) *Social Workers: Their Role and Tasks* (Bedford Square Press) at para. 4.21.
174. Ainsworth, F. (1982) 'Private Lives' *Social Work Today* vol.14, no.7 at p.13.
175. *Williams v. Gwent Area Health Authority (1982)* Cardiff Crown Court (unreported), June 16th.
176. Jones, B. (1976) 'Social Workers at Risk' *Social Work Today* vol.6, no.25 at p.780.
177. *AC 465.*
178. Rogers, W. V. H. (1984) *Winfield and Jolowicz on Tort* (Sweet and Maxwell) at p.280.
179. ibid., at p.283.
180. See Unfair Contract Terms Act 1977, s.3.

181. See Supply of Goods and Services Act 1982,

182. Bartlett, H. and Brook, R. (1986) 'Terms of a C
Community Care January 2, 1986, pp.14-16.

183. Furmston, M. P. (1986) *Cheshire and Fifoot's Law
Contract* (Butterworths) at p.341.

184. Watts, J. K. (1988) 'Arduous Relatives' *Community Care*
February 11, 1988, at p.13.

185. Shaw, B. (1988) 'Relatives not bound by contracts for
residential care' *Community Care* March 10, 1988.

186. As reported in the *Guardian* May 18, 1988.

5.1.1   HEALTH AND THE ELDERLY

Anxiety about illness and disability often accompanies the process of growing old.[1]   In fact, most people over retirement age enjoy good health and a high degree of mobility, although the likelihood of suffering from an acute or chronic illness increases after the age of 65, and deterioration in health is more rapid after the age of 75.[2]   As a result, the elderly are heavy users of health care provision.[3]   But self-referral rates can be misleading indicators of need, since a condition may be well advanced before a doctor is consulted.[4]   It has been suggested that because of a commonly held stereotype of old age, people tend to expect ill-health and decrepitude to occur as they grow older. It may not be surprising, therefore, that they refuse, for as long as possible, to be labelled as sick.[5]   They may also believe that in old age, medical conditions are less likely to respond to care and treatment.[6]   Information, advice and support, as well as access to preventive, curative and rehabilitative services, are important in overcoming such problems, and in helping to achieve the more general aim of ensuring secure, dignified, and fulfilled lives for those who are elderly.[7]   The elderly should be encouraged to seek medical care at an early stage and helped to do so, if necessary. It is of equal importance, however, that care and treatment should not be imposed. A dilemma can arise, in some circumstances, in balancing the rights of individuals to control over their bodies, and to take risks with their lives, against society's concern to protect those deemed unable to protect themselves. The difficulty is to avoid intrusive paternalism, which can lead to loss of dignity and choice, without leaving individuals to suffer neglect, discomfort, or pain.   This issue is of growing significance as the number of those suffering from mental infirmity increases.[8] There may be no simple answers to the complex problems which can arise in this field; but that is no excuse for riding rough-shod over the rights of those who are vulnerable. The general legal principle, to which there are few exceptions, is that medical care and treatment can be given only with the consent of the patient.(see para. 5.10.1 below)

5.2.1   ENTITLEMENT TO HEALTH CARE

Most people over retirement age are automatically entitled, as UK residents, to free and comprehensive care and treatment in the NHS and will, therefore, be subject only to such general NHS charges as are in force from time to time. Problems can sometimes arise, however, for individuals who have only been in this country for a short period of time. In October 1982, overseas visitors lost their previous entitlement to free hospital care.[9] They are now liable to pay statutory charges for most hospital care, except treatment given in an emergency, accident, or casualty out-patient department; treatment for certain notifiable diseases; and, compulsory treatment for a mental disorder, all of which remain free. There are no charges, either, for such services as domiciliary nursing, or for ambulance transport. In general, a person is classified as an 'overseas visitor' if he/she is not ordinarily resident in the UK. The residence test depends upon whether a person is living in this country 'lawfully and voluntarily and for a settled purpose as part of the regular order of his/her life for the time being'. There must exist a recognizable purpose for residing here plus a sufficient degree of continuity for that purpose to be described as 'settled'.[10] The Department of Health (DH) advises health authorities to treat as ordinary residents those intending to remain in this country for six months or more. Establishing residence should be a question of fact in each case, however, using the judicial test set out above. A stay of less than six months could, in some circumstances, be sufficient to qualify an individual as ordinarily resident here.[11]

The relevant regulations also contain a list of those with complete or partial exemption from the rules. For example, a person who has lived in the UK for at least twelve months should receive all hospital treatment free of charge (even if he/she has been absent from the country for up to three months), as should anyone who has come here to take up residence permanently, including former residents returning to live in this country after an absence abroad, and immigrants who have come to this country with the hope of settling here. War disablement pensioners and war widows receiving a UK pension are also exempt, as are refugees and anyone who has applied for asylum or refuge. In all such cases, the husband or wife, and any child of that person, is also wholly exempt. Pensioners (and members of their families) from an EC country are exempt unless they came to this country expressly for treatment. If so, prior authorization is needed before exemption will be granted. Those granted only partial exemption include nationals of EC countries and their dependants, UK state pensioners living abroad, and the nationals of countries such as Austria or Sweden with which the UK has reciprocal arrangements. They have exemption only with respect to 'treatment the need for which arose during the visit'. The main category with no exemption at all from having to pay hospital charges in full are short-term visitors from a country, such as India, Pakistan, or the United States, with which the UK has no reciprocal agreement in this respect. Since the test to be applied is residence and not nationality, some British nationals may find themselves subject to charges for the treatment they receive. Individuals, in need of hospital treatment, who are uncertain about their residential status in the UK would be well advised to check carefully whether or not they are classed as 'overseas visitors' under these regulations.

5.2.2 Health care is also available in the private sector of medicine but here entitlement is determined by the terms of the agreement under which a course of treatment is to be provided. The nature and extent of a person's rights in the private sector depend largely upon the terms and conditions of that agreement. There has been considerable growth in this sector of medicine since the late 1970s. By 1983, private care accounted for eight per cent of all patient care in hospital, with five per cent of acute beds being located in private hospitals or nursing homes.[12] Between 1984 and 1985, the number of beds available in Registered Nursing Homes (see Chapter 4 at para. 4.8.9) rose by 15 per cent. In Wales the trend continued in 1986, with a 40 per cent increase. Nevertheless, only 13 per cent of all beds in England and Wales in 1985 were in private hospitals and nursing homes.[13]

5.2.3 Speed and convenience are two of the reasons why individuals may opt for care in the private sector rather than in the NHS. Hospital care can often be obtained more quickly in the private sector, and may, therefore, seem an attractive alternative for those needing acute care and treatment. Taking out private medical insurance in order to cover costs is now becoming more common. By the end of 1986, 5.25 million people, consisting of about nine per cent of the population, were covered by private medical insurance.[14] The nature and extent of care and treatment covered by an insurance policy will depend upon its terms and conditions. Not every type of care and treatment will necessarily be included and, in any case, some medical insurance schemes do not accept as first time contributors those who are aged 60, or 65 and over. Those falling into this age group may also find that their premiums are increased substantially within the scheme to which they already belong. Without insurance cover, the cost of private care falls on the individual and could prove prohibitive.

5.2.4 In some areas, NHS health authorities enter into contractual arrangements for the use of private and voluntary hospitals and nursing homes for their long-term patients. The government currently encourages co-operation of this kind and is hopeful that further developments will take place in future.[15] In any case, because of the degree of overlap in clientele between local authority residential accommodation, private and voluntary homes, nursing homes, geriatric wards, and psycho-geriatric wards in mental hospitals, it has been suggested that all these institutions should be considered as part of a composite 'market' which in 1984 covered 3.7 per cent of the elderly population.[16]

5.3.1   ACCESS TO HEALTH CARE

Although long-term institutional care is of growing importance, only a relatively small proportion of the elderly population is in need of this form of care at any one time. Most of those who are elderly live at home and their main need is for access to health care in the community. (see Chapter 3 at para. 3.1.1) There has been increasing emphasis recently upon the importance of enabling elderly people to remain independent, healthy, and in their own homes for as long as possible.[17] Consequently, greater stress is placed upon care in the community as a means of preventing or deferring the need for long-term care in residential homes or hospitals.[18] The primary health care services are seen as having a particular role to play in providing elderly people with skilled help in dealing with the health problems and disabilities which may develop with age. There are difficulties in establishing and maintaining care in the community, however. As a result, some elderly people enter residential care when, with more help and support, they could possibly remain at home.(see Chapter 4 at para. 4.1.3)

5.3.2 PRIMARY HEALTH CARE

Primary health care in the NHS is provided by the Family Practitioner Services (FPS) organized and administered by local Family Practitioner Committees (FPCs), and by the Community Health Care Services, organized and administered by the District Health Authorities (DHAs) and including, for example, the services of community nurses and Health Visitors. Since April 1985, FPCs have functioned as health authorities in their own right.

Access to the NHS normally takes place by means of self-referral to a family practitioner working for the FPS, that is, to a GP, to a dentist or to an opthalmic practitioner. The other health professionals who make up the FPS are pharmaceutical chemists. Although their main function in the NHS is to dispense and supply drugs and appliances, usually as prescribed by GPs or dentists, they also offer advice to members of the public on request, especially to individuals uncertain whether or not to consult a doctor about a particular problem.

Family practitioners are independent contractors working for the FPS on the basis of service agreements entered into with the local FPC. The main terms of these service contracts are agreed nationally, and are contained in the relevant regulations. Other terms relating, for example, to the location and times of surgeries, are negotiated between individual family practitioners and their local FPC.

5.3.3 It may be too readily assumed that the elderly, as a group, have little difficulty in gaining access to family practitioner care. The problem of access to the NHS at this level is relatively under-researched but data currently available suggests that some elderly people experience difficulty in obtaining the care which they need.[19] Difficulties can arise in a number of ways: from lack of information and advice, for example, or because the availability of family practitioner services in the NHS varies from place to place. For instance, access to GP care may be more difficult in inner city areas where there is often a shortage of doctors, and where those working in such areas tend to be older and in single handed practice, whereas group practice would be more effective.[20] Because of pressure of work, GPs in such areas may limit the number of patients on their list. At present, there are more than 500 family doctors aged 70 or over in general practice, of whom a small proportion are over 85. Rightly or wrongly, the government proposes to introduce a compulsory retirement age of 70 for GPs, although, exceptionally, an FPC would be allowed to continue the contract of a doctor aged 70 or over, where the doctor's retirement would adversely affect the continued provision of an adequate service to the public.[21] In other parts of the country, problems arise not so much from a general shortage of family practitioners as from the fact that many of them offer private care only. In some areas, this is particularly true in relation to dental and optical services.

5.3.4 Lack of information can also be a problem, especially for particular groups of elderly people, such as those who came here originally as refugees, or who are members of ethnic minorities. They may have language problems or suffer from cultural isolation or separation from their wider families.[22] Currently, FPCs are only required to keep lists of family practitioners in their area (with particulars such as their addresses and surgery times). These lists should be available at places other than the offices of the FPC, for example, at main post offices, public libraries, Citizens Advice Bureaux (CABx), and police stations. The evidence of one study of a London borough shows, however, that in practice the likelihood of finding a list varied significantly from place to place.[23] The most reliable locations were the reference sections of public libraries, and CABx, but elsewhere the response to a request to be shown a list was not encouraging. For example, chemists were often unable or unwilling to produce a list although they were found to be helpful in giving general information about local doctors.

5.3.5 It has been suggested that FPCs, as the bodies responsible for ensuring that the population in their area receives adequate care and attention from the FPS, should be far more active and innovative in helping the public by providing them with information and advice.[24] The government is anxious for this to happen and for patients to be given more information and be given greater freedom in their choice of doctor. In one recent White Paper, the government proposed that FPCs should be required to provide more comprehensive information about practices in their area. In addition to names and addresses, a doctor's year of qualification, sex, and qualifications would have to be included, along with other essential practice information such as opening hours, services offered and arrangements for emergencies and night calls. The government's intention is that such lists should be made more widely available in each locality.[25] It also intends to discuss with representatives of the medical profession the feasibility of requiring practices to submit annual reports to the FPC on the range of services they offer and the workload undertaken by them during the year. By such means, the government hopes to encourage doctors to focus more clearly on the provision of high-quality patient-orientated services and on the need to plan and set objectives for their development and improvement.[26] The White Paper welcomed a number of initiatives by professional bodies to encourage practitioners themselves to disseminate information by means of practice booklets for their patients, setting out useful information about the GPs in their practice, its organization, and the services they provide.[27]

5.4.1 GENERAL MEDICAL CARE

The general medical services (GMS) provided in the community by GPs are an important aspect of the FPS. In most instances, GPs are an individual's first point of contact with the NHS and they treat the vast majority of the problems brought to them without referring the patient elsewhere. As family doctors, GPs are responsible for providing a comprehensive and continuous system of care. Because of the nature and extent of their responsibility towards their patients, registration is normally a pre-requisite of the doctor-patient relationship. Registration is of particular importance for those who are elderly. It has been suggested that non-registration should be treated as a possible pointer to other unmet social need.

In theory, the relationship of doctor and patient is the result of the exercise of choice by both parties. The individual wishing to become a registered patient can approach any GP in the area in which he/she is living and ask to be accepted as an NHS patient. Should the individual be incapable of making a personal approach, possibly because of old age, sickness or some other infirmity, the request can be made by a relative or a carer on his/her behalf.[28] If the GP agrees to accept the patient, the applicant's medical card or, if that is unavailable for some reason, the appropriate application form should be sent to the local FPC so that the patient's name can be added to the doctor's list. The Merrison Committee recognized that for some people the right to choose a doctor was theoretical only, yet its existence was felt to be highly valued.[29] It has also been pointed out that the practice by some local authorities of paying a retainer to a particular GP for accepting *all* the elderly residents of a residential home as his/her patients is inconsistent with freedom of choice.[30] This practice may also be widespread in the private residential sector.

5.4.2 An elderly person who intends to live in a district for not more than three months, perhaps during a short-term stay in a residential home, can apply to be accepted as a temporary resident without being removed from the list of the doctor with whom he/she is already registered. Should he/she stay in the district for longer than three months, however, this temporary arrangement can be brought to an end. The FPC for the area where the individual was previously living can remove his/her name from the GP's list. If practicable, a patient should be told that this has been done and should be informed of his/her right to apply to be put on the list of a doctor in the area where he/she is now living. The patient could ask to be placed on the list of the GP who has been treating him/her as a temporary resident.[31]   If the GP agrees, the patient is then to be treated as that GP's registered patient.

5.4.3   For various reasons referred to above, some elderly people may have particular difficulty in registering with a doctor, perhaps because they live in an inner city area, or have personal characteristics which result in their being rejected by the GPs they approach. One study of an inner London area has highlighted the difficulties in obtaining GP care experienced by some single elderly people.[32]   Since everyone resident in this country is entitled to be registered with a doctor, although not to be on a particular GP's list, individuals in difficulty should be encouraged to contact their local FPC. The FPC will try to find a practitioner-doctor to accept him/her as a patient. Failing that, the individual can ask to be allocated by the FPC.

FPCs delegate this task to an Allocation Joint Committee (AJC).[33]   In deciding to allocate a patient to a doctor, the AJC must take a number of factors into account, such as the distance between a person's residence and the practice premises of doctors in their area; whether the person has been removed from another doctor's list during the previous six months; and the size of GP lists in the area.

A GP can appeal to the FPC against having a person allocated to his/her list.   Whatever the outcome, the GP remains responsible for the allocated patient for up to seven days after the hearing of the appeal.   Similarly, if the patient needs treatment at intervals of less then seven days, the GP's responsibility continues until no further treatment is needed, or until the patient has been accepted by, or allocated to another doctor.

Doctors can ask to be exempt from having patients allotted to them.   In reaching its decision, the AJC must have regard for the doctor's age, state of health, and the number of patients already on his/her list.[34]

5.4.4   IMMEDIATELY NECESSARY TREATMENT

In exceptional circumstances, GPs are responsible for individuals who are not on their lists.   According to their terms of service, they must give 'immediately necessary treatment for up to 14 days to anyone who is without a doctor in the area in which they practise, unless, in the meantime, the person has been accepted by, or allocated to another doctor'.[35] GPs are also normally obliged to treat anyone needing immediate treatment as the result of an accident or an emergency occurring within their practice area.[36]

5.4.5   Some elderly people may be reluctant to approach their GPs with complaints they regard as either too trivial to bring to the attention of a doctor, or as an inevitable part of growing old. Some doctors pay particular attention to the needs of patients who are elderly, and stress the importance of preventive care. They may make special arrangements, such as providing 'well-elderly' clinics, or annual check-ups, or they may keep registers of those likely to have the greatest need, or to be at particular risk.[37]   It has been suggested, however, that more should be done to prevent incapacity and in assisting the elderly maintain a healthy life-style, which together with regular and frequent assessment should be part of a continuing programme of care. The government proposes to change the remuneration system so to encourage GPs to provide comprehensive and regular care for elderly people.[38]

5.4.6   *A GP'S DUTY TO PROVIDE SERVICES*

A GP's main responsibility towards his/her patients is set out in para. 13 of the terms of service. Patients must be provided with 'all necessary and appropriate personal medical services of the type usually provided by general medical practitioners'.[39] In doing so, he/she is not expected to exercise a higher degree of skill, knowledge and care than general practitioners as a class may reasonably be expected to exercise,[40] a standard which is similar to that operating under the rules of negligence at common law.[41]   The tautology in para. 13 makes it difficult, however, for patients to know precisely what services are 'necessary' and 'appropriate'.   This, coupled with their independent contractor status, allows GPs considerable professional freedom, whether, for example, to work single-handed or in a group practice; whether or not closely with other health care professionals; whether or not to be part of a primary health care team; whether or not from their own premises or from a health centre; and whether or not to employ staff, such as a practice nurse. There are other terms of service, however, which give patients a greater degree of guidance as to the nature and extent of their doctor's obligations towards them. These are discussed below.

5.4.7 ATTENDING PATIENTS

Most GPs working in the NHS are contracted to provide their patients with a 24 hour service[42] which they must usually provide in person.[43] They can divest themselves of this obligation only so long as they take reasonable steps to ensure continuity of treatment by another doctor acting as their deputy.[44] The deputy will often be a partner or an assistant, or if clinically reasonable, any person authorized by the GP, and competent to treat the patient. Local FPCs must be told of any standing deputizing arrangements (unless the deputy is the GP's assistant, or has his/her name on the FPC's medical list) and of any intention to enter into arrangements with a commercial deputizing service. Commercial services are used more and more frequently, particularly by doctors in single-handed practices in inner city areas.[45] The FPC must give its consent to arrangements of this kind, and, in order to ensure they are adequate, can impose any conditions considered reasonable or expedient.[46]

The Merrison Committee received complaints over the use of deputizing services, and, in particular, that doctors working for such services had neither personal knowledge of the patients, nor access to their medical records. It was said that deputies were often slow in responding to emergencies and that their standards were sometimes unsatisfactory.[47] In the Committee's opinion, however, there were advantages in having a deputizing service available, especially for the single-handed doctor.[48] A Code of Practice was introduced by the DHSS in 1978 designed to ensure that the services used by GPs are of a satisfactory standard.[49] FPCs now have to ensure that commercial deputizing services offer proper care and are not used to an unreasonable extent.

GPs are generally responsible for the acts and omissions of their deputies, except where the deputy's name is also on the FPC's medical list, in which case, the deputy will be personally responsible for his/her acts and omissions. Should grounds for complaint arise in such circumstances, the complaint must be brought against the deputy, and not the patient's own GP.[50]

On occasion, a GP can be relieved of all responsibility for his/her patients, for example, during a period of study leave. The FPC must give its approval, and will only do so if it can make other satisfactory arrangements.[51] The GP remains obliged to give treatment in certain circumstances, for example, if he/she is asked to give treatment which is immediately required because of an accident or other emergency occuring within his/her practice area.

5.4.8 TREATING PATIENTS

A GP's foremost obligation is to treat patients at his/her practice premises. The place and times of consultation must be approved by the FPC, or, on appeal, by the Secretary of State. An FPC can require a doctor to inform patients about any special arrangements for running the practice and any substantial changes in those arrangements.

Unless prevented by an emergency, or unless adequate cover has been arranged, a GP must be available to attend and treat patients during surgery hours. A system for seeing patients by appointment is permissible, however. If an appointment system is in operation, a GP is not obliged to treat patients who attend without having made a prior arrangement to be seen, unless delay would jeopardize the patient's health, and provided he/she is offered another appointment within a reasonable time. A GP must, however, take reasonable steps to ensure that a consultation is not deferred without his/her knowledge. The use of appointment systems has increased substantially of recent years.[52] They may cause particular problems for some elderly patients since, as a group, the elderly are less likely to be on the telephone.[53] Some practices operate both an appointments system and 'open' surgeries at which patients can simply turn up and wait to be seen.

Most GPs employ a receptionist who is usually the patient's first point of contact with the doctor. The Merrison Committee received complaints from patients, and from a number of Community Health Councils (CHCs) that some receptionists were over-protective of the GP for whom they worked and appeared to make it difficult for patients to see their doctor. The Committee recognized the demanding nature of the work and recommended that they should receive more training.[54]

5.4.9 The importance for the elderly of contact with their GP can be seen from the fact that nearly a quarter of all those over 65 interviewed as part of the General Household Survey in 1983 had seen a doctor at the surgery during the previous month.[55] This may underestimate need, however, since evidence indicates that elderly people are often discouraged from visiting the surgery because they have difficulties with transport, because of an appointments system, or because of the likelihood that they might not be seen by their 'own doctor', but by another doctor in the practice. Although most of those interviewed in this particular study realized that they could make an appointment to be seen by their own doctor, they were easily deflected by receptionists who seemed to be putting them off by offering consultation at a different time, or with a different doctor from the one they had anticipated they would see.[56] Some practices attempt to overcome some of these problems by providing 'off-peak' surgery hours specifically for elderly patients.[57]

5.4.10 PRACTICE PREMISES

Responsibility for the provision of proper and sufficient practice premises rests primarily with GPs as independent contractors.[58] Sometimes, particularly in rural areas, GPs also hold branch surgeries. If main or branch surgeries need improvement, there are grants available for the purpose. Nevertheless, the standard of practice premises varies, and the government is concerned that, in some areas, a substantial proportion is below minimum standards. One of its major objectives is to improve premises, particularly in deprived areas, by increasing the assistance available to GPs by way of improvement grants, and under the cost rent scheme.[59] Some elderly people interviewed in one study mentioned that one of the constraints in visiting their GP, was that they found the waiting room at the doctor's practice premises to be depressing.[60] The Merrison Report recommended FPCs to use their powers, including their right of inspection, in order to press for better standards generally. The government is now proposing to review its minimum standards for practice premises.[61]

5.4.11 Over 6,000 GPs practice from health centres, that is, from premises provided for them by the FPC or district health authority. These are often purpose-built and, therefore, more likely to be suitable in providing a range of services, some of which may be delivered to the patient by other primary health care professionals who either visit or work at the health centre. One development, to which the government remains firmly committed,[62] is the setting up of primary health care teams consisting of doctors, health visitors, nurses, and sometimes other professionals such as social workers, physiotherapists, and chiropodists, and possibly practice managers. The government is anxious to strengthen team work in this way, and so ensure a more efficient delivery of care in the community.[63] Not all primary health care teams are based at health centres, but it is suggested that if they work from such premises, the quality and accessibility of primary care is improved.[64] The Merrison and Acheson Committees[65] recommended,as a matter of urgency, that more health centres should be built in inner city areas. The government's response has been more cautious: it currently offers higher improvement grants to practices in inner city areas, encourages the development of projects in primary health care, and has allocated additional funds to train district nurses and health visitors. In its recent White Paper, the government committed itself to improving primary care services in the inner cities. One of its proposals was a 'deprived areas' allowance to support doctors working in such localities.[66]

5.4.12 For the elderly, there are both advantages and disadvantages in being registered with a GP working from a health centre. One advantage is the likelihood of closer co-operation between doctors, community nurses, and the other professionals providing health care in the community. The possibility of better preventative, and all-round care is likely to exist. Purpose-built premises may also be easier to use for those with limited mobility, as well as being better equipped and more welcoming for the patient. One disadvantage is that when a practice moves to a health centre, a local surgery may close and patients may have further to travel and, as a result, it may be more difficult for them to get to see their GP.

5.4.13 HOME VISITS

Patients wishing to consult their doctor are normally expected to attend the surgery. A GP is required, however, to attend a patient elsewhere within his/her practice area, or at the address where the patient was living when accepted by the doctor, or at any other place at which the GP has agreed to visit, if the patient's condition requires it.[67]

The number of consultations held at the home of the patient increases with age, from around eleven per cent for those aged 65 to 32 per cent at the age of 85, a likely reflection of the increasing frailty and more restricted mobility of this age group. Some GPs make regular visits to older patients, or arrange for a Health Visitor or district nurse to call.(see para. 5.5.1 below) There seems to be no particular consistency, from practice to practice, in either the frequency or pattern of such visits.[68] Regular contact with a GP or another health service professional, although helpful, does not necessarily result in the elderly person revealing all his/her symptoms. Deferential attitudes towards doctors and other professionals, and a reluctance to complain are characteristic of many in this age group.

5.4.14 PRESCRIBING

One function for which a GP is responsible is to issue prescriptions for drugs, medicines and appliances to be dispensed by a chemist, although they must themselves supply any drug needed for a patient's immediate treatment.[69] Since 1985, GPs can prescribe only from a restricted list of drugs and substances.[70] They are issued with two lists, one listing drugs which cannot be prescribed at all, and another listing drugs which can be prescribed only in certain circumstances. These regulations reflect attempts by the government to control the high cost of drugs prescribed in the NHS. GPs can continue to prescribe privately any items they choose. Although GPs may not charge for issuing a private prescription, the full cost of purchasing the drug will be borne by the patient.

An aspect of prescribing practice which causes continuing concern is the issuing of repeat prescriptions without the patient being re-examined by the doctor. Individual GPs vary in the extent to which they allow the practice to continue without further consultation. A high incidence was reported by those interviewed by Wenger in her sample of elderly people.[71] In several instances, patients had not been seen by a doctor for over a year, but were continuing to take drugs on a repeat prescription. In one case, possibly extreme, the practice had continued unchecked for five years. Unpleasant side-effects were often reported and endured by elderly patients who perceived their doctor as unsympathetic and authoritarian, and were, therefore, reluctant to ask whether the prescription should be repeated.

5.4.15 DISPENSING DRUGS, MEDICINES, AND APPLIANCES

GP prescriptions are normally dispensed by pharmaceutical chemists. FPCs are responsible for compiling lists of community pharmacists dispensing NHS prescriptions in their area, with the addresses and opening times of each chemist's shop. In general, opening hours are a matter for the proprietor(s), but the FPC must ensure that at least one chemist's shop is open at all reasonable times in each district.[72] Most FPCs also organize a rota so that pharmaceutical services are made available outside normal opening hours, for example, in the evenings, to coincide with local surgery times, as well as for a period on a Sunday and during bank holidays. In an emergency, a pharmacist may issue drugs (except for those on a special list) without a prescription as long as the GP making the request supplies the pharmacist with a prescription within 72 hours.[73]

The Merrison Committee received evidence expressing concern over the reduction, of recent years, in the number of chemists's shops. The Committee concluded that getting to a chemist's shop was not, as yet, a major difficulty for most people, but recognized that if this trend continued, problems already existing in rural areas, particularly for the elderly disabled, and for non car-owners, were likely to become more widespread.[74] The government recognizes that, as with general practitioner services, pharmaceutical services are often at their poorest in inner city and other deprived areas. It proposes to establish a fund to be used by FPCs to help attract pharmacists to such areas and to help improve the standard of available services.[75] A GP may, in some circumstances, be given permission to dispense drugs directly to those living in a rural area who suffer serious difficulty in obtaining drugs, medicine and appliances from a chemist because of distance, and problems with transport.[76] A new contract for community pharmacists was introduced in 1987. This gives financial support to pharmacies, not otherwise financially viable, which provide a service to a small population.

A particular difficulty for elderly patients may arise from the way in which medicines and drugs are labelled, for example, 'as directed' or 'as needed'. Lack of information or a breakdown in communication between doctor and patient via pharmacists seem common[77] with too much of the responsibility being placed upon patients. Following a recommendation in the Nuffield Report,[78] the government proposes to pay an allowance to pharmacists who maintain a substantial number of records of medicines prescribed for or purchased by elderly or confused patients on long-term medication. Such arrangements might be particularly useful where elderly patients take a number of different medicines and regularly use the same chemist's shop.[79]

Community pharmacists also often give advice on minor ailments to those who call at their shop. The Merrison Committee wished to encourage this within limits and suggested that setting up pharmacies at health centres would be a step in the right direction.[80] An extension of the advisory role of pharmacists in health education and health promotion is also mentioned in the recent White Paper.[81] The Nuffield Report[82] recommended that pharmacists should be encouraged to become more active in the continuing education of other community health workers, such as those responsible for residential homes for the handicapped and the elderly. Supervision of the supply and safe-keeping of medicines in residential homes is seen by the government as particularly important, and it is intended to introduce an allowance for those providing this service.[83]

5.4.16 CHARGES

There are no charges for GP care and treatment in the NHS. Prescription charges are also waived for those over retirement age, that is, 65 for men and 60 for women. Some services provided by GPs fall outside the NHS scheme, however, and these charges are normally made. They include medical examinations requested by insurance companies, and the issue of international certificates of vaccinations. In general, however, elderly people in this country are relieved of financial anxiety when consulting their doctor.

5.4.17 REFERRAL

GPs are also obliged to refer patients, as necessary, to other parts of the NHS, such as specialist and hospital services. Failure or refusal to refer a patient could form the basis of a complaint to the FPC. (see Chapter 6 at paras. 6.3.3 to 6.3.12) The complainant would need to establish that referral was necessary in the particular circumstances of the case. The more usual practice is for the patient to change doctors and then ask again for a referral.

There might be grounds for an action in negligence at common law as the result of a doctor's failure to refer a patient.[84] In this case the action is available whether a patient is being treated either privately or on the NHS. The plaintiff would need to show that the doctor's failure to act was unreasonable and that he/she had suffered loss as a consequence.

General practitioners must also advise their patients so as to enable them to take advantage of local authority social services.[85] Advice of this kind may be of particular importance to elderly people since it may enable them to obtain services, such as home help, which will assist them to remain in the community.

5.4.18 CHANGING DOCTORS

In general, patients only rarely change doctors. It usually happens only because they have changed their address or because the GP has moved his/her practice premises.[86] Patients can then apply in the usual way to be accepted onto another GP's list. (see para. 5.4.1 above).

Sometimes, however, patients wish to change doctors because they are dissatisfied with the care and attention they were receiving. They may ask to be transferred to another doctor's list, although finding another GP to accept them may not always be easy. No reason for wanting to change need be given but some patients may worry about being labelled as 'difficult' especially where they have also complained officially to the FPC against their GP.[87] There are two ways by which a patient can change doctors. First, the patient, having found another doctor willing to accept him/her, can ask his/her GP to sign Part B of the medical card which is then sent to the FPC. Alternatively, the patient may write directly to the FPC, enclosing his/her medical care and expressing a wish to change doctors. In this case, it takes 14 days from the date upon which the letter is received by the FPC before the patient is re-registered.[88]

Where a person who wishes to change doctors is unable to find another GP to accept him/her, the FPC must refer the matter to their AJC which will then allocate the patient to a GP's list. (see para. 5.4.3 above)

The government is proposing to make it easier for patients to change doctors. Under the new system, patients would no longer have to approach the FPC or their current GP before registering with a new doctor. It is hoped that when coupled with more comprehensive and accessible information, this will make people more discriminating in their choice of practice and doctor, thus introducing a degree of competition which should further encourage doctors to improve the quality of their services.[89]

5.4.19 REMOVAL FROM A GP'S LIST

On occasion, a GP may ask the FPC to remove a patient from his/her list. No reason need be given.[90] Removal is effective after seven days, or from the date upon which the patient is accepted by another GP, or if necessary, allocated to another doctor's list (see para. 5.4.3 above) whichever is the sooner. There is one proviso, however, in that a patient, who is receiving treatment which is needed at intervals of less than seven days, remains the GP's responsibility until accepted by another doctor, or until the end of one week after the need for treatment has come to an end, whichever is the sooner.[91]

In some circumstances, removal from a GP's list can present very real problems. A patient may, for example, live in a rural area, where there are few or no other practices within reasonable distance. Since, on the whole, the elderly are uncomplaining patients, they are, perhaps, the least likely to find themselves in this position. Nevertheless, some 'awkward' individuals, possibly suffering from a form of mental disorder or from dementia, may find themselves removed from a GP's list. The system of allocation can be important in ensuring that such patients are not left without a doctor.

5.5.1 THE COMMUNITY NURSING SERVICES

Community nursing services (particularly district nurses and Health Visitors) make an important contribution to the care of elderly people. Although employed by a DHA, they are often attached to a health centre, or to one or more general practices, sometimes as members of a primary health care team. Better teamwork at primary health care level is seen as important in raising the standard of the services available to elderly patients in the community. The Cumberlege Report[92] proposed that community nursing services should be planned, organized and delivered on a neighbourhood basis. While recognizing the advantages of this proposal in providing an effective service, the government does not believe there is only one way of organizing nursing services. The decision should rest with the local DHA.[93]

District nurses are qualified Registered General Nurses (RGNs) who have undertaken additional training to enable them to provide skilled nursing care in the community, including residential homes.[94] They should also give general advice to elderly patients on how to care for themselves and offer particular help over such problems as incontinence.[95] They may act as leaders of a district team which can include State Enrolled Nurses (SENs) and auxiliaries who carry out certain tasks such as bathing and dressing frail ambulant patients.[96] District nurses often assess and, if necessary, re-assess the needs of patient and family, as well as monitoring the quality of care.[97]

Health Visitors are primarily concerned with promoting better health and preventing illness and disability by giving advice, education, and support. Their training should enable them to understand relationships within the family and the effects upon these of normal human processes, such as ageing.

5.5.2   Both district nurses and Health Visitors may themselves initiate visits, or may be asked to see a patient by a hospital doctor, a social worker, or a relative or by the patient him/ herself. Often, however, it is a patient's GP who will refer an elderly person to them. Community nurses often pick up problems which then need to be referred to a GP, or to a social services department, or to a voluntary organization. Because of the increasing number of elderly people in the community, with more of them also frail or infirm, the community nursing services may be over-burdened and unable to visit patients as often as they might wish. Wenger found that visits from district nurses were, however, more likely to be regular than from any other health professional. Their support of elderly people and the carers of those who are very dependent was much appreciated.[98]   The introduction, into primary care, of nurse practitioners has been under discussion recently. The government intends to look at possible further developments in that field.[99]

5.6.1   GENERAL DENTAL SERVICES

Another aspect of the FPS which has a bearing on the health care of elderly people is dental care. It might not be supposed that, in general, elderly people are in need of such care, but in fact, about one-quarter are said to have at least some teeth of their own needing regular attention. Dentures, too, will need replacing or adjusting from time to time. This should be done before the need becomes urgent.[100]   Access to dentists is on the same basis as access to GPs, that is, individuals are free to approach any dentist whose name appears on the dental list compiled by the local FPC[101]   and dentists are free to accept or refuse patients. Where a person is incapable of applying in person, the application can be made on his/her behalf by a relative or carer.[102]   Unlike GPs, dentists are not responsible for a registered list of patients. The dentist-patient relationship exists only for as long as is necessary to render the patient dentally fit, that is, to such reasonable standard of dental efficiency and oral health as is necessary to safeguard a person's general health.[103] When that has been achieved, the dentist's obligation to the patient comes to an end. Individuals are free to approach another dentist if, and when, further treatment is required. In fact, many people return to the same dentist, and most dental practices send out appointment cards at regular intervals to those they regard as their patients.

5.6.2 Obtaining dental care under the NHS is not always easy and elderly people may face particular difficulties.[104] They may lack information about the availability of NHS treatment in the area where they live, or they may have difficulty in finding a dentist offering either NHS treatment, or, alternatively, the full range of treatment which they need, and, in particular, items such as dentures.[105] There is also considerable local variation in the number of practising dentists. The government proposes to introduce measures which will help alleviate the current situation as well as providing better choice and information for patients.[106] Where elderly people have difficulty in obtaining care, they should contact the local FPC for advice on which dentist(s) might be prepared to accept them as patients although the FPC cannot go further and ensure dental care for the patient under the NHS. Indeed, in some areas, individuals may find that private care only is available. On occasion, complaints arise over the boundary between NHS and private care.[107] It should be established from the start whether or not treatment is being offered on the NHS, and this should be re-established each time a new course of treatment is offered. Patients should give the dentist their NHS card or number and be sure to sign the dental estimate form which constitutes a contract between them and the dentist to do all that is necessary on the NHS to make them dentally fit. Signing the form also signifies the patient's agreement to be inspected by a Dental Officer from the DH or the Welsh Office whose function is to check a random selection of patients who have received NHS treatment. Dentists are not allowed to give part of the treatment within the NHS and part of it privately; but they have the right to offer privately any treatment which is also available on the NHS, for example, supplying new dentures.

5.6.3 Most NHS treatment is now subject to charges which the dentist may ask for wholly or partly in advance. Dentists can charge any amount they wish for each course of treatment but only up to the prescribed maximum. Anxiety over cost may deter elderly people from seeking dental care. It is important, therefore, that those eligible for free or cheaper treatment should receive it. All NHS dental treatment is free for certain groups including those receiving income support (IS) or family credit or whose partner is in receipt of either, as well as for those on a low income. Even where an elderly patient's income or that of his/ her partner is of such an amount that he/she does not qualify for free care, it may be low enough to be eligible for help with part of the cost. An application should be made on form AG1. After assessment, the DSS will issue a certificate, valid for six months, which can be used to get free or cheaper dental treatment. Where a person is not eligible for free or cheaper treatment, about three-quarters of the cost must be paid. The maximum charge is now £150 for any one course of treatment. Charges for dentures and bridges can include any minor adjustment which may be needed after they have been fitted. Major alterations more than a few months after the fitting must be paid for by the patient.

5.6.4 Dental check-ups have been a universally free service, but under government proposals, to take effect in January 1989, charges will be levied on all adults apart from those individuals who are fully or partially exempt from payment.[108] Treatment to stop bleeding will continue to be free of charge, as will any repair made to dentures. No charge can be made for calling out a dentist to the surgery in an emergency, although there is a charge for any treatment which the dentist might then give, except if the person is entitled to free treatment. Dentists are not obliged to give treatment out of hours, although some health authorities and FPCs organize a rota of dentists to attend surgeries to deal with emergencies. In other areas, dentists themselves may operate a rota privately or under the NHS.

5.6.5 Getting to the dentist's surgery can be a problem for elderly people and they may need help with transport. The GP, a district nurse, Health Visitor or community dentist may be able to offer advice and assistance. Dentists should visit and treat a patient at any place (including a residential home) within five miles of the surgery if the patient's condition requires it,[109] but otherwise dentists do not make domicilary visits. In some areas, community dentists employed by the DHA visit handicapped people who may be unable to attend a surgery and also make annual visits to residential establishments to give the residents a dental examination. The government proposes that community dental services should, in future, mainly provide treatment for children, and for those adults who experience difficulty in obtaining treatment from a general dental practitioner.[110]

5.6.6 Where a patient needs various kinds of more expensive treatment, the dentist must first obtain permission from the Dental Estimates Board (DEB) before the work is carried out. Such treatment includes the supply or repair of a denture, or supplying a bridge which is more expensive than is clinically necessary to secure dental fitness.[111] If the DEB refuses to approve the proposed treatment the patient may have cheaper treatment done on the NHS, or may appeal to the DEB, within four weeks, against its decision. An alternative would be to pay for the work to be done privately. Where the DEB approves the more expensive treatment, the additional amount is added to the normal cost of the treatment.

If a patient requires treatment which cannot be carried out by the dentist but could be given by another dentist, or which forms part of the hospital or specialist dental services, the dentist must inform the patient and, if requested, refer him/her so that he/she can receive the treatment.

5.6.7 At the end of the course of treatment, the patient signs the NHS form once more. In effect, this brings to an end the dentist's obligation to treat the patient.

5.7.1 OPTICIANS

General opthalmic services (GOS) also form part of the FPS. Their primary function is to provide sight-testing and, where necessary, issue prescriptions for spectacles. Should a problem be diagnosed which needs further or different care or treatment, individuals should be referred to the hospital eye service, for example, or, possibly, to a social service department. Although a high proportion of the population wear spectacles, the Merrison Committee received few complaints about this aspect of the NHS. Since 1984, the government has introduced greater competition and suggests that the benefits of this, both to the patient and to the profession, have been greater than were expected, and also realized more quickly.[112]

5.7.2 Since eyesight tends to deteriorate with age, most elderly people need regular attention from an optician. There may also be specific problems which can lead to loss or impairment of vision. Poor vision can have an adverse effect on mobility, with greater dependency and social isolation. As people grow older, they should have regular eye-sight tests so that suitable glasses can be prescribed and any incipient problems diagnosed as quickly as possible. They should also see an optician or their GP as soon as possible after noticing any particular difficulty or discomfort.

5.7.3 Annual sight tests have been available free of charge but the government is to extend its policy of increased competition in the opthalmic services by charging for this service from April 1, 1989, except for certain groups, such as those on low incomes, and those registered blind or partially sighted.[113]

Eye-sight tests can be given only by a registered opthalmic medical practitioner or a registered opthalmic optician (optometrist). Lists of these must be compiled and held by the local FPC and should also be available elsewhere in the community.[114]

NHS spectacles are no longer available and a prescription can be made up by an unregistered supplier, except if a person is registered blind or partially sighted. Elderly people needing new glasses or lenses must pay for them unless they, or their partner, are eligible for free glasses because they are receiving IS or family credit, or on grounds of low income.[115]

In such cases, vouchers are issued which can be used to obtain spectacles in the private market either free of charge or at a lower cost. Those needing complex/powerful lenses will be eligible for help with part of the cost, as will those on a low income which is above the limit for free treatment. Those entitled to free or cheaper glasses on the grounds of low income should apply to the DHSS on form AG1. After assessment, the DSS will send back a certificate entitling the patient to free or cheaper treatment. This is valid for six months. In reviewing voucher values, the government is to pay particular attention to the needs of those requiring complex and expensive lenses, for whom the current voucher rates may not be adequate.[116] Those who are eligible should tick the voucher entitlement box when signing the eye-sight test form. If new spectacles are needed, the optician should then issue both a prescription and a voucher. Vouchers are valid for a single transaction only, and must be used within six months of the date of issue.[117] The government intends to amend the relevant regulations to allow vouchers to be used for the purchase of contact lenses. It also proposes to extend the voucher system to include those suffering from a mental or physical disability whose spectacles are frequently damaged as a result.[118]

5.7.4 In some parts of the country it may be difficult to locate an NHS optician whose practice is conveniently close to an elderly person's residence. Opticians are not obliged to make home visits but might be prepared to visit if a person was unable, for some good reason, to make the journey to their premises. Opticians may charge for a home visit. Alternatively, an elderly person could ask to be referred for a sight test given by the hospital eye service. Concern has been expressed over the lack of domiciliary sight test services for the housebound. The government is to discuss with the relevant professions the provision of such a service for those entitled to a NHS sight test. In such cases, an additional fee might be charged.

5.8.1 CHIROPODISTS

Problems connected with mobility are particularly significant in old age. Services offered by chiropodists help elderly people to keep active and independent. Unlike most other NHS services, chiropody is available only to certain priority groups, including women over 60, and men over 65, except that a GP can refer an individual who is below that age. Chiropodists work mainly at clinics run by the local DHA, although about a quarter of their contacts with patients take place at the person's home with a further one-eighth at the chiropodist's surgery. The principal drawback in obtaining chiropodist care in the NHS is the length of waiting lists in some areas. As a result, many elderly people may have no alternative but to opt for private care.

5.9.1   ACCESS TO HOSPITAL

As individuals grow older, they are more likely to need hospital care and to stay in for longer. Only two and a half per cent of elderly people are in hospital at any one time, but they occupy nearly one half of all NHS beds, and about 40 per cent of all acute beds, with departments of general medicine, orthopaedic surgery, general surgery, urology and opthalmology being particularly heavily used.[119]   Most elderly people become hospital patients by way of referral from their GP to a hospital consultant's out-patient clinic.   The time-lag between referral and consultation will vary but where a GP believes the matter to be urgent, that should be stated in the letter of referral so that the waiting time is kept as short as possible.   The waiting list for non-urgent cases is often very long.   In some areas, for example, a patient may have to wait for up to three years before seeing a consultant about a possible hip replacement. Some patients turn to the private sector rather than wait for care to become available in the NHS.   Waiting lists are likely to become longer as a result of current cut-backs and ward closures.   In September 1986, 61 per cent of urgent cases had been on a list for more than a month, whereas 26 per cent of non-urgent cases had been waiting for more than a year.[120]   The 'Guide to Hospital Waiting Lists' is useful in providing information about the length of NHS lists for various treatments in different areas of the country.[121]

5.9.2   GETTING TO HOSPITAL

For various reasons, such as limited mobility, transport difficulties, or cost, elderly people may find it difficult to make their own way to and from hospital either to see a consultant, or for admission as an in-patient.   In such circumstances, the patient's GP or the hospital itself should be asked whether transport can be arranged, either by ambulance or hospital car. For those using public transport, or some other means of getting to hospital, financial help may be available if they (or their partner) are receiving IS or family credit, or if they receive a war or Ministry of Defence disablement pension and are being treated for that disability in an NHS hospital. Help with hospital travel costs for NHS treatment may also be available on grounds of low income. The claim for travel expenses can be made on arrival at the hospital. Evidence must be produced to show that the person is eligible for financial help. Proof of entitlement as a result of low income can be obtained by sending form AG1 to the Agencies Benefits Unit (ABU) in Newcastle upon Tyne for an assessment to be made. The ABU will then send back a certificate stating whether full or partial entitlement can be claimed. The certificate is valid for six months. If travel costs have already been paid by an individual falling into either of the above groups, a refund can be claimed within one month of the payment. Those unable to travel to hospital, because they do not have sufficient funds, should ask the local DHSS office for a Crisis Loan from the Social Fund.

A person visiting a patient in hospital may be able to obtain help with fares from the Social Fund if the patient is a war or Ministry of Defence disablement pensioner being treated for that disability, or is a close relative receiving income support.

5.9.3   *THE CONSULTATION*

NHS patients have no right to insist that they see a particular consultant, not even the one to whom they were referred by their GP. The consultant decides whether or not to examine patients personally, or whether to delegate the task to another doctor working in his/her team. The consultant carries the ultimate responsibility, however, for the decision whether or not to admit the patient for treatment and care.

An elderly person may be suffering from an acute or from a chronic condition. In the latter case, admission could be to a geriatric or psycho-geriatric hospital or unit. In some areas, patients may be referred by a consultant (and sometimes by a GP) to a geriatric day hospital for nursing care or rehabilitation.[122]

A consultant may refer a patient for outpatient treatment, such as physiotherapy. In such cases, the same arrangements as above can be made for transport to and from a clinic and for the payment of fares.

5.9.4 *ADMISSION TO HOSPITAL*

Admission to hospital normally takes place as a result of referral followed by a consultant's decision to admit. In certain circumstances, however, a patient may be admitted to hospital without following the normal route.

In an emergency - if, for example, an elderly person has a heart attack while out shopping, or is involved in a road accident - he/she may be taken straight to an accident or casualty department at a hospital, and, if necessary, be admitted for in-patient treatment. Not all hospitals have such departments, however, and even if they do, the department may be open at certain times only and not at all at the weekend.

If the situation is not urgent, the patient's GP should be contacted. If the GP decides the patient needs to be admitted, he/she has authority to do so should a bed be available locally. The GP will, if necessary, contact the ambulance service. If it is not possible to contact the GP or he/she will not visit, but it is still felt that immediate treatment is needed, an elderly person may be taken direct to an accident or casualty department for attention and possible admission to hospital. Only in a serious emergency should a 999 call be made to the ambulance services. In any case, the ambulance services are likely to try to contact the person's GP first, and will usually come direct to the patient's house only where they have failed to contact the doctor.

NHS hospitals and doctors are allowed to charge a fee for emergency treatment following a road traffic accident. The charge, levied against the user of any vehicle involved in the accident, is usually paid by the insurance company.

5.9.5 *ADMISSION TO HOSPITAL UNDER*
THE MENTAL HEALTH ACT 1983

Apart from an emergency where a person's consent could not be obtained, agreement is normally required before a patient can be admitted to hospital and be given treatment. The other main exceptions to the rule relating to consent arise under s.47 of the National Assistance Act 1948 (NAA 1948)(see Chapter 4 at paras. 4.10.2-4.10.7) and in relation to the compulsory admission to hospital of mentally disordered patients as defined by the Mental Health Act 1983 (MHA 1983).[123] Most mentally disordered patients, in fact, enter hospital informally. Indeed, s.131 of the MHA 1983 states that nothing in the Act should be construed as preventing a person needing treatment for mental disorder from being admitted in that way. Mental disorder is defined by s.1(2) as 'mental illness, arrested or incomplete development of mind, psychopathic disorder and any other disorder or disability of mind'. There are four specific categories: mental illness, severe mental impairment, mental impairment and psychopathic disorder, each of which is further defined by the Act.

5.9.6 An application for compulsory admission to hospital under the MHA 1983 can be made only by an approved social worker,[124] or by the 'nearest relative' of the patient, as defined in s.26 of the Act. Before making an application, an approved social worker must interview the patient in a suitable manner in order to satisfy him/herself that detention in hospital or mental nursing home is, in all the circumstances of the case, the most appropriate way of providing the care and medical treatment which the patient needs.[125] In all cases, whether application is being made by the approved social worker or by the patient's nearest relative, it must comply with either s.2, (admission for assessment); s.3, (admission for treatment); or s.4, (admission for assessment in an emergency) and with the other statutory provisions in the 1983 Act which relate to medical recommendations and other related matters. If the application is for admission for treatment under s.3 of the Act, the patient's nearest relative may object. It is possible, however, for any other relative, or any person with whom the patient is residing, or any approved social worker to apply to the county court for the functions of the patient's nearest relative to be exercisable by the applicant or any other proper person willing to act.

5.9.7 A person appearing to be mentally disordered can be detained in hospital under other sections of the Act. Under s.136, a police constable is authorized to remove to a place of safety any person found in a public place, who appears to be

221

mentally disordered and in immediate need of care and control, if that is thought necessary in his/her own interests or for the protection of other people. The purpose of detention, which may last no longer than 72 hours, is in order for the individual to be examined by a doctor and interviewed by an approved social worker so that any necessary arrangements can be made for his/her treatment or care. A place of safety under the Act includes, apart from a hospital, local authority social services accommodation, a police station, a mental nursing home, a residential home for mentally disordered persons or any other suitable place the occupier of which is prepared temporarily to receive the person.

5.9.8 Section 135 also contains a 'place of safety' provision. Under this section, a magistrate can issue a warrant authorizing a police constable to enter premises, if necessary by force, and without the consent of the occupant, in order to remove a person thought to be mentally disordered, with a view to making an application for admission to hospital, or for making other arrangements for his/her treatment or care. Detention under s.135 cannot exceed 72 hours.

Before issuing a warrant, the magistrate must first receive information, given on oath by an approved social worker, that there is reasonable cause to suspect that a person believed to be mentally disordered has been, or is being ill-treated, neglected or kept otherwise than under proper control; or being unable to care for him/herself, is living alone. An approved social worker and a doctor must accompany the constable when executing the warrant.

5.9.9 A criminal court can order a person brought before it in relation to an alleged offence to be admitted to hospital in circumstances and on conditions set out in ss.35-40 of the MHA 1983.

5.10.1 CONSENT TO TREATMENT

The general rule is that however elderly, frail, or infirm the patient, he/she must freely consent to being medically treated, otherwise a tortious and actionable wrong is committed against that person.[126]   A patient's consent is often given expressly, by signing a consent form. It usually describes what operation it is intended to perform but may contain the additional phrase 'and proceed'. This permits the surgeon to carry out any further surgery deemed immediately necessary. A question arises, however, whether consent is real unless it is given on the basis of full knowledge. Does the doctor have to explain to the patient all the possible consequences of the treatment which is to be given? In *Sidaway v. Bethlehem Royal Hospital Governors [1985]*[127] the House of Lords held that the law of this country does not recognize the doctrine of 'informed consent', namely, that a patient has a right to be informed of all possible risks involved in the proposed treatment. The doctor is required to act only in accordance with the practice accepted as proper at the time by a reasonable body of medical opinion.

Consent may not always be given expressly, but may be implied from a patient's conduct. For example, if a person with backache attended a physiotherapy department, agreement to receive treatment which is reasonable for that condition, could be assumed from the individual's conduct, unless the contrary was then clearly expressed or implied by the patient.

5.10.2 TREATMENT WITHOUT CONSENT

At common law, treatment can be given without consent only in cases of urgent necessity, for instance, operating to save a person's life, or to prevent an individual acting in ways dangerous to him/herself or to others. Even so, the treatment must be only that which is reasonable and sufficient in the circumstances of the particular case.

5.10.3 Where an elderly person is mentally confused, but not detained as a mentally disordered patient within the meaning of the MHA 1983, the legal position on consent to treatment is far from clear. To comply with the law it would seem that the patient's consent must be obtained, unless treatment is urgently required on the grounds of necessity. Does good medical practice allow further intervention? Doubt has been cast on that proposition[128] but no real guidance is currently available either from judicial decisions or legislative provision. This has the effect of giving proper protection neither to those who give treatment, nor to those who receive it. In practice, treatment which is reasonable, given the elderly person's condition, is often administered without consent if it would appear that the elderly person is not unwilling to receive it.[129]

In its second Biennial Report, the Mental Health Act Commission discusses the difficulties in using the MHA 1983 to detain elderly patients, especially those suffering from dementia. The Commission notes the delicate balance to be maintained in such circumstances. Staff may be understandably reluctant to employ formal detention under the Act, even in respect of a difficult elderly patient. On the other hand, where a patient is not detained and not subject to the provisions of Part IV of the MHA 1983, staff may hesitate to give positive treatment. How the law might be developed to give non-volitional informal patients a measure of protection similar to that for detained patients is being actively considered by the Commission.[130]

5.10.4 The position on consent to treatment by detained mentally disordered patients (other than those in hospital for very short periods of time) has been made much clearer by Part IV of the MHA 1983. In effect, the patient's consent is not required for treatment given for the mental disorder under s.63 of the Act, by the responsible medical officer, that is, by the doctor in charge of the patient's treatment, except in relation to certain categories of treatment as set out in the Act. In the case of psychosurgery, and the surgical implantation of hormones, treatment can be given to a detained (and, in this case, an *informal*) patient only with his or her consent *and* the agreement of an independent doctor specifically appointed for the purpose, who in accordance with s.57 of the Act, has also consulted with two other persons concerned with the patient's treatment. Where ECT treatment is proposed, or where a course of medication has continued for three months during a period of detention, treatment can be given or continued only with the detained patient's consent and the issue of a certificate given by the RMO, or an independent doctor specifically appointed for the purpose, which confirms that the patient's consent is real and valid. But, in this case, if the patient refuses his/her consent or is incapable of giving it, an independent doctor appointed specifically for this purpose may, after consulting in accordance with s.58 with two other persons concerned with the patient's treatment, certify that the treatment should be given since it is likely to alleviate or prevent a deterioration in his/her condition.

The procedures under s.57 and s.58 apply to treatment given on a single occasion, or to a plan of treatment.[131] Because of the danger of consent to treatment being without limit of time, s.61 provides a procedure for reporting and reviewing treatment given under s.57 or s.58, and for the cancellation of any certificates granted under those sections.

Sections 57 and 58 do not apply to *urgent treatment* given under s.62 of the Act, that is, treatment immediately necessary to save the patient's life. Urgent treatment includes treatment which is immediately necessary to prevent serious deterioration to the patient's condition or which is immediately necessary to alleviate serious suffering; or which is immediately necessary, but is the minimum interference necessary to prevent the patient for behaving violently or being a danger to him/herself or others. If the proposed treatment would also be irreversible or hazardous, however, the patient's consent and/or a second opinion in accordance with s.57 or s.58, would have to be obtained, however urgent the circumstances.

5.10.5 WITHDRAWAL OF CONSENT

Under general rules of law, a patient, including an informal mentally disordered patient may withdraw his/her consent to treatment at any time, unless the doctrine of necessity applies. (see para. 5.10.2 above) Where a *detained* mentally disordered patient has given consent to treatment under s.57 or s.58, he/she may withdraw consent at any time before the treatment, or plan of treatment is completed (unless the treatment is urgently needed, under the provisions of s.62, to save his/her life). If it is then proposed to continue the treatment, the procedures under ss.57 and 58 would have to be followed once more, unless the responsible medical officer considered that to discontinue the treatment would cause serious suffering to the patient.[132]

5.10.6 LIVING WILLS

In some parts of the United States, a form of 'anticipated' consent by means of a 'living will' is permitted. This is a document drawn up by a person who is rational and lucid at the time, in anticipation of an event, such as serious illness. The 'living will' sets out the person's wishes should he/she become unable to give consent, or to refuse treatment. A document of this kind enables patients to declare that they do not wish to be kept alive by the use of medical technology, such as a life support machine, if their condition deteriorates and is no longer reversible. In practice, it seems that there is no legal obligation to give treatment which is unlikely to benefit a patient who may be near to death. Yet insensitive practices apparently continue in some hospitals.[133] 'Living wills' are not legally recognized in this country and there are mixed feelings about their possible use, both from an ethical point of view, and because of anxiety that pressure could be placed upon particularly vulnerable people to sign a document of this kind.[134]

5.11.1 LEAVING HOSPITAL

In general, patients may leave hospital at any time even during a period of treatment although such behaviour might well be unwise, and could result in a deterioration to physical or mental health for which the staff of the hospital could not be held responsible. Normally, patients should wait to be discharged by the consultant in charge of their case. In the case of an elderly patient, arrangements for domicilary care may also be needed.

In certain circumstances, however, a patient can be prevented from leaving hospital. There are common law powers which can be used if a patient is a danger to him/herself or to other persons. Patients suffering from one of the notifiable infectious diseases, such as tuberculosis or infectious jaundice can also be prevented from leaving hospital;[135] as can persons admitted to hospital under s.47 of the NAA 1948 (see Chapter 4 at paras. 4.10.2-4.10.7), and patients detained under the MHA 1983. Statutory powers can also be used to prevent *any* patient from leaving hospital if it is thought that an application for admission as a detained patient under the MHA 1983 ought to be made. (see para. 5.11.2 below)

5.11.2 DETAINING INFORMAL PATIENTS UNDER THE MENTAL HEALTH ACT 1983

Under s.5(2) of the MHA 1983, the doctor in charge of a patient's treatment, or the doctor nominated to act in his/her absence, can report to the hospital managers that in his/her opinion an application for the patient's compulsory detention in hospital ought to be made under the Act. The delivery of the report to the managers of the hospital authorizes the patient's detention in hospital for a period of up to 72 hours during which time an application for admission for assessment or admission for treatment can be made.[136] This section could be used if, for example, it was felt that an elderly patient who had perhaps entered a general hospital for the treatment of a physical ailment was suffering from a mental disorder which justified detaining him/her for assessment or treatment in a psychiatric hospital or ward, and the patient was unwilling to be admitted informally.

An informal patient in hospital *receiving treatment for mental disorder*, can be detained in hospital if the criteria set out in s.5(4) of the MHA 1983 exist. This section enables the patient to be detained for up to six hours by a first level nurse qualified in mental nursing if he/she considers the patient to be mentally disordered to such a degree that it is necessary for the patient's health or safety or the protection of others for him/her to be restrained from leaving, and it is not practicable to secure the immediate attendance of the doctor in charge of the patient's treatment. A record of the circumstances of the case must be made by the nurse in writing and in the prescribed form and be delivered to the hospital managers. The nurse's power lapses at the end of the six hour period, or upon the arrival on the ward of a doctor with authority to make a report to the managers under s.5(2), whichever is the sooner.

5.11.3 THE END OF DETENTION

The right to detain a patient admitted to hospital under the MHA 1983 can come to an end in one of several ways. First, a patient can be detained only for the period specified in the section under which an application for detention was made,[137] unless a subsequent application under a different section of the Act, or an application for renewal of detention has been made as appropriate under the Act.[138] Secondly, the managers of the hospital or the medical officer responsible for his/her treatment or the nearest relative of the patient can bring detention to an end in accordance with the provisions of the Act.[139] Discharge by the nearest relative may be prevented, however, by the operation of procedures contained in s.25(1) of the Act. Thirdly, a patient may apply, and in some circumstances, must be referred to the Mental Health Review Tribunal (MHRT) which has power to release the patient. The nearest relative whose right to discharge the patient has been prevented may also apply to the MHRT in accordance with s.66 of the Act. A patient who is absent from hospital with or without leave becomes automatically discharged after the lapse of a specified period of time.[140]

5.12.1 AFTER-CARE

For many elderly patients, their families, and carers, leaving hospital can present difficulties in relation to continuity of care and adequacy of support in the community. No general statutory provisions are in force to enable or oblige social services authorities to provide after-care as such, although they may, and on occasion must, make arrangements for promoting the welfare of certain groups of disabled and handicapped persons.(see Chapter 3 at paras. 3.7.1-3.8.4) The only current provision for after-care as such applies to those who are mentally disordered. Under the provisions of s.21(1)(b) and para. 2(1) of Sched. 8 of the National Health Service Act 1977 (NHSA 1977):

> A local social services authority may, with the Secretary of State's approval, and to such extent as he may direct shall, make arrangements for the purpose of the prevention of illness and for the care of persons suffering from illness and for the after-care of persons who have been so suffering.

Approval by means of DHSS Circular 19/74 has, so far, been given only to arrangements made for those who are, or have been, suffering from mental disorder. Paragraph 4 directs authorities to provide centres (including Training Centres and Day Centres) or other facilities (including domiciliary facilities), whether in premises managed by the local authority or otherwise, for training or occupation of persons suffering from, or who have been suffering from, mental disorder.

The powers and duties set out in the Circular have been extended, with respect to certain mentally disordered patients leaving hospital, by s.117 of the MHA 1983. This section is restricted to those patients detained under s.3, or s.37 of the Act, (and to prisoners transferred to hospital under ss.47 and 48) who have ceased to be detained and leave hospital. The duty, in this case, is placed upon both the DHA and local social services authority. They must, in co-operation with relevant voluntary agencies, provide after-care services for any person to whom the section applies until such time as they are satisfied that the person concerned is no longer in need of such services. Current provisions will be extended if and when s.7 of the Disabled Persons (Services Consultation and Representation) Act 1986 (DP(SCR)A 1986) is brought into effect. Section 7 will apply to mentally disordered patients, whether detained or informal, who have been receiving hospital treatment as in-patients for a continuous period of six months or more. Hospital managers will be required to inform the health and social services authorities for the area where the patient lives that a patient to whom the section applies is to be discharged. This will enable the two authorities to assess the patient's need for any of the services for which they are responsible.

In all other circumstances, the provision of after-care continues to depend upon an assessment of need, coupled with availability of resources.

Notes

1. Hunt, A. (1978) *The Elderly at Home*, OPCS, Social Survey Division, (HMSO).

2. op.cit.

3. DHSS (1978) *A Happier Old Age*, A Discussion Paper, (HMSO); Royal Commission on the NHS. *Report*, (1979) Cmnd. 7615, (HMSO) at p.61 (The Merrison Committee); DHSS (1987) *Promoting Better Health*, Cm 249, (HMSO), at p.14.

4. Johnson, M. (1972) 'Self-perception of need among the elderly', *Sociological Review*.

5. Tinker, A. (1984) *The Elderly in Modern Society*, 2nd edition, (Longman), at p.59.

6. Wenger, C. (1988) *Old People's Health and Experience of the Caring Services* The Institute of Human Ageing, Occasional Paper 4, (Liverpool University Press).

7. DHSS (1981) *Growing Older*, Cmnd.8173, (HMSO), at p.64.

8. DHSS (1978) op.cit., at p.9.

9. National Health Service (Charges to Overseas Visitors) (No 2) Regulations 1982 S.I. 1982 No.863.

10. *Akbarali v. Brent LBC [1982] QBD 688*; see also *R. v. Barnet LBC ex parte Shah [1983] 2 WLR 16.*

11. See discussion in Carty, H. 'Overseas Visitors and the NHS' in the *Journal of Social Welfare Law*, September 1983, pp. 258-64.

12. CSO (1983) *Social Trends*, (HMSO); see also 1987 edition.

13. CSO (1988) op.cit., at p.127.

14. ibid.

15. DHSS (1981) *Care in Action*, (HMSO).

16. Laing, W. (1985) *Private Health Care*, (OHE) at p.27.

17. Royal Commission on the National Health Service (1979), op.cit., at p.62.

18. DHSS (1981) op.cit., at p.43.   Griffiths, R. (1988) *Community Care: Agenda for Action*, (HMSO).

19. Lovell, A. et al. (1981) *An Exploration of Non-Registration With General Practitioners in Attenders at an Accident and Emergency Department*, South Bank Occasional Paper, Health Series 1 (Polytechnic of the South Bank).

20. DHSS (1987) op.cit., at p.17.

21. op.cit., at p.19.   See also powers to make regulations, in this respect, in the Health and Medicines Act 1988, ss. 8 and 9 (not in force).

22. DHSS (1978) op.cit., at p.9; DHSS (1981) op.cit., at p.1

23. Lovell, A. (1981) op.cit., at pp.65-72.

24. ibid., at pp. 84-8.

25. DHSS (1987) op.cit., at p.17.

26. ibid., at p.23.

27. ibid., at p.17.

28. National Health Service (General Medical and Pharmaceutical Services) Regulations 1974 S.I. 1974, No.160 reg 32.

29. Royal Commission on the National Health Service (1979),

op.cit., at p.72.
30. DHSS/WO (1980) *Residential Homes for the Elderly. Arrangements for Health Care*, A Memorandum for Guidance, 4th impression at para. 8.
31. National Health Service Regulations 1974, op.cit., at reg 21.
32. Bloomsbury Community Health Council (1982) *Finding a Doctor in Bloomsbury.*
33. National Health Service Regulations 1974, op.cit., at reg 15.
34. reg 16(3).
35. Sched 1, Part 1 at para. 4(3).
36. Sched 1, Part 1 at para. 4(1)(h).
37. DHSS (1981) op.cit., at p.47.
38. DHSS (1987) op.cit., at p.15.
39. National Health Service Regulations 1974 op.cit., Sched 1, Part 1 at para. 13.
40. Sched 1, Part 1 at para. 3.
41. See Chapter 6 at para. 6.4.1.
42. Royal Commission on the National Health Service Regulations 1974, op.cit., Sched 1, Part 1 at para. 16(1).
43. National Health Service Regulations 1974, op.cit., Sched 1, Part I at para. 16(1).
44. National Health Service Regulations 1974, op.cit., Sched 1, Part I at para. 16(2).
45. Royal Commission on the National Health Service (1979) op.cit.
46. National Health Service Regulations 1974, op.cit., Sched 1, Part 1 at para. 19(1).
47. Royal Commission on the National Health Service (1979) op.cit.
48. ibid., (1979) at p.74.
49. Circular HC(FP)(78)1.
50. See Chapter 6 at paras. 6.3.3 - 6.3.10.
51. National Health Service Regulations 1974, op.cit., Sched 1, Part 1 at para. 15(2).
52. Royal Commission on the National Health Service (1979) op.cit., at p.74.
53. Tinker, A. (1984) op.cit., at p.71.
54. Royal Commission on the National Health Service (1979) op.cit.
55. CSO (1986) *Social Trends* (HMSO).

56. Wenger, C. (1988) op.cit.
57. DHSS (1981) op.cit., at p.47.
58. National Health Service Regulations 1974 op.cit., Sched 1, Part 1 at para. 24.
59. DHSS (1987) op.cit., at p.21.
60. Wenger, C. (1988) op.cit.
61. DHSS (1987) op.cit., at p.49.
62. ibid., at p.20.
63. ibid.
64. Royal Commission on the National Health Service (1979) op.cit., at p.87.
65. ibid.; see also The Acheson Report (1981) *Primary Health Care in Inner London* - Report of a Study Group commissioned by the London Health Planning Consortium.
66. DHSS (1987) op.cit., at p.19.
67. National Health Service Regulations 1974 op.cit., Sched 1, Part 1 at para. 13.
68. Wenger, C. (1988) op.cit.
69. National Health Service Regulations 1974 op.cit., reg 29(b) inserted by National Health Service (General Medical and Pharmaceutical Services) Amendment Regulations 1982 S.I. 1982 No.1283.
70. NHS Regulations 1974 op.cit. Sched 3A as inserted by NHS (General Medical and Pharmaceutical Services) Amendment Regulations 1985 S.I. 1985 No.290, amended by NHS (General Medical and Pharmaceutical Services) Amendment (No.2) Regulations 1985 S.I. 1985 No.540. See also NHS (General Medical and Pharmaceutical Services) Amendment Regulations 1987 S.I. 1987 No.5; NHS (General Medical and Pharmaceutical Services) Amendment (No.4) Regulations 1987 S.I. 1987 No.1425.
71. Wenger, C. (1988) op.cit.
72. National Health Service Regulations 1974 op.cit., reg 29.
73. National Health Service Regulations 1974 op.cit., Sched 1, Part 1 at para. 36 as substituted by the National Health Service (General Medical and Pharmaceutical Services) Amendment Regulations 1985 op.cit.
74. Royal Commission on the NHS (1979) op.cit., at p.94.
75. DHSS (1987) op.cit., at p.36.
76. National Health Service Regulations 1974 op.cit., reg 30.
77. Wenger, C. (1988) op.cit.
78. DHSS (1987) op.cit., at p.37.
79. ibid., at p.36.

80. Royal Commission on the NHS (1979) op.cit., at p.96.

81. DHSS (1987) op.cit., at p.36.

82. The Nuffield Foundation (1986) *Pharmacy: The Report of a Committee of Inquiry.*

83. DHSS (1987) op.cit., at p.36.

84. See Chapter 6 at para. 6.4.2.

85. National Health Service (General Medical and Pharmaceutical Services) Regulations, 1974 op.cit., Sched 1, Part 1 at para.13.

86. Cartwright, Ann (1967) *Patients and their Doctors* (Routledge & Kegan Paul) at p.21.

87. See Association of CHCs for England and Wales (1988) Annual Report 1987/88 (ACHEW).

88. National Health Service (General Medical and Pharmaceutical Services) Regulations 1974 op.cit., reg 18

89. DHSS (1987) op.cit., at p.18.

90. NHS (General Medical and Pharmaceutical Services) Regulations 1974 op.cit., Sched 1, Part 1 at para. 10.

91. ibid.

92. DHSS (1986) *Neighbourhood Nursing - A Focus for Care (The Cumberlege Report)* (HMSO).

93. DHSS (1987) op.cit., at p.41.

94. DHSS (1977) Circular CNO(77)8 *Nursing in Primary Health Care.*

95. DHSS (1981) op.cit., at p.48.

96. DHSS (1977) Circular CNO(77)8, op.cit.; DHSS (1981) op.cit., at p.48.

97. DHSS (1977) Circular CNO(77)8, op.cit.

98. Wenger, C. (1988) op.cit.

99. DHSS (1987) op.cit., at p.41.

100. Fox, B. and Maddick, I. H. (1985) 'Making the most of the dental service', *New Age*, Winter, 1985.

101. National Health Service (General Dental Services) Regulations 1973, S.I. 1973 No.1468, reg 4.

102. reg 17.

103. Sched 1, Part 1 at para. 2(b).

104. Fox, B. and Maddick, I. H. (1985) op.cit.

105. ibid.

106. DHSS (1987) op.cit., at p.28.

107. Royal Commission on the NHS, (1979) op.cit., at p.111.

108. Health and Medicines Act 1988 (Commencement No.1) Order 1988. S.I. 1988 No.2102.

109. National Health Service (General Dental Services) Regulations op.cit., Sched 1, Part 1 at para. 4.

110. DHSS (1987) op.cit., at p.27.

111. National Health Service (General Dental Services) Regulations op.cit., reg 20.

112. DHSS (1987) op.cit., at p.33.

113. op.cit. See Hansard H.C., November 15, 1980, and also Health and Medicines Act 1988, s.14 (not in force).

114. See paras. 5.3.4 and 5.3.5.

115. National Health Service (Payment for Optical Appliances) Regulations 1986, S.I. 1986 No.976.

116. DHSS (1987) op.cit., at p.34.

117. National Health Services (Payment for Optical Appliances) Regulations 1986, op.cit.

118. DHSS (1987) op.cit., at p.33.

119. DHSS (1981) op.cit., at p.50.

120. CSO (1988) *Social Trends* at p.125.

121. Published by the College of Health, 18 Victoria Park Square, London E2 9PS.

122. DHSS (1981) op.cit., at p.53.

123. Mental Health Act 1983, s.1.

124. s.114.

125. s.13(2).

126. See Chapter 6 at para. 6.4.4.

127. *1 All ER 643.*

128. Gostin, L. (1983) *A Practical Guide to Mental Health Law,* (MIND) at p.48.

129. Age Concern (1986) *The Law and Vulnerable Elderly People,* (Age Concern England).

130. Mental Health Act Commission (1987) *The Second Biennial Report 1985-87,* (HMSO) at p.56.

131. Mental Health Act (1983), s.59.

132. s.62(2).

133. Norman, A. J. (1980) *Rights and Risks,* (National Corporation for the Care of Old People) at pp.71-4.

134. Age Concern (1986) op.cit., at pp.70-3.

135. Health Services and Public Health Act 1968, s.47.

136. Mental Health Act 1983 s.2 and s.3.

137. s.2, s.3 and s.4.

138. s.5(1) and s.20(1).

139. s.23.

140. s.18 and s.17.

Chapter Six

COMPLAINTS AND REDRESS OF GRIEVANCES IN HEALTH CARE

6.1.1 HEALTH CARE PROBLEMS

The issues relating to health care which most often give rise to complaints by patients can be categorized in three main ways. First, there are complaints which relate to gaps, deficiencies, and delays in the provision of service, often arising from lack of resources; second, there are complaints over the way in which services are organized and delivered and/or the standard of care provided; and, third, there are complaints which allege actual harm or injury to a particular individual which may amount to the torts of negligence or trespass to the person. These different types of complaint gives rise to different procedures which are examined below.

6.2.1 COMPLAINTS ABOUT GAPS, DEFICIENCIES, AND DELAYS

A major cause of complaint in the NHS is that gaps, deficiencies, and delays in the provision of service have a detrimental effect upon patients in need of care and treatment. There is often a shortage of geriatric beds in local hospitals, for example, or long waiting lists for operations such as hip replacements. In such circumstances, what action can an individual take in order to try to obtain the services which are needed?

Three kinds of legal action may be available, although on existing evidence, success is uncertain and often unlikely. The legal possibilities are: to sue for breach of statutory duty; to apply to the courts for judicial review of an administrative decision; and to request the Minister concerned to exercise his default powers.

6.2.2 BREACH OF A STATUTORY DUTY

The NHS is available to its users as a result of duties placed upon the Secretary of State by ss. 1 and 3 of the National Health Service Act, 1977 (NHSA, 1977). Section 1 of the Act places a duty upon the Minister to promote a comprehensive health service designed to secure improvement in the physical and mental health of the people of England and Wales, and in the prevention, diagnosis, and treatment of illness. The Minister also has a duty under s.3 of the NHSA 1977 to provide accommodation facilities and services for the prevention of illness and for the care and after-care of people suffering from illness, to such extent as he considers appropriate and necessary.

One possible course of action is to sue for alleged breach of one or more of these statutory duties. The primary task of the person bringing the action is to show that the duty relates to him/her, either as an individual, or as the member of a specific group, and is not owed to the public in general. Success, therefore, depends upon the court's interpretation of the presumed intention of Parliament when enacting the legislation. Judicial attitudes in this context can be illustrated by the (unreported) decision of the Court of Appeal in *R. v. Secretary of State for Social Services, and others, ex parte Hincks (1981)*.[1] Four individuals, including three elderly persons, who had been on a waiting list for orthopaedic surgery for up to three years, brought an action against the Secretary of State, the regional health authority and the local health authority, alleging breach of statutory duty because plans to build an extension to a particular hospital had been abandoned as the result of financial cutbacks. The applicants sought a declaration that the respondents were in breach of the duty set out in s.1 of the Act to continue to promote a comprehensive service designed to secure improvements in health and the prevention of illness, and were also in breach of their duty under s.3 to provide accommodation, facilities and services in order to fulfill those purposes. The plaintiffs also sought damages for the pain and suffering which they had suffered as a result of the time spent in waiting for treatment, and an order to compel performance of these statutory duties. (see para. 6.2.3 below)

The applicants' attempt failed since they were unable to establish a right of action for breach of statutory duty. The Court of Appeal held that the terms of s.3(1)(a), which specifically relates to the provision of hospital services, required the Secretary of State to provide accommodation, facilities and services only 'to such extent as he considered necessary to meet all reasonable requirements.' The duty was not absolute and Lord Denning suggested that for an action to succeed, the way in which the Minister had exercised the discretion given to him had to be so unreasonable that no reasonable Secretary of State would have acted, or not acted, in that particular way. According to Lord Bridge, current government policies in the economic and financial fields were to be regarded as proper limitations on a Minister's statutory duties to provide services. It would seem that the question of how much is to be made available by way of resources, and of how these resources are then to be allocated to particular services, is regarded as a matter of political decision-making lying outside the jurisdiction of the courts. Action for breach of statutory duty is, therefore, of limited value and unlikely to be of much use to elderly people unable to secure the services they need because of financial stringency unless it could be shown, perhaps, that the Minister's decision was so unreasonable as to be *ultra vires* and possibly open to judicial review. Subsequent attempts at using actions for breaches of statutory duty have been no more successful in their outcome than they were in the Hincks case.[2]

6.2.3   JUDICIAL REVIEW

Another possible course of action available to an aggrieved patient would be to invoke the supervisory jurisdiction of the High Court by making use of a procedure known as judicial review. This is the means by which the High Court exercises control over the wrongful administrative acts or omissions of public authorities and officials by the use of the prerogative orders of *mandamus, certiorari,* and prohibition. The procedure for applying for judicial review is now governed by Order 53 of the Rules of the Supreme Court, and by s.31 of the Supreme Court Act 1981 (SCA 1981).

Applicants for one or more of these prerogative orders - to quash, restrain, or to require the performance of a public duty - must first obtain the leave of the court which will only be granted if the court considers the applicant has shown a 'sufficient interest in the matter to which the application applies.' An order can be refused if the court considers that a suitable alternative remedy is available to the applicant, such as a statutory right of appeal to the Minister, appeal to some other court, or the use of default powers. (see para. 6.2.4 below) If these hurdles can be overcome, judicial review is one of the main methods by which the decision of a public body, such as a health authority, can be controlled by the courts.

6.2.4 DEFAULT POWERS

Another possible course of action is to ask the Secretary of State to exercise the default powers set out in s.85 of the NHSA 1977. Under that section, the Secretary of State can declare a Regional Health Authority (RHA), or District Health Authority (DHA), or a Family Practitioner Committee (FPC) or a Special Health Authority (SHA), plus a number of other bodies, to be in default for failing to discharge any duty placed upon them by the Act. (This power parallels default procedures available under local government legislation.) If the Minister exercises his power, members of the authority are dismissed, and others are appointed in their place. It is rare, however, for Ministers to exercise such powers, and the procedure is, therefore, of limited value in itself. The threat of drawing the attention of a Minister to a particular problem by asking him to exercise his default powers has, however, been used by a number of groups seeking to obtain services for disabled people.[3]

If the Secretary of State refuses to exercise his default powers, is it then possible to take legal action in the courts? The position is not clear since judicial opinion seems divided on this point. It has been suggested that legal action can be brought if a public body had apparently acted *ultra vires*, that is, beyond the powers granted to it by statute, or where the decision affects an individual who is a member of the class of individuals to whom the statutory duty is owed.[4] In such cases, the courts might be prepared to require the authority to act in a reasonable manner in relation to that person and his/her needs. It seems unlikely, however, that elderly persons *per se* would be regarded as members of a particular class of individuals to whom a statutory duty is owed.

6.3.1 COMPLAINTS ABOUT THE ORGANIZATION AND STANDARD OF SERVICES

The second category of complaints are those concerned with the way in which a service is organized and delivered, and/or the standard of care provided. Complaints of this kind can fall to be dealt with by any one of a number of procedures. Complaints against family practitioners and complaints about hospital care and treatment are dealt with in different ways. This can create particular problems for those who may be unsure which procedure to use, or whose complaint relates to several parts of the NHS. For example, a complaint might relate to the organization and standard of care in services received both in hospital and from a GP. The reason for the diversity of procedures in this field is to be found in the history of health care rather than in a rational development of an appropriate and suitable complaints system.[5]

6.3.2 Patients can seek help and advice from their local Community Health Council (CHC) when bringing a complaint. In some areas, members and/or officers of the local CHC will also assist individuals in presenting their complaints to the appropriate body but there is apparently wide variation in the willingness and/or ability of members and officers to carry out this role.[6] If an individual changes his/her mind and decides not to proceed with the alleged grievance, the CHC might, however, use the case as an example of poor standards of service. It could then make its views known to the relevant authorities since one of the main responsibilities of a CHC is to keep health services in its locality under review. Community Health Councils have a statutory right to be consulted by the local DHA whenever that body proposes 'any substantial development of health services in the Council's district or .... any substantial variation in the provision of such services',[7] although, in exceptional circumstances, an authority may take a decision without consultation, in the interests of the service. In that case, the CHC must be notified immediately and be given reasons for the lack of consultation. A CHC can also require a DHA to give it such information as it reasonably requires about the way in which services are being planned and operated. A CHC also has rights of access for the purpose of inspecting premises controlled by a DHA. Given that it has such powers and duties, and given that it has representatives from the local community serving on it, contacting a local CHC can be of advantage to a patient with a possible grievance.

6.3.3   COMPLAINTS AGAINST
FAMILY PRACTITIONERS

The current system for complaining about family practitioner services has been criticized in that it works unevenly from one part of the country to another; is complex and long-drawn out; does not deal adequately with some of the problems which most worry patients; is weighted in a number of ways against the complainant; is not widely known or understood and does not, therefore, provide adequate consumer safeguards.[8]   A particular cause for misunderstanding is that the system, which originated with the health insurance scheme of 1911, is designed not so much as machinery for the redress of grievance by patients, but as a means of ensuring that family practitioners comply with their contractual terms and conditions of service.[9]   In essence, the system is concerned with enabling the FPC to sanction those practitioners who have breached their terms of service with the Committee.   Many of the complaints brought against family practitioners have to do with matters which fall outside the terms and conditions of service, however, such as allegations of discourtesy, brusqueness or rudeness, or the way in which a practice is organized and the effect that has upon the delivery of the service to the individual complainant.

Some of the weaknesses of the current complaints system were recognized by the Government in its White Paper on the primary health care services.[10]   The main proposals for amending the regulations are referred to in the discussion that follows.

6.3.4   Most complaints brought against family practitioners in fact relate to GPs.   What is mainly discussed below is how the procedure works in relation to complaints against them. Parallel procedures exist for bringing complaints against the other family practitioners (that is, against dentists, opticians and pharmacists) who also have contracts with FPCs. These procedures are discussed briefly at para. 6.3.14.

6.3.5   COMPLAINTS AGAINST GPs

A complaint against a GP must, at present, be brought within the rather short period of eight weeks from the alleged breach of the terms of service.[11]   The government now proposes to extend this period to 13 weeks.   In doing so, it recognizes that eight weeks can be an unreasonably restrictive time limit in some cases but that the time-scale has to be considered against the strain imposed upon the practitioner when a complaint is outstanding. A complaint brought outside the time-limit may be allowed, but only on the grounds that the complainant was or is ill, or for some other reasonable cause, and only with the consent of the doctor concerned, or the Secretary of State.   If the FPC does not allow a late complaint, the patient may appeal to the Secretary of State against this refusal.[12]   The government proposes that oral, as well as written complaints should be permitted, subject to certain conditions aimed at securing impartiality; and that complaints should be regarded as properly lodged if received by an RHA or DHA within the proper time limits, since there may be confusion in the complainant's mind as to the proper channels for making a complaint.   In such cases, the health authority which had received the complaint would be required to pass it on immediately to the appropriate FPC for action to be taken.

Complaints must normally be made by the patient him/herself, although someone else can be authorized to act on the complainant's behalf.   There is a similar concession where a person is incapacitated by age, sickness, or some other infirmity.   Examples exist of complaints being made by social services authorities on behalf of elderly residents living in residential homes for the elderly.   A complaint may also be brought in relation to a patient who had since died.

As soon as practicable after receiving a complaint, the FPC administrator must send a copy of the complainant's statement to the chairman of the Medical Services Committee (MSC) which is the body set up by the FPC to oversee medical services in the area.[13]   Having considered the complaint, the chairman must decide whether, in his/her opinion, the GP has failed to comply with one or more of the terms of service.[14] If the chairman decides that the complainant's statement does not disclose a breach of service, the administrator must inform the complainant of that fact and invite him/her to submit, within fourteen days, a further statement amplifying the complaint. If no further statement is received, or if, after giving it further consideration, the chairman is of the opinion that no hearing is necessary, that decision must be brought before the MSC which may either dismiss or uphold the chairman's decision.

If the chairman considers there are reasonable grounds for believing a breach of the terms of service has occurred, however, the GP must be told and asked for his/her comments within four weeks or such longer period as the MSC allows. Any comments received from the GP must be sent to the complainant who is given not less than fourteen days, or such longer period as the MSC may allow, to make observations on them. If the chairman, after further considering the GP's comments, decides a hearing is unnecessary, that decision, too, must be brought before the MSC. Where the MSC agrees with the chairman's decision, no further action will be taken. The complainant may, however, appeal to the Secretary of State within 14 days of being denied a hearing.

Should no comments be received, or if, notwithstanding any which are received, the chairman considers a hearing to be necessary, or where there is a material difference between the parties over the facts of the case, the administrator must be instructed to arrange a hearing, to inform the parties, and to send them copies of the relevant correspondence, comments or observations which are to be produced as evidence at the hearing. If the complaint concerns a GP's deputy who is also on the FPC's medical list, the complaint is deemed to have been made against both doctors. If, in the chairman's opinion the evidence shows no personal failure to comply with his/her terms of service by the patient's doctor, the MSC may limit its investigation to the complaint against the deputy.

6.3.6 *THE HEARING*

Both patient and the doctor (or doctors) (see para. 6.3.5 above) must be given 21 days' notice of their right to attend the hearing. Hearings are held in private although the secretary of the local medical committee (which represents all doctors in the area) may attend as an observer. The MSC consists of a lay chairman, three lay members of the FPC and three doctors. At present, there need not be an equal number of lay men and professionals attending the hearing, provided that at least one lay and one professional member attends. The government proposes to amend the regulations so to ensure that apart from the Chairman, an equal number of lay and professional members are present at the start of the hearing. If a member were to leave during a hearing that would, however, not invalidate the proceedings. It is also proposed to increase the quorum from one lay and one professional member to two of each.

At present only the chairman of the MSC is subject to annual re-appointment. The government intends to extend this provision to all service committee members, recognizing that the quality of decisions also reflects the effectiveness of members. The deputy chairman of the MSC is entitled to attend but takes no part in the proceedings, except when chairing a hearing in the absence of the chairman. This restriction is likely to be lifted so as to empower the deputy chairman to participate in the proceedings as a lay member of the committee. The deputy chairman will be appointed from amongst the lay members.

6.3.7 Before the start of the hearing, the chairman must ask members if they have any direct or indirect interest in the matter to be discussed. If any person declares an interest he/she cannot take part in the hearing although a deputy may act in his/her place. The White Paper speaks of impartial treatment of complaints as essential if they are to be fairly and properly resolved. It can be difficult to achieve impartiality in areas where members of the service committee may be acquainted with one another or with the parties to a complaint. It could happen that the respondent practitioner is a member of the FPC. In such cases, the regulations will be amended to ensure that the complaint is transferred for investigation by another FPC.

Both sides may be assisted in presenting their case before the Committee, for example, by a friend, or by a member of a CHC[15] (see para. 6.3.2 above), but neither a barrister, nor a solicitor, nor any other paid advocate may appear as representative, although they may attend to give advice.[16] Some FPCs have interpreted this rule so as to exclude secretaries of CHCs from acting as representatives on the grounds that they are paid officials. The new regulations will make it clear that the secretary of the local representative committee or a local CHC can represent a party at a service committee hearing.

Both parties may give and call relevant evidence and put relevant questions to the other party, and to any witnesses, either directly or, if the service committee directs, through the chairman. The conduct of the hearing is otherwise at the discretion of the MSC. The chairman may postpone a hearing on the application of either party if it is not reasonably practicable for them or any witnesses to attend because of the date fixed, or for any other reason. If either party fails to appear at the hearing it may be adjourned if the committee is satisfied that absence is due to illness or some other reasonable cause. The committee may also adjourn the hearing for any reason as it thinks fit. Before doing so, it must invite the observations of any party who is present.

6.3.8 THE DECISION

At the end of the hearing, the MSC must decide whether or not a breach in the terms of service has occurred. A majority decision is possible if the committee is not unanimous.[17] In the event of a tie, the chairman has a casting vote. A report containing the committee's recommendations must then be prepared for submission to the next meeting of the FPC. On hearing the report, the FPC may a) dismiss the complaint; b) recommend to the Secretary of State that the GP be warned to comply more closely with his/her terms of service in future; c) limit the number of patients which the GP may have on his/her list; d) recommend to the Secretary of State that an amount should be withheld from his/her remuneration; or e) refer the GP to a NHS Tribunal with a recommendation that the continued inclusion of the GP on the medical list would be prejudicial to the efficiency of the service.[18]

Although an FPC may recommend to the Secretary of State that expenses incurred by the patient as a result of the GP's breach be deducted from the doctor's remuneration, the primary purpose is to ensure that GPs comply with their contractual terms of service and not to award damages or compensation to the complainant.

The government proposes to simplify this complaints procedure. It believes that FPCs can and should act independently and therefore proposes to make them responsible for determining the outcome of complaints and the action to be taken. The decision of the FPC would then be final, except where an appeal was made to the Secretary of State (see para. 6.3.9 below) or where the FPC believed that withholding fees above a certain level (to be reviewed periodically) was desirable.

The parties to the complaint must be informed of the FPC's decision, and a copy of the MSC's report should also be sent to them, as soon as possible after the decision is reached. The White Paper proposes that, at the request of any party, FPCs should be required to send a copy, together with the FPC's decision, to any member of either House of Parliament at any time.

6.3.9   APPEALS

Either party can appeal to the Secretary of State within one month from the date upon which the party to the complaint receives notification of the decision. It is now proposed that the time limit should run from the date upon which the party is given, or served with notification of the FPC's decision. Proof of posting to the party's usual or last known address would be accepted as proof of service. The appeal must be accompanied by a statement of the facts, and of the arguments forming the basis for the appeal. On appeal by the patient, the Secretary of State may dismiss it without a hearing on the grounds that the patient had no reasonable grounds for the appeal, or that it is otherwise vexatious or frivolous. On appeal by a practitioner, however, an oral hearing must be held, unless the appellant does not require it. The appeal, at which the parties and their representatives appear in person, takes the form of a hearing before three officers of the DH. In this case, barristers or solicitors can represent the parties, as can officers or members of any organization of which the appellant is a member, and any member of his/her family or a friend. The tribunal reports its decision to the Secretary of State who then informs the parties in writing.

6.3.10 Complaints to FPCs often allege failure to make a home visit when requested and when the condition of the patient required it; or refusal to refer a patient's case to a consultant when the patient's medical condition required it. The MSC cannot review a reasonable exercise of clinical judgement by a doctor, but can be asked to adjudicate on whether or not the practitioner took all reasonable steps in the exercise of that judgement, for example, whether or not the diagnosis was made without proper and necessary examination of the patient.

One complaint, upheld by an MSC, concerned a GP who twice visited a patient and, on the second occasion, diagnosed gastroenteritis and gave appropriate treatment. Two days later, the patient's condition worsened and his wife asked for a further visit which was refused. She was told, however, to contact the GP again if the patient's condition continued to give cause for concern. Later on the same day, another request was made, and the GP arranged for a deputy to call on his behalf. The patient died from a burst appendix shortly after the deputy arrived. The MSC recognized the difficulties of making an early diagnosis of the patient's condition and that the GP sincerely believed in the correctness of the diagnosis which had been made. Nevertheless, it held that a visit ought to have been made, although it also recognized that the GP had been influenced by a history of unnecessary requests for visits made by the patient over the years. The committee also accepted that the GP had in the past given satisfactory service to both the patient and his wife.[19]

Another complaint, made on behalf of an 86 year old patient, alleged failure to visit and treat a patient whose condition required it. A telephone call had been made at 11.45 a.m. on a Monday as a result of which medicine was made available and collected for the patient but the doctor did not call. A further call was made at 6.45 a.m. the following day, followed by another at 7.30 a.m. At 10.30 a.m. on the same day, the doctor's wife was told that a doctor from another practice had attended and treated the patient. The MSC considered that the GP, following the telephone calls and with knowledge of the patient's previous medical history of a heart complaint, should have made a visit. He was, therefore, in breach of his terms of service which obligated him to render to his patient all necessary and appropriate medical services, and to visit if the patient's condition required it.

6.3.11 THE INFORMAL PROCEDURE

Some FPCs currently operate an informal procedure in an attempt to reach a satisfactory conclusion without involving the statutory procedure described above. If the parties agree, the FPC appoints two members of the Committee, that is, a lay member assisted, where necessary, by a doctor to discuss the matter informally with the patient and his/her GP. This is usually done within two weeks of the complaint being received. The informal procedure does not preclude holding a formal hearing later if the matter remains unresolved.

The government recognizes the value of this procedure and proposes to amend the regulations to make it available, where appropriate, for dental, pharmaceutical, and general ophthalmic services as well as for general medical services. Since the statutory complaints procedure described above cannot be used where the complaint is concerned not with breaches of a practitioner's terms of service, but, for example, with a general practitioner's attitude or manner, the government believes that informal conciliation on an extra-statutory basis may be appropriate in such cases.

6.3.12 A relatively recent development, in the field of primary health care, is the setting up of a patients' committee in some group practices and health centres to act as a forum for expressing patients' opinions about the organization and running of the practice or health centre, and as a means of communicating with the doctors working there the problems raised by patients in the context of service delivery. A National Association for Patient Participation was formed in 1978 to support the work of individual Patient Participation Groups, to share information and experience between groups, and to spread the idea and practice of patient participation generally. The establishment of a group will depend upon the interest and encouragement of the doctors within the practice or health centre. At present, only about 50 of these groups exist throughout the country.

6.3.13 NHS TRIBUNALS

NHS Tribunals are bodies, separate from FPCs and MSCs, set up to consider recommendations, primarily from FPCs, that a GP should be removed from the list of those practising in the NHS. A Tribunal consists of a chairman who must be a practising barrister or solicitor of at least ten years' standing, and two members appointed by the Secretary of State, one of whom must be a lay person and the other a member of the medical profession. A decision in favour of the practitioner is final, but if the decision goes against him/her, there is right of appeal to the Secretary of State.

6.3.14 COMPLAINTS AGAINST DENTISTS, OPTICIANS, AND PHARMACISTS

FPCs also deal with complaints against other family practitioners. In relation to dentists, complaints must be made within six months of the completion of treatment, or eight weeks of the patient becoming aware of grounds for the complaint, whichever is the sooner. The Dental Service Committee is the body set up to hear complaints of this kind. Some FPCs have Denture Conciliation Committees whose function is to listen to complaints about dentures.

Complaints against opticians must at present be made within eight weeks. They are heard by the Opthalmic Service Committee consisting of a Chairman and up to ten other persons, of whom four are lay members of the FPC, two are opthalmic medical practitioners, two are opthalmic opticians, and two are dispensing opticians. Complaints against pharmaceutical chemists must also be made within eight weeks and are heard by the Pharmaceutical Service Committee. In these cases, the procedure is similar to that described above in relation to GPs. The government proposes to extend the time limit to allow complaints to be made within 13 weeks of the matter coming to the complainant's attention.

6.3.15 COMPLAINTS ABOUT HOSPITAL SERVICES

Until recently, no statutory procedure existed in relation to complaints about the organization and standard of services in hospitals managed by a DHA or SHA. In consequence, procedures varied from one authority to another. The Hospital Complaints Procedure Act 1985 (HCPA 1985) required the Secretary of State to direct health authorities on the complaints procedure to be set up in hospitals in their area for which they are responsible. Following circulation of a Consultation Document, the Secretary of State has now issued directions to health authorities on the arrangements to be made for dealing with complaints made by, or on behalf of those who are, or have been, hospital patients. Such arrangements were to be brought into effect by each authority by July 29, 1988.[21]

6.3.16 In accordance with these directions, a health authority must designate one officer at each hospital or group of hospitals to receive and be accountable for all formal complaints made by or on behalf of a patient. If the patient is dead, or is unable to act, the complaint may be made by a close relative, friend, or suitable representative person or body.

6.3.17 A formal complaint must be made, or be recorded, in writing. According to Circulars HC(88)37 and WHC(88)36, issued at the same time as the directions, where a complainant cannot put the complaint in writing, the designated officer should ensure that a record of the complaint is made and should ask the complainant to sign it. Refusal to sign the record should not delay the investigation. The complaint ought normally to be made within three months of the event which gave rise to it, although the designated officer should, if satisfied that there was good cause for the delay, have discretion to allow a longer period.

6.3.18 INVESTIGATING FORMAL COMPLAINTS

Arrangements for dealing with formal complaints must allow the complainant, and any hospital staff involved in the matter, an opportunity to bring any relevant information or comments which they wish to make to the designated officer's attention. After carrying out the investigation, he/she must prepare a report for the complainant, for any person involved in the complaint, and for any other person, as required by the authority. Where appropriate this might include the manager of another department or service. The Circulars suggest that the report detailing the results of the investigation should be informative on the reasons for any failure in the service. They should also refer to any steps taken to prevent a recurrence and should contain an apology where appropriate. If the complainant remains dissatisfied, he/she should be advised to refer the matter to the Health Service Commissioner (HSC) unless the complaint clearly falls outside the HSC's jurisdiction, or the complainant proposes to take further action through the courts.

Arrangements made under these provisions may provide for a designated officer to be assisted by other officers, who may, with his/her permission, act on the designated officer's behalf.

6.3.19 INFORMAL COMPLAINTS

Arrangements must also exist for staff at a hospital to seek to deal informally with any complaints which are made. A complainant may also ask for the designated officer's assistance in dealing with a complaint which it is likely to be dealt with informally. Informal complaints need not be in writing but the Circulars mention the importance of making a note in cases where the complaint is not readily settled and where a dispute as to the precise nature of the complaint might arise, particularly when a formal investigation is likely. If an informal complaint is not dealt with to the satisfaction of the patient, staff should advise the complainant to make a formal complaint to the designated officer for that hospital.

6.3.20 Designated officers are not responsible for investigating complaints which fall into the following categories: (a) those concerning the exercise of clinical judgement by a hospital doctor or dentist which cannot be resolved by discussion with the consultant concerned; (b) those relating to serious untoward incidents involving harm to a patient; (c) those relating to the conduct of medical or hospital staff and requiring the holding of disciplinary proceedings; (d) those giving reasonable grounds for police investigation as to whether a criminal offence has been committed. The designated officer's duty in such circumstances is to bring the matter to the authority's attention for appropriate action to be taken.

6.3.21 Authorities are required to take all necessary steps to ensure that patients, visitors and staff, as well as the local CHC, are fully informed about the arrangements set up to deal with complaints, the designated officer's identity and his/her location. According to the Circulars, publicity is essential for improving public perception of the complaints procedure. The various methods of publicising it referred to in the Circulars are: admission booklets; leaflets; notices placed in health authority premises, including reception areas; and training to ensure that staff are made aware both of the complaints procedure, and of the name and location of the designated officer. Authorities are asked to consider the need to make leaflets available in ethnic minority languages.

6.3.22 Health authorities are required to make arrangements for reports to be prepared every three months so as to make it possible to monitor progress, to consider trends, and to take remedial action as necessary.

6.3.23 COMPLAINTS ABOUT CLINICAL DECISIONS

In 1981, a new procedure was set up by the DHSS and the Welsh Office (WO) to investigate complaints made by, or on behalf of, a patient about a doctor's clinical judgement. If the patient has since died, or has limited competence to deal with the matter because of physical or mental disability, the complaint may be made by a relative. At the first stage, the complaint should be made, either orally or in writing, direct to the consultant concerned, to the health authority or to one of its officers. Where a complaint which contains a clinical element is made to the authority or to one of its officers, the DGH should show it to the consultant concerned and refer the clinical aspects to him. In either case, it is the consultant's responsibility to look into the clinical aspects of the complaint. The consultant must also involve any other medical staff concerned with the care of the patient. It may be helpful to discuss the matter with the patient's GP. The consultant should try to resolve the complaint within a few days, preferably by offering to see the complainant in order to discuss matters and attempt to resolve the patient's anxieties. If there be any delay, the consultant should get in touch with the complainant and explain the reason. A brief, strictly factual record of the discussion should be made by the consultant in the patient's hospital notes. If the consultant feels there is a significant risk of legal action, he/she should bring the matter to the attention of the District General Manager. (DGM). Where there are non-clinical aspects to a complaint, the consultant should inform the DGM so that these aspects can be dealt with by the appropriate member of staff.

Normally, it will be the DGM who sends the complainant a written reply on behalf of the authority, having agreed any reference to clinical matters with the consultant concerned. On occasion, however, the consultant may wish to send a letter directly to the complainant referring to the clinical aspects of the complaint.

If the patient is dissatisfied with the outcome at this stage, he/she may renew the complaint either to the authority, one of its administrators, or to the consultant. If the complaint has not yet been put into writing, the patient should be asked to do so before it is considered further. The next step is for the consultant to write to the Regional Medical Officer (RMO) in England, or the Medical Officer (Complaints) (MO(C)) in Wales, informing the DGM that this step has been taken. The RMO or MO(C) will discuss the matter with the consultant who may then indicate that he/she wishes to discuss the matter with professional colleagues. The consultant may consider that a futher talk with the complainant might resolve the complaint. If this fails, or if it is felt that no purpose will be served by a meeting with the complainant, the RMO and MO(C) should discuss with the consultant the value of offering the complainant an independent professional review of the circumstances of the complaint. If the matter is not satisfactorily resolved at this point, and if the RMO or the MO(C) feels the seriousness of the complaint justifies it, an independent professional review can be set up involving two consultants working in the same speciality, one of whom is from another health region. This will not be done, however, if the matter is likely to be subject to more formal action by the health authority or if the patient is likely to initiate legal action at this stage. The independent professional review will involve discussions with the medical staff concerned with the patient's care and treatment, as well as with the patient him/herself. If the independent professional review up-holds the complaint, the DGM must write giving the patient an assurance that action has been taken which will ensure that the same problem will not arise again. The patient obtains no further remedy or recompense under this procedure.

6.3.24 PUBLIC INQUIRIES

The Secretary of State can hold statutory public inquiries[22] in relation to matters of particular public concern. Several were held in the late 1960s as the result of scandals in a number of long-term hospitals, some of which contained geriatric patients. These inquiries led to the establishment of what is now known as the Health Advisory Service (HAS). Its terms of reference include the scrutiny, maintenance, and improvement of overall standards in certain areas of the NHS. Included in its current remit are geriatric and psychiatric services both in hospital and in the community. After a visit by a team from HAS, reports are prepared, and sent to the Secretary of State and the health authority concerned, and summaries of any recommendations are also sent to local CHCs. It should be noted, however, that the main influence of HAS is persuasive, since it cannot ensure that its recommendations are put into effect, nor that individual grievances will be remedied.

6.3.25 The absence of a single complaints procedure within this sector of the NHS is clearly unsatisfactory and may explain the relatively low number of complaints.[23] The Ministerial directions, issued under the HCPA 1985, may alleviate some of these difficulties, but they hardly go far enough to make the process less daunting for patients wishing to register dissatisfaction with this part of the service. The position of those who are vulnerable, such as the elderly in long-term care, whose dependence upon staff may make them less likely to criticize standards of care, gives rise to particular concern. The public inquiries referred to above showed how easily mistreatment of patients could remain hidden within the institution. It is important, therefore, that staff should feel able to bring complaints on behalf of patients. A useful model procedure for staff complaints and for managers in handling them is to be found in the publication *Protecting Patients* available from the National Association of Health Authorities (NAHA).

6.3.26 REFERRAL TO THE HEALTH SERVICE COMMISSIONER

An elderly patient, or if he/she is incapable of doing so, a member of his/her family, or if he/she has died, his/her personal representative, or some other individual body, such as a DHA, may take a complaint to the Health Service Commissioner (HSC) (or Ombudsman) whose function is to investigate allegations of injustice or hardship suffered either as a result of the failure of a relevant body (which includes RHAs, DHAs and FPCs) to provide a service which it is under a duty to provide, or as the result of a failure in the way in which a service was made available. The HSC can also investigate allegations of maladministration resulting from any other action taken on behalf of an authority. There is no statutory definition of 'maladministration' but it has been said to include 'bias, neglect, inattention, delay, incompetence, ineptitude, arbitrariness and the like'.[24]

A complaint must normally be made in writing not later than one year from the day on which the matter came to the notice of the complainant, although the HSC has powers to extend the time-limit if that is considered reasonable. The HSC must be satisfied that the relevant body has been given notice of the complaint and had reasonable opportunity to investigate it and to give a reply.

Certain matters are excluded from the HSC's remit. The HSC cannot usually investigate matters which would come within the jurisdiction of the courts or a tribunal, unless it is considered unreasonable to expect the complainant to make use of such procedures. Nor can the HSC investigate matters which concern the actions or omissions of a family practitioner in providing a service (see paras. 6.3.3 to 6.3.14 above) although the administrative failures of an FPC, alleging, for example, poor communication or delays in dealing with a complaint could be examined by the HSC. Also excluded from the HSC's juris-diction are matters concerned solely with clinical judgement in relation to diagnosis and treatment, an omission which led to much public and official disquiet[25] and resulted eventually in the introduction of the procedure referred to at para. 6.3.22 above.

The HSC can interview any person if it is thought he/she could provide information on the matter complained of, and can also examine any relevant documents. On completing an investigation, the HSC submits a report of the findings to the patient and to the relevant body, but cannot ensure that any changes are made as a result of the investigation. The HSC's powers are limited to investigating and, if necessary, to publicising the complaint and the findings and trying to persuade the relevant body to act on the suggestions and recommendations made by him in his report. If the HSC decides not to conduct an investigation a statement, with the reasons, must be sent to the complainant, to the relevant body, and to any Member of Parliament who may have assisted in making the complaint.[26]

6.3.27 The following are examples of cases where a complaint to the HSC has been upheld.

The HSC severely criticized the failure of a Community Nursing Service (CNS) to make a visit to assess the needs of a patient, in his eighties, suffering from the effects of a stroke. Hospital staff had asked for home nursing and incontinence laundry services to be provided. The patient was not visited until three days after his discharge from hospital, and laundry services had not been provided before he died two days later. The CNS was also criticized for the inaccuracy of the record of visits made to the patient which indicated that the patient had been visited two days earlier than was the case.[27]

Another complaint[28] concerned an elderly diabetic man who was taken to an accident and emergency department in a coma. Because of severe weather conditions, he could not be taken home after treatment and stayed the night in hospital. His MP complained that the patient's care and treatment had been totally inadequate; that a serious failure in communication led to the patient receiving a fatal dose of insulin; and that the patient's relatives became aware of the wrong injection only when a report of the subsequent inquest was published. The HSC found a serious failure in the care provided for the patient; that a senior registrar had failed to help a nurse who sought his advice; and that a failure in communication had led to an incorrect dose of insulin being given. The HSC held that the authority had a duty to inform relatives of any serious accident in hospital without delay and criticized them for not doing so. But the promptness with which the authority took action following the tragic incident was commended and it was hoped that other health authorities would note the steps taken.

The HSC also upheld a complaint concerning an 84 year old man who had been living an independent life but who was admitted to hospital and died there. He had recently been a patient in a different unit at the hospital where it was known that his niece, who was close to him, was also his next- of-kin. He died and was cremated, but it was two months before his niece found out. The HSC found the cause of this error was the fact that the records of the hospital were not integrated or cross-checked, and that external inquiries made to trace next-of-kin had been unsuccessful. Steps had since been taken to improve the hospital's records system and the authority apologised to the complainer.[29]

6.3.28 *THE MENTALLY DISORDERED*

The Mental Health Act Commission (MHAC) was set up to protect the interests of those detained under the Mental Health Act 1983 (MHA 1983) The Commission can visit and interview detained patients in private and investigate any complaints made by them. The powers of the Commission do not extend to protecting informal patients who, in fact, are the majority of those in mental hospitals or mental nursing homes at any one time.[30] Under s.121(4) of the Act, the Secretary of State could, if he so wished, direct the MHAC to review any aspects of the care and treatment of informal patients. In its first Biennial Report,[31] the Commission stated that the members had become increasingly concerned about the position of two categories of informal patients, that is, long-stay patients not detained under the Act but who were incapable, and those patients who, for one reason or another, were subject to *de facto* detention in a locked ward or room. The MHAC has now asked for an extension of its remit to cover three aspects of the care of informal patients. These are: (i) any restraints, other than those arising under s.5 of the Act (see Chapter 5, para. 5.11.2) which prevent informal patients from leaving the hospital or any part of it, including medication or the denial of clothing; (ii) intentional deprivation of the company of other patients or deprivation of amenities normally enjoyed by the patient; and (iii) any form of medical treatment which includes the imposition on a patient of a stimulus which it is intended that he/she should find unpleasant or uncomfortable, other than treatment for physical illness or disability.[32]

In relation to detained patients, the MHAC must, at present, investigate two kinds of complaint. First, a patient may complain, either at the time of detention or later, about any matter which occurred while he/she is, or was, detained under the Act in a hospital or mental nursing home, and which he/she considers has not been satisfactorily dealt with by the managers of the hospital or mental nursing home. Secondly, the MHAC may receive complaints from any person in relation to the exercise of powers, or the discharge of duties, conferred in respect of detained patients by the Act.[33] According to the First Biennial Report, the normal route for complaints, in the first instance, should be the hospital's own complaints procedure, although a primary investigative function is not ruled out in some cases. In the period between July 1, 1985 and June 30, 1987 the Commission received 1,231 oral or written complaints, of which it was judged that 277 needed investigation by a team of two Commissioners. In the period September 30, 1983 to June 30, 1985, the comparable figures were 1,549 complaints, of which 533 were followed up by investigation by two Commissioners.[34] The decision to investigate a complaint rests with the Commission, which could refer it to another agency.

6.3.29 PROFESSIONAL MISCONDUCT

Where a complaint alleges professional misconduct occuring either in the NHS or in private practice, it should be directed to the relevant Council or Board concerned with the maintenance of standards in that particular profession. Complaints about the conduct of doctors are made to the General Medical Council (GMC) which has statutory powers to discipline registered medical practitioners under the Medical Act 1978 (MA 1978). Disciplinary proceedings are now governed by the Statutory Regulations of 1980[35] and the procedure to be followed is described in a GMC publication *Professional Conduct and Discipline: Fitness to Practice.*[36]

A complaint must allege 'serious professional misconduct', a term which is not statutorily defined but which has been judicially described as 'no more than serious misconduct judged according to the rules, written or unwritten, governing the profession'. Such behaviour might include abuse or disregard of the doctor's responsibilities for the care and treatment of patients. If the complaint is upheld, the GMC has a range of powers open to it, including the removal of the doctor's name, subject to a right of appeal, from the list of those entitled to practice.

6.3.30 COMPLAINTS AGAINST OTHER HEALTH SERVICE PROVIDERS

In relation to services provided by chiropodists, complaints often arise as the result of delays between assessment of need and treatment being made available. Referring the problem to the DGM may help to secure care more quickly but other action, such as alleging breach of statutory duty, is not likely to succeed (see para. 6.2.2. above). Complaints concerning the standard of any services given by a chiropodist should be directed to the DGM in the first place. Where maladministration is alleged, a complaint can also be made to the HSC.

The body which regulates the professional conduct of chiropodists is the Chiropodists Board of the Council for Professions Supplementary to Medicine, to which any complaint concerning professional misconduct should be directed. The Disciplinary Committee of the Board has power, in serious cases, to remove a person from the list of those registered to practice. Only state registered chiropodists may work within the NHS.

6.3.31 COMMUNITY NURSES

Complaints about the provision of services by District Nurses and Health Visitors lie initially to the DGM. There is also a right of access, where appropriate, to the HSC. The National Boards for Nursing, Midwifery and Health Visiting handle serious complaints of a professional nature. Reference may be made by a Board to the General Council for Nursing, Midwifery and Health

Visiting which can remove a practitioner found guilty of a serious breach of conduct from the register of those permitted to practice.

6.4.1 ACTIONS IN NEGLIGENCE OR TRESPASS TO THE PERSON

The third category of complaint which may arise in relation to health care concerns harm or injury suffered by an individual which, it is alleged, amounts to the tort (or civil wrong), either of negligence or of trespass to the person. A patient may seek financial compensation for an injury suffered as the consequence of the act or omission of someone involved in his/her care. Such actions are available to patients in either the public or the private sector of medicine. For NHS patients, the various complaints procedures described above are, generally, no bar to taking action in the courts as well. The possibility of using the judicial process will, however, normally prevent a complaint being made to the HSC (see 6.3.26 above). For private patients, an action in tort, or possibly an action for breach of an express or implied term in the contractual agreement entered into for the provision of care and treatment, may be their single form of redress. Actions for breaches of statutory duty, or for judicial review, and requests to the Minister to exercise statutory default powers are not available. Nor is the complaints machinery of the NHS open to them.

Mentally disordered patients detained under the MHA 1983 cannot bring a legal action in relation to acts committed under the provisions of the Act without first obtaining the leave of the High Court, and no liability will arise unless the act complained of was done in bad faith or without reasonable care.[37]

6.4.2 NEGLIGENCE

The three essentials of the tort of negligence are that the defendant owes a legal duty of care to the plaintiff; that there was a breach of that duty; and that, as a consequence, harm was suffered by the plaintiff. The standard of care expected of a defendant is that of a reasonable person, so that, for example, a doctor must conform to the standard which can reasonably be expected of a person fulfilling a doctor's role or function. If there is a standard practice in a particular field, deviation from it could be regarded as evidence of negligence. Action which did not observe accepted practice might, however, be held to be warranted because of the special circumstances of the case. It will be for the plaintiff to show what would have been normal or usual practice; second, that the defendant did not follow such practice; and third, that the alternative course which was, in fact, followed was one which no professional person of that status or experience, displaying reasonable skill and ability, would have taken in acting with reasonable care. In *Bolam v. Friern HMC [1957]*[38] it was said that a doctor must 'exercise such care as accords with the standards of reasonably competent medical men at the time', and that the test 'is the standard of the ordinary skilled man exercising and professing to have that special skill'. This could be subject, however, to the exercise of a higher duty if the practitioner had knowledge of special risks. The defendant is not expected to avoid all possible risks, nor will he/she be negligent because of an error of judgement where all reasonable care was taken, nor because of some of mischance.

In some circumstances, the rule *res ipsa loquitur* - the thing speaks for itself - may apply. In such cases, if injury can be shown by the plaintiff, negligence will be presumed, and it will be for the defendant to rebut the presumption. If the defendant succeeds, the burden of proof then shifts back to the plaintiff to show that the injury was caused by the defendant's negligence. Although *res ipsa loquitur* has been successfully pleaded in a number of cases of alleged medical negligence, it has been suggested,[39] that judges are generally resistant to its application in this field.

There may be a particular duty of care towards patients who present special risks, such as elderly persons who are mentally confused. In such cases, suitable precautions should be taken if there is a danger that they may injure themselves or other persons. Their mental state might be such that constant supervision is necessary to ensure that they come to no harm.

6.4.3   VICARIOUS LIABILITY

Where it is alleged that a tort has been committed by an employee, it may be possible to bring the action against the employer as well as, or as an alternative to, suing the employee. This is not possible where the person concerned is an independent contractor, such as a family practitioner, or a doctor in private practice. In those cases, action can only be brought against the person who is alleged to have committed the tort.   The rules relating to vicarious liability are not discussed in detail here but the rationale is that an employer, such as a DHA, should be made liable for any wrong suffered as the result of the actions of those who are its employees and acting within the scope of their employment, because this gives economic advantage to the individual claiming damages.   In *Cassidy v. Ministry of Health [1951]*[40]   the plaintiff lost the use of his left hand and suffered severe pain as a result of negligent post-operative treatment.   The Court of Appeal held the hospital liable because the negligent act was carried out by those employed by the hospital authority. Similarly, in *Roe v. Ministry of Health [1954]*[41] it was held that, had negligence been proved, the defendants would have been vicariously liable for the actions of an anaesthetist who at the time of the alleged tort was working part-time for the NHS, although the rest of the time was spent in private practice.

6.4.4   TRESPASS TO THE PERSON

Another possible form of legal action is to sue in the tort of trespass to the person, either for assault or battery.   Such action would be possible where it is alleged that medical treatment was given without the consent of the patient,[42] or where a patient is wrongfully restrained, or detained against his/her will and prevented from leaving the premises. The most difficult cases are again likely to arise where the patient is mentally disordered or mentally confused.   The statutory position in relation to consent to treatment by detained mentally disordered patients is discussed elsewhere (Chapter 5 at para. 5.10.4), but in relation to informal mentally disordered patients and patients who are elderly and confused, the common law principles will, generally, apply.   As indicated, the common law position concerning treatment for those incapable of giving consent is not well defined. Treatment can be justified only in cases of 'urgent necessity' to save life or to prevent serious harm to the patient or others, but any action which is taken must be reasonable in the circumstances. It seems doubtful if treatment is permissible in any other circumstances, even though the patient is permanently incapable of giving consent.

The common law powers of restraint or detention are similar to those relating to treatment. The defendant would need to show that the action taken was on the basis of reasonable belief that the patient was a danger to him/herself or to other people, and would continue to be so if allowed to leave the premises. The restraint or detention must only be such as necessary in the circumstances. In other circumstances, the defendant may be held liable in the tort of false imprisonment.

6.4.5 SUMMARY

The purpose of this chapter has been to indicate the main processes and procedures for making complaints and seeking redress in the field of health care. These are often complicated for patients to understand and to use. The present situation may present particular difficulties for elderly people since, as a group, they may not find complaining easy, especially against those in positions of authority or power over them. Yet many elderly people, because of their social, psychological, and physical status, can be particularly vulnerable when they enter the health care system, whether in the public or in the private sector. In such circumstances, they may not only need information about their rights, but advice and support in bringing complaints and in seeking redress of grievances. There seems a clear case for strengthening consumer rights in this field and for setting up better systems for registering complaints and for securing more effective remedies. A balance needs to be struck between protecting patients and protecting professionals from frivolous or even malicious complaints. It seems doubtful, however, whether at present the balance is satisfactory from the point of view of the consumer. The Merrison Committee felt that what was needed was a 'simple and well understood mechanism through which people who use the

NHS can suggest how it can be improved and complain when things go wrong'.[43] Since 1979 when that report was published, there has been only one statutory change to the complaints system which has only recently been brought into effect.[44] Although the government proposes to modify the complaints system relating to family practitioners, far more comprehensive and radical change is needed. The low number of recorded complaints is probably misleading, given the cultural and structural constraints which currently exist.[45]

Notes

1. *123 S.J. 436, (1981)*, C.L.Y. unreported cases, 274; see also the *Lancet,* November 24, 1984 at pp. 1224-5; Braham, D. 'A Doctor's Justification for Withdrawing Treatment', *New Law Journal* vol.135, 1985 at pp.48-9.

2. See, e.g., news items in the *Independent,* November 23, 1987, January 5, 1988 and January 6, 1988 and in the *Guardian,* January 7, 1988. An attempt at judicial review was similarly unsuccessful.

3. See, e.g., RADAR, (undated) *Putting Teeth into the Act.*

4. See Hoggett, B. (1984) *Mental Health Law* (2nd ed.) (Sweet and Maxwell) at pp.288-9.

5. Stacey, M. (1974) 'Consumer Complaints Procedure in the British National Health Service', *Social Science and Medicine,* vol.X, p.429.

6. Welsh Office (1981) *Community Health Councils in Wales.*

7. Community Health Councils Regulations 1985 S.I. 1985 No.304, reg 19(1).

8. Stacey, M. (1974) op.cit. See also Health Service Commissioner's Third Report, Sessions 1983-84, (HMSO) 1984.

9. Klein, R. (1973) *Complaints Against Doctors: A Study in Professional Accountability,* Charles Knight.

10. *Promoting Better Health* (1987) Cm 249 (HMSO), 1987.

11. National Health Service (Service Committees and Tribunal) Regulations 1974 S.I. 1974 No.455, reg 4.

12. National Health Service (Service Committees and Tribunal) Regulations 1974 op.cit., reg 5.

13. Sched 1 at para. 1(1).

14. Sched 1 at para. 1(2).

15. But see *The Health Service Journal*, March 27, 1986 at p.411.

16. National Health Service (Service Committes and Tribunal) Regulations 1974 op.cit., reg 7.

17. Sched 1 at para. 1(15).

18. reg 10.

19. *The Family Practitioner Services*, vol.5 no.5 1985.

20. op.cit., vol.9, no.5, 1982.

21. HC(88)37; WHC(88)36.

22. National Health Service Act 1977, s.84.

23. Royal Commission on the NHS *Report* (1979) Cmnd.7615, (HMSO) at p.150.

24. The Crossman Catalogue 734 HC Deb. Col. 51, October 18, 1966.

25. Select Committee Report HC 45, 1977-78; HC 665, 1979-80, (HMSO). See also Birkinshaw, P. (1985) *Grievances, Remedies and the State*, (Sweet and Maxwell) at p.149.

26. Parliamentary and Health Service Commissioners Act 1987, s.5.

27. Health Service Commissioner, First Report, Session 1981-2, Case W. 231/79-80.

28. Health Service Commissioner, Third Report, Session 1983-4, HMSO, 1984, Case W. 483/81-82.

29. op.cit., case SW 54/81-82.

30. 110,000 'resident' informal patients as compared to 6,500 informal patients.

31. First Biennial Report of the Mental Health Act Commission 1983-5, (HMSO).

32. Second Biennial Report of the Mental Health Act Commission, 1985-7, (HMSO).

33. Mental Health Act 1983, s.120.

34. Second Biennial Report, op.cit., at p.13.

35. S.I. 1980 No.858.

36. August 1983.

37. Mental Health Act 1983, s.139.

38. *2 All ER 118*.

39. Samuels, A. (1983) 'Medical Negligence Today - An Appraisal', *Social Science and Medicine*, vol.23, no.1 at p.31.

40. *2 KB 343*.

41. *2 All ER 131*.

42. See Chapter 5 at paras. 5.10.1-5.10.5.

43. Royal Commission on the National Health Service, Cmnd.7615, (1979) op.cit., at p.150.

44. Hospital Complaints Procedure Act 1985.

45. Stacey, M. (1974) op.cit., at p.429.

Chapter Seven

FAMILY MATTERS

7.1.1   MARRIAGE BREAKDOWN

A relatively lower proportion of divorces now take place late in
married life as compared with 1971. Nevertheless, the overall
figure is up, reflecting the rising trend in divorce figures
generally.[1] Those who experience marriage breakdown in old age
face particular problems. Some of the issues relevant to their
position are discussed below.

7.2.1   DIVORCE

The only ground upon which divorce can be granted is that a
marriage has broken down irretrievably. Irretrievable breakdown
must be evidenced, however, by the existence of one or more of
the following facts: that the respondent has committed adultery
and that the petitioner finds it intolerable to live with the
respondent; that the respondent has behaved in such a way that
the petitioner cannot reasonably be expected to live with
him/her; that the respondent has deserted the petitioner for a
continuous period of at least two years immediately preceding
the presentation of the petition; that the parties have lived
apart for a continuous period of two years immediately preceding
the presentation of the petition and that the respondent
consents to the granting of the decree; that the parties have
lived apart for a continuous period of at least five years
immediately preceding the presentation of the petition.

   In calculating whether or not the parties have lived apart
for the requisite length of time, any cohabitation for a period
or periods not exceeding six months in total is ignored. A
similar six-month rule applies where the parties continue to

live together after the discovery of an act of adultery, or after the occurrence of the incident incidents giving rise to a petition based upon the respondent's behaviour. Cohabitation for more than six months is a bar to presenting a petition based upon adultery, but no specific statutory restriction exists in relation to a petition based upon the respondent's behaviour.

Divorce petitions founded upon five years separation can be refused where it is shown that the dissolution of the marriage would cause grave financial or other hardship to the respondent.(see para. 7.2.4)

7.2.2 The vast majority of divorce petitions are now undefended. Nevertheless, the need for the petitioner to show irretrievable breakdown of the marriage has resulted in considerable litigation over the years. Some of the reported cases have particular relevance for those who are elderly. For instance, what must a spouse reasonably be expected to endure where a husband or wife's difficult behaviour arises from deteriorating health? In *Thurlow v. Thurlow [1976]*,[2] the wife's mental deterioration arising from epilepsy led her to being progressively unable to perform domestic tasks. She 'threw items', caused damage to household equipment, and wandered in the street causing distress and worry to her husband. She also became incontinent and had to be admitted to hospital when her husband could no longer cope. The evidence indicated that her condition was unlikely to improve. The husband's petition, alleging it was not reasonable to expect him to continue to live with her, was successful. The judge acknowledged the existence of a marital duty to accept and share the burdens of a spouse's illness but the length of the wife's illness had to be taken into consideration as well as the ability of the petitioner to bear the stress which it had imposed upon him. It was implied, however, that relying on this ground might not be possible where the respondent's behaviour was merely passive. Should a person be permanently comatose, the only available remedy might be a decree based upon evidence of five years separation.

Another relevant issue in this context is the mental element necessary in order to establish desertion. Even where *de facto* separation exists, there can be no desertion unless one spouse intended to remain permanently separated from the other. Where, for example, separation had resulted from the poor health of one of the spouses, that, in itself, would not constitute desertion unless coupled with evidence that the respondent wished to have nothing more to do with the petitioner.[3]   A person suffering from mental illness might be incapable of forming the necessary intention to desert.   If, however, it could be shown that the respondent had formed an intention to desert prior to becoming mentally ill, the petition might succeed even though the respondent had become ill before the beginning of the two-year period of separation necessary to establish desertion.   Section 2(4) of the Matrimonial Causes Act 1973 (MCA 1973) provides that:

> ... the Court may treat a period of desertion as having continued at a time when the deserting party was incapable of continuing the necessary intention if the evidence before the court is such that, had that party not been so incapable, the Court would have inferred that his desertion continued at that time.

Where one spouse behaves so unreasonably that he/she effectively drives the other from the matrimonial home, there may be grounds for bringing a petition against that person for 'constructive' desertion.   In effect, the spouse remaining in the home is deemed to be in desertion because of his/her behaviour.

7.2.3   In order to establish grounds for divorce on the basis of having lived apart, the parties may be treated as living separately even though they live in the same house.   The courts have distinguished between living in the same accommodation and living in the same household.   In *Fuller v. Fuller [1973]*,[4] the wife had left her husband for another man.   Sometime later she took in the husband as a lodger, because he was suffering from a serious heart condition and was too ill to live by himself.   It was held that the couple were to be treated as if they were living apart.   It is not clear whether this distinction would be applied by the court in circumstances where the couple were living within the same residential establishment.   It might be necessary to show more than that the couple were no longer sharing the same bedroom.

7.2.4   Where a petition is based upon the fact of five years separation, (see 7.2.1 above) the defence of 'grave financial hardship' may be available to the respondent.   It could be used, for example, where a marriage had been in existence for many years, and the wife, being the respondent, would lose the benefit of her husband's occupational pension were a divorce to be granted. The defence can, however, be met by the petitioner making alternative financial arrangements which satisfy the court, such as providing a compensatory insurance policy.[5] A spouse's entitlement to social security benefit might be sufficient to overcome the statutory defence.[6] Where 'other hardship' is alleged that, too, must be 'grave.'[7] In practice, the courts have been reluctant to accept this defence and only in exceptional circumstances have they refused to grant a decree.

When it was suggested that divorce should be allowed on this basis, it was labelled a 'Casanova's Charter' by critics who believed it might be used by some husbands to divorce a wife who was becoming less physically attractive in their eyes. In fact, more women than men have used this ground of recent years, as the basis for divorce.[8]

7.2.5 Less than one per cent of divorce petitions presented in 1985 were defended. Petitions which are undefended are now dealt with under a special procedure, first introduced in 1973, which allows evidence to be presented in written form. Much of the trauma associated with court proceedings is removed since neither party need be present in court.[9] If the divorce court registrar is not satisfied that the petitioner has proved his/her case, further evidence can be submitted, also in writing.

7.3.1 JUDICIAL SEPARATION

A spouse may decide to petition for judicial separation rather than divorce. This might arise from adherence to a particular religious faith which prohibited or frowned upon divorce, or it might be based upon hope of eventual reconciliation. It may also be used as a remedy by those experiencing marital problems during the first year of marriage when divorce is not possible. The grounds for judicial separation are the same as those for divorce.

7.3.2 Where a decree of judicial separation is granted, the court's power to make various financial awards can be invoked.(see paras. 7.4.1 and 7.4.2) The decree terminates the duty to cohabit, and removes consent to sexual intercourse which is implied by the existence of marriage, so that a husband who had intercourse with his wife against her will might be guilty of rape.[10] So long as the decree is in force, it cannot be alleged that either spouse has deserted the other. The existence of a decree of judicial separation also affects a spouse's right to inherit under the rules of intestacy (see para. 7.9.1) although he/she could apply for reasonable provision under the Inheritance (Provision for Family and Dependants) Act 1975 (I(PFD)A 1975). (see para. 7.12.1) An undefended petition for judicial separation is also dealt with under the 'special' procedure. (see para. 7.2.5 above)

7.4.1   FINANCIAL MATTERS

Divorce and judicial separation often lead to disputes about money and property. On application, a divorce court can order lump sum payments to be made by one spouse to the other as well as award maintenance payments to an ex-spouse or to support any dependent child.[11] The Matrimonial and Family Proceedings Act 1984 (MFPA 1984) amended the previous provision contained in the MCA 1973 that the court was to place the parties, as far as practicable, in the position they would have been in had no divorce taken place. As amended, the MCA 1973 sets out new guidelines for the court in making financial arrangements. The court's duty is to have regard to all the circumstances of the case, first consideration being given to the welfare of any child under 18. Particular regard must also be given to a number of other matters, including the income, earning capacity, property and other financial resources of either of the parties to the marriage, as well as any which they are likely to possess in the forseeable future. Other matters which must be taken into account by the court include: (i) the age of each party and the duration of the marriage; (ii) any physical or mental disability of either of the parties; (iii) the contribution which each has made or is likely, in the forseeable future, to make to the welfare of the family, including any contributions by looking after the home and caring for the family; (iv) the conduct of each of the parties, if that conduct is such that it would, in the opinion of the court, be inequitable to disregard it, and the value to each of the parties to the marriage of any benefit (for example, a pension) which the party will lose the chance of acquiring.

Another change introduced by the MPFA 1984 is that the court must now consider whether it would be appropriate for the financial obligation of each party towards the other to be terminated as soon after the grant of the decree as the court considers just and reasonable.[12] If it is thought an order for periodical maintenance payments would be appropriate, the court must then consider whether these should be sufficient only to enable the spouse receiving them to adjust without due hardship to the termination of his/her financial dependence on the other party.[13]

Where a settlement is not limited by the 'clean break' principle, the courts can vary a maintenance arrangement at any time on the grounds that circumstances have changed. In *Re W (deceased) [1975]*, an ex-wife's claim was upheld 29 years after the divorce. She had been granted a divorce on the basis of her husband's desertion in 1946, but following professional advice, did not claim maintenance because of her earnings. The husband resisted his ex-wife's later efforts to obtain maintenance and was thereby able to amass capital which should have gone towards his wife's maintenance. On his death, he left an estate worth £28,000. The wife, then aged 75 years, had very limited resources. It was held that, having regard to her age, it would be just for her to receive £11,000.[14]

In deciding the quantum of the sum to be awarded, the courts have used as a guideline the so-called 'one-third rule', as set out in *Wachtel v. Wachtel [1973]*.[15] It must be emphasized, however, that the rule has been used flexibly, and that its application will vary according to the circumstances. There will be some situations where more than one-third is appropriate. In other circumstances, where the marriage was brief, or the wife is qualified and able to earn a reasonable living, a lesser amount may be awarded.

The age of the parties could be a significant factor in deciding questions of maintenance, particularly where there is a considerable age gap between the husband and wife. In *Compton v. Compton [1985]* the Court of Appeal was influenced by the fact that the wife was only 40 years old and had good earning

capacity, whereas the husband was over 60 years and had
retired.[16]   In *S. v. S. [1977]*[17] it was held that where a
marriage was short-lived, and particularly where the parties
were not young, the primary consideration was the needs of the
wife.   Regard should be had to the effects of the marriage,
mainly on the wife, but also on the husband. The resources and
obligations of the parties should be ascertained and balanced
against each other in relation to all the circumstances of the
marriage.

7.4.2 Divorce can have important implications for social
security and private pension rights. A woman under 60 must build
up her own national insurance record, but on reaching pensionable age can rely, if that is to her advantage, upon
contributions paid by her former husband during the marriage.
If a woman re-marries before reaching the age of 60, she can no
longer rely upon her ex-husband's contribution record. A woman
divorced after the age of 60 can rely, if necessary, on her ex-
husband's record in claiming a state pension.[18]   The DHSS has
produced a special leaflet (NP32A) outlining a person's
entitlement to a pension after divorce.   Special rules enable
divorced women to claim short-term benefits such as sickness or
unemployment benefit if they have not been in paid work or have
not paid full national insurance contributions.

Private pension schemes rarely provide for an ex-spouse. In
this respect, provision in Britain lags behind that of some
countries, such as the Netherlands, where an ex-wife has a legal
right to a proportion of her previous husband's occupational
pension and to a proportion of the state widow's pension,
depending on how many years they were married. In Britain, an
ex-wife might be advised to consider making provision for
herself from her own resources. There are several possibilities,
but the simplest and cheapest way of securing a degree of
protection is probably to take out a term life assurance policy
on the life of her former husband. As mentioned above, a divorce
court can always make financial orders to compensate for loss of
state benefits. The value of occupational pension schemes are
rarely taken into proper account by solicitors or judges,
however, possibly because their potential value is not fully
appreciated.[19]   Should there be cause for concern, it might be
appropriate to consult a pensions consultant or an actuary.[20]

7.4.3 THE MATRIMONIAL HOME

One of the most important settlements on divorce is in relation to the matrimonial home, which may be sold (if owner/occupied), or surrendered (if a tenancy), or one party may remain in it. Arrangements of this kind can result from an agreement between the parties, or can be ordered by the court, which has wide powers to apportion legal interests in the home as it sees fit.[21] The court order might provide for sale of the property to be postponed, contingent upon some event, or it might transfer the property to either of the parties.[22]

It is common practice for solicitors, prior to the actual divorce or judicial separation, to draw up 'Consent Orders' to deal with any interim arrangements which may be needed. In effect, these amount to legal contracts between the parties. It seems, moreover, that if one of the spouses should die, the right to enforce a Consent Order vests in the deceased person's estate. The leading case in this context involved an agreement that the husband should pay his wife a lump sum, and that she, in turn, would transfer her interest in the matrimonial home to him. The husband honoured his part of the agreement but died before his wife had completed hers. Although there was no apparent legal authority, the court declared that the husband's executors could enforce the agreement against the surviving spouse.[23] No such discretion exists where the parties are unmarried. In those circumstances, the court can uphold existing legal interests only, but might be prepared to recognize an implied trust which would protect, as beneficiary, a non-owner who had contributed to the acquisition of a capital asset.[24]

7.5.1 FINANCIAL PROVISIONS IN THE MAGISTRATES' COURT

Under the Domestic Proceedings and Magistrates' Court Act 1978 (DPMCA 1978), a magistrates' court (sitting as a domestic court) has jurisdiction to order financial provision to be paid by one party to the other while a marriage is in existence. The grounds are (i) that the respondent has failed to provide the applicant with reasonable maintenance; (ii) that the respondent has failed to provide, or make reasonable contribution towards reasonable maintenance for a child of the family; (iii) that the respondent has behaved in such a way that the applicant cannot reasonably be expected to live with the respondent (see para. 7.2.2); and (iv) that the respondent has deserted the applicant.(see paras. 7.2.2 and 7.2.3)

7.6.1   DOMESTIC VIOLENCE

Should one of the parties to a relationship be the victim of domestic violence, the law can provide a degree of protection by means of orders and injunctions. Where the parties are married to each other, application can be made either to a magistrates' court or to the County Court, but where they are unmarried, only the County Court has the necessary jurisdiction.[25]

To succeed in a magistrates' court, it is necessary to show physical violence was used or threatened against the applicant, and that the order is necessary for his/her physical protection. If so, a protection order may be granted. In the County Court, it is necessary to show only that the individual suffered 'molestation', which can include 'pestering', 'harassment', or 'mental torment'.[26] In such cases, the County Court may grant an injunction protecting the other party from molestation. Orders are available in both courts to exclude the offender from the matrimonial home, and to provide for the arrest and, where necessary, the detention of the violent partner. Difficulties, leading to acts of domestic violence, sometimes occur when elderly couples find themselves spending almost every hour in each other's company.[27]

7.7.1   GRANDPARENTS AND GRANDCHILDREN

Grandparents have no vested powers and responsibilities vis à vis their grandchildren. Normally, this lack of status - which can be contrasted with the position of parents in relation to their children - is unlikely to cause grandparents difficulty. In certain circumstances, however, they may perceive links formed with their grandchildren as under threat because of some change, either contemplated or already in existence, in arrangements for the child's custody or care. They may then wish to acquire legal rights, the nature of which will depend upon the particular circumstances of the case.

7.7.2 ACCESS TO GRANDCHILDREN

Sometimes, all that grandparents wish to ensure is that they can keep in touch with their grandchildren and see them from time to time. In general, however, they cannot themselves initiate access proceedings but can only apply for leave to intervene in other proceedings relating to the child. This can be done in divorce court hearings, as well as in other proceedings relating to the custody of a child.[28] Should one of the child's parents be dead, however, the parents of the deceased person may themselves apply for access.[29] Where an order for access has been made, grandparents can apply for it to be varied or discharged, as can the parent of the child and other specified parties. These rights apply equally to a child who is illegitimate.

On making an adoption order, the court can impose 'such conditions as it thinks fit'.[30] This power has been held to be wide enough to enable the court, in exceptional circumstances, to make an access order in favour of any relative, if that is in the best interests of the child.[31] Access can also be granted to grandparents in custodianship proceedings. (see para. 7.7.4 below) Where a child is in care, the local authority has complete discretion whether or not it allows access to the child's grandparents. The courts will not intervene in matters which the legislature has left to the discretion of the authorities, unless an authority has acted in ways which are contrary, or beyond the powers granted to it. (see Chapter 6 at paras. 6.2.2 and 6.2.3)

7.7.3 CUSTODY

A number of legal procedures exist which might help grandparents obtain custody over a grandchild. A person who is neither a parent nor a guardian of a child has no legal standing (*locus standi*) in a dispute over custody, but it is possible to ask to be made a party (that is, be enjoined) in proceedings ancillary to divorce as well as in other proceedings. The court might, in exceptional circumstances, award custody to that person where, for example, a grandparent was already caring for the child. In reaching a decision on custody, the courts must have regard for the welfare of the child as the first and paramount consideration. It should be noted that, under the provisions of the Children Bill, the welfare of the child is to be the court's *paramount* consideration, the word 'first' having been removed.

It is always open for any person having 'sufficient interest' in the welfare of a child to apply to make him/her a ward of court if that appears necessary for the child's protection. A claim to custody of the child in wardship proceedings by a grandparent who seemed intent upon severing all contact between a child and a parent might be resisted (because of the welfare principle) even if the parent in question was of dubious character. In *Re F (a minor) (wardship: appeal) [1976]*, the grandmother's hostile attitude towards the child's father was seen as crucial, even though the father had been convicted of crimes of dishonesty and of indecent assault.[32]

7.7.4 CUSTODIANSHIP

Custodianship is another procedure which might be used by grandparents seeking custody over a child for whom they are already the caretakers. Under s.33(3) of the Children Act 1975 (CA 1975), a relative with whom a child has had his/her home for three months preceding the making of the application can apply to a court, with the consent of the person having legal custody of the child. No consent is needed where the applicant, whether a relative or not, has been looking after the child for a period, or periods, of at least three years, including the three months preceding the application.

If granted, a custodianship order vests 'legal custody' in the custodian, that is, 'so much of the parental rights and duties as relate to the person of the child (including the place and manner in which his/her time is spent)......' Certain rights are not, therefore, transferred, including the right to administer any property belonging to the child; the right to change the child's name; the right to withhold consent to the child's adoption; and the right to arrange for the child's emigration from the United Kingdom.

In deciding whether or not to make a custodianship order, the court must currently have regard for the welfare of the child as the first and paramount consideration.(see para. 7.7.3 above) If granted, a custodianship order (unlike an adoption order) is revokable since it suspends, rather than terminates, parental rights. It is also possible, and often appropriate, for a court to grant one or both parents access to the child. In certain circumstances, the court must make a custodianship order in other proceedings brought in relation to a child. This could happen if the application is for adoption.(see para. 7.7.5 below) Similarly under the DPMCA 1978, the court may direct that a person to whom it wishes to transfer legal custody should be treated as if he/she had applied for a custodianship order, even where the applicant would not otherwise be qualified to make such application.[33]

7.7.5   ADOPTION

A child's caretaker(s) may wish to adopt him/her. Grandparents can apply as 'relatives of the child', although in such cases the court must treat the application as one for custodianship if satisfied that the child's welfare would not be better safe-guarded and protected by the making of an adoption order in favour of the applicant, than it would be by the making of a custodianship order.[34] Should the court, nevertheless, consider adoption as appropriate, the grandparents would have to qualify as adopters in accordance with the other relevant statutory requirements.

7.7.6 The legal position of grandparents wishing to obtain custody of a grandchild may be much weaker where a local authority is involved in the care of the child. If, for example, a grandparent wished to foster a grandchild, prompt action may be needed before long term plans have been made for his/her future. If approached early enough, a social services authority might have been persuaded that the grandparents were appropriate carers for the child. Unfortunately, if the request is delayed, their position may be prejudiced by the time proceedings are heard, or because other action has been taken, such as the passing of a parental rights resolution under s.3 of the Child Care Act 1980 (CCA 1980), in relation to a child in care under s.2 of the Act.

In *T L v. Birmingham City Council (1985)*,[35] a Chinese grandmother from Hong Kong, had cared for her granddaughter on her own for six years. She later joined her son and daughter-in-law in England. Some twelve months later the granddaughter was taken into care as a result of bruising, allegedly caused by the mother. Rehabilitation with the parents was attempted but the child suffered further non-accidental injuries when home on trial. Long-term foster parents and potential adopters were sought by the local authority and access by the family, including the grandmother, was terminated. The parents, who retained care of three younger children, accepted that there was no prospect of the child returning to them. The grandmother, who proposed to go back to live in Hong Kong, sought custody by initiating wardship proceedings. The judge decided against intervention stressing that the court would intervene in exceptional circumstances only, with the decision of a local authority in relation to a child in care. The decision apparently hinged on the fact that the grandmother spoke very little English, whereas her granddaughter (who by the time of the court case had been in a children's home for almost two years) spoke English very well and had forgotten much of her Chinese. In the judge's opinion, the circumstances were not exceptional although the grandmother had been the *de facto* guardian of the child for the first six years of her life. The care order had been granted, in fact, only some twelve months after the girl had left the care of her grandmother. On her admission into care, the local authority could quite properly have placed her with the grandmother. Indeed, it has been suggested[36] that the local authority was under a duty to consider this step and that failure to give reasonable consideration to that possibility amounted to a breach of statutory duty which could have been challenged on principles of administrative law.[37]

In any case, local authorities have a duty under s.18(1) of the CCA 1980, in reaching any decision in relation to a child in their care to give first consideration to the need to safeguard and promote the welfare of the child throughout his/her childhood. The authority must also, as far as practicable, ascertain the wishes and feelings of the child regarding the decision and give due consideration to them having regard to his/her age and understanding.

It should also be noted that where a child has been received into care under s.2 of the CCA 1980, it is the duty of the local authority, where it appears to be consistent with the welfare of the child, to endeavour to secure that his/her care is taken over either by the child's parent or guardian, or by a relative or friend.[38]

The Children and Young Persons (Amendment) Act 1986 (CYP(A)A) 1986) may be helpful to grandparents wishing to persuade a court that they should be a child's carer. It inserts into the Children and Young Persons Act 1969 (CYPA 1969), a provision for making grandparents (and guardians) parties to care proceedings, whenever an order has been made for the child to be separately represented and for the appointment of a guardian *ad litem* under s.32A of the CYPA 1969. The court may give leave for a grandparent to be made a party to the proceedings if satisfied that he/she had a 'substantial involvement in the infant's upbringing at any time during the infant's lifetime'. It must also be satisfied that such a step is likely to be in the interests of the child's welfare.[39] The court may order that a grandparent be eligible for Legal Aid when granted party status.[40]

7.8.1   WILLS AND INTESTACY

Some 550 women are widowed every day and some 120 husbands lose their wives.[41] In addition to experiencing the trauma of bereavement, many of those who are widowed face financial uncertainty as a result of the spouse's death. A simple way of reducing stress for the surviving spouse is to execute a will. Where no will exists, the rules of intestacy will apply in distributing the deceased's estate. Many people mistakenly believe that, should they die intestate, everything will automatically go to their husband or wife. This is not necessarily so. If the estate is of sufficient value, other relatives may benefit, thus reducing the amount available for the surviving spouse.[42] Another problem is that cohabitees have no automatic right to inherit under the rules of intestacy. It may, therefore, be vital to make specific provision for the other partner.[43]

The only occasion upon which a widow or widower is guaranteed the whole of a deceased person's estate on an intestacy is where there are no children or other relatives, such as parents, brothers and sisters.

For many people, it will be of little concern to learn that their children have an automatic right to share in their estate in certain circumstances. They might react differently, however, on learning that, where there are no surviving children, the deceased spouse's parents could possibly benefit. If there are no surviving parents, their share will be distributed to other specified relative(s) in the order set out in the statutory provisions.(see para. 7.9.1)

However much or however little a person owns, there are good reasons for making a will. An added advantage is that one or more suitable person(s) can be chosen to act as executor(s)/trix, with the responsibility of proving the will and of carrying out its directions. On an intestacy, those appointed as administrators are invariably entitled to a share in the estate. The cost of administering an estate could be greater than the cost of proving a will. The powers granted to administrators are relatively limited, and sometimes inadequate, whereas executor(s)/trix can be given wide powers to insure, invest or otherwise manage the deceased person's assets.

7.8.2 MAKING A WILL

A valid will can be executed quite simply and easily. In general, it has to be made in writing but otherwise need not be in any particular form, nor use any special terminology. A word of warning is needed, however. The wording of a will could affect its legal meaning and it is always wise to seek professional advice if the drafter is uncertain of the effect of what is proposed. The Legal Advice and Assistance Scheme can be used to engage a solicitor to draft a will if the financial criteria are met. In any event, for a simple transaction such as this, the cost of professional services should be relatively low. The Law Society, in its pamphlet, *Making a Will Won't Kill You*[44] suggests that, as a rough guide, the fee for a straight-foward will should be between £20 and £30. It recommends individuals to ask at the outset how much the service will cost, and suggests that solicitors are always prepared to give estimates. If difficulties arise, it might be advisable to quote from this pamphlet.

Alternatively, standard form wills with instructions are available from newsagents and elsewhere. The disadvantage of these is that they may not provide the individual with the formula necessary to give effect to his/her wishes. Another danger, in drafting a will, is that the testator/trix may use ambiguous language. For example, if a testator states that: 'I give everything equally to my wife and three sons', it is not clear whether he means to give one half to his wife and for the other half to be shared amongst his three sons, or whether he means to give them all one quarter each. A similar problem arises where a will creates an unintended life interest with such words as 'I leave everything to my wife and after her death to my children'. According to the Law Reform Committee[45] this type of provision, which frequently occurs in home-made wills, has usually been interpreted as restricting the wife's inheritance to a life interest. In other words, the wife would not be entitled to the capital but only to interest arising from it. In many cases, this may not have been the testator's intention. The Law Commission recommended a change in the law, which has since been enacted in s.22 of the Administration of Justice Act 1982 (AJA 1982). This provides that:

> Except where a contrary intention is shown it shall be presumed that if a testator devises or bequeaths property to his spouse in terms which in themselves would give an absolute interest to the spouse, but by the same instrument purports to give his issue an interest in the same property, the gift to the spouse is absolute notwithstanding the purported gift to the issue.

Under this provision, therefore, the wife would get everything. It should be noted, however, that the circumstances to which the section applies are limited and that it will help resolve only the second of the two situations referred to above.[46]

7.8.3 There are few limitations on what may be disposed of by will. Testators should, however, give careful consideration to whether they wish to provide specific or general legacies. A specific legacy is the gift of a specific object, such as 'My Ford Escort car'. A general legacy is a gift to be provided from the testator's general estate. It is irrelevant whether its subject matter forms part of the testator's property at his death. Usually a general legacy is in the form of a gift of money. The problem with specific gifts is that they may no longer be available at the testator's death, with the result that the intended beneficiary will receive nothing. In the example given above, it might have been better for the will to have simply provided the gift of a car.

If the words 'tax free' are added to specific gifts, this ensures that, subject to there being sufficient monies available, any liability for tax will come out of the estate and will not be deducted from the gift. Where appropriate, the will should also make clear whether or not property is being left free of any liability for mortgage re-payments.

After making individual legacies, it is important for the testator to leave the residue of the estate to a particular person or body. If that is not done, a partial intestacy will arise and part of the deceased's estate will be governed by the rules of intestacy rather than by the terms of his/her will.

7.8.4 Once made, a will is valid unless and until revoked by the person making it, or altered by a codicil, or declared invalid by a court. The marriage of a testator/trix usually revokes a will previously made, except where it is clear from its terms that marriage to a particular individual was not intended to have that effect. Recent legislative reform may mean that more wills made in contemplation of marriage will be treated as valid.[47]

Another important change in the law means that the granting of a divorce will in most cases revoke an existing will insofar as it applies to a former spouse.[48] It is not possible to predict how many will be affected by this change but the number is likely to be substantial. It has been suggested that many more intestacies will result since it is not uncommon for wills to provide for a spouse to be the sole beneficiary.[49] An ex-spouse, disinherited by divorce, who has not remarried can, however, apply for provision to be made for him/her under the I(PFD)A 1975 (see para. 7.12.1-7.12.5 below) although success is by no means certain.[50]

7.8.5   CHOOSING EXECUTOR(S)/TRIX

Persons of 18 years of age or over can be appointed executor(s)/trix of a will. It is possible, therefore, (and not uncommon) for a husband and wife to name each other as executrix and executor, either alone or in conjunction with others. If one of the executors/trix is a professional person, such as a solicitor, he/she must be authorized by the terms of the will to charge for any services undertaken as a result of this appointment. Otherwise only reasonable expenses can be recovered. The will does not become invalid if it provides for an executor/trix to receive a bequest. Those with an interest of this kind must not, however, act as witness, nor must their spouse.

Some bank managers encourage the practice of appointing a bank to act as executor. Banks have specialist departments dealing with this kind of work and are experienced in investment and trust management. Some charge an 'acceptance fee' when they agree to act as executor which can be as much as five per cent of the value of the estate. All banks make additional charges for work to be carried out which vary in amount from one bank to another. A 'withdrawal fee', which could be as much as two per cent, may be charged on completion of the work. Banks invariably appoint a solicitor to do some of the work. As a result, it may also be necessary to pay a solicitor's fee from the assets.

7.8.6 CAPACITY

In order for a will to be valid, the person executing it must be *compos mentis*, that is, mentally competent. The well-established test of mental capacity is that the testator/trix understands the nature of the act, the extent of his/her property, and any moral claims he/she ought to consider. In other words, an individual must know that he/she is making a will, the broad extent (though not the value) of his/her property as well as those individuals he/she ought to bear in mind.[51] Although the general rule is that a person must be competent at the time of executing the will, it may be sufficient to show that mental capacity existed when the testator/trix was giving instructions. It will be valid if the testator/trix was lucid at the time even if generally confused.[52] This rule can be of practical importance where a person is ailing.[53] Being deluded does not automatically deprive a testator/trix of the necessary mental capacity. In the leading case of *Banks v. Goodfellow (1870)*[54] the testator suffered from delusions of being persecuted by a particular individual (who, in fact, was dead), as well as by devils and spirits. The court held that since the delusions had no influence upon the will's contents, it could be treated as valid. Where only a part of a will is affected by a delusion, it might be possible to show that the remainder is valid.[55]

Proving mental capacity can be difficult. Where problems could arise, it may be advisable to ensure the will is witnessed by a medically qualified person. It is common practice to include in a will a statement to the effect that the person making it fully understands its effect. That should also be done if a testator/trix has an obvious impediment, such as a visual handicap or if he/she is hard of hearing.

Fraud and/or undue influence can also affect validity. It has been said that in executing a will a testator/trix 'can be led but not driven'.[56] In other words, persuasion, appeals to the affection, or to the ties of kindred, or pity for future destitution, or the like, are all legitimate. On the other hand, pressure of a kind which overpowers the testator's judgement would invalidate the will. Talking incessantly to a feeble person might be sufficient to affect a will's validity.[57] It need not be shown that physical force was used. Litigation is not common since the burden of proof falls upon the person alleging fraud or undue influence. Where the person benefiting from the will or the gift stands in a special relationship to the donor,[58] however, there is a presumption of undue influence. The burden of proving that the will was freely made then rests with the beneficiary. These special relationships, known as 'fiduciary relationships', include those of doctor and patient; solicitor and client; and priest and parishioner. The courts have stressed that the list of such relationships is never closed.[59] It is not established whether or not the staff of a residential home are regarded as having a fiduciary relationship towards those who are resident there.

A presumption of undue influence can also arise where no recognized category of special relationship exists but there are special social or domestic circumstances which could affect the will's validity. *Re Craig (deceased) [1971]* concerned the will of an eighty-four year old man who had made substantial gifts to his secretary-companion. The gifts were set aside by the court, even though the medical evidence confirmed the testator was not lacking in mental capacity, but rather a 'very gentle, dependent and vulnerable old man'.[60]

Where a fiduciary relationship exists or there are special circumstances, the gift may be set aside unless it can be shown that the donor received proper independent advice, which was given with knowledge of all the relevant circumstances. In *Inche Noriah v. Shaik Allie Bin Omar [1929]*[61] an elderly Malayan woman executed a deed of gift in favour of her nephew who had been responsible for managing her affairs for some time. Although she had the benefit of independent advice, the lawyer who gave it, was unaware of all the facts of the case. The court held that the gift should be set aside on the grounds that the presumption of undue influence had not been rebutted.

7.8.7   DEPOSITING THE WILL

Once executed, a will should be deposited in a safe place and the executor(s)/trix told of its location. If it cannot be found on the death of testator/trix it may be presumed to have been destroyed with the intention of revoking it.[62] If it were to be found some time afterwards, complex problems could arise. Those who had already benefited from the estate, either on the basis of an earlier will, or according to the rules on intestacy, would be liable to return that which had been already received.[63] This could cause financial difficulty if, for example, a gift had been disposed of by the beneficiary. Testators/trix would be well advised to deposit the will at a bank or with a solicitor. The safest procedure, however, is to deposit the will with the Principal Registry of the Family Division of the High Court at Somerset House. This should ensure that there are no problems since a search will be automatically carried out to see if a will had been placed there on the death of the testator/trix. A registration fee of £1 is charged for this service.

It is also useful to compile a list of personal documents for use by the executor(s)/trix. Age Concern has published a guide which sets out the information which should be included.[64] The list should be shown to the executor(s)/trix before being deposited in a safe place.

7.8.8 *DISPOSAL OF ONE'S BODY*

One reason for making a will is that the testator/ trix wishes to arrange for the disposal of his/her body. A clause can be inserted in a will specifying whether the body is to be buried or cremated, although instructions of this kind do not normally have any legal force.[65] It is possible, however, to bequeath part of one's body for medical research.

7.8.9 An alternative method of achieving that objective is set out in the Anatomy Act 1984 (AA 1984). This makes it possible for a person's body to be used for medical research on the basis of a request made orally, or in writing, during a person's last illness and in the presence of two or more witnesses.[66] The phrase 'last illness' is not defined in the Act, and a dispute over its designation could arise in particular circumstances. The AA 1984 also permits a body to be used for anatomical research if there is no reason to believe that the deceased, his/her surviving spouse, or his/her relatives had expressed any objection to the body being used in this way. Individuals who do not wish their body to be used for anatomical research should object in writing, or orally before two witnesses.[67]

7.8.10 It is not uncommon for wills to include directions as to the conduct of the deceased's funeral. Individuals with particular wishes in this regard would be well advised, however, to make other arrangements to ensure they are known, since a will may not be made public until after the funeral has taken place. It would be better, therefore, to prepare a separate letter containing specific instructions. A number of organizations exist to help ensure a person's wishes are carried out. Salford Age Concern's Funeral Manning Society, for example, enables individuals, on payment of a small fee, to register their instructions. When a person dies, his/her relatives can telephone the society and be given the relevant information. The society will also undertake to negotiate the price of a funeral with firms of undertakers and will give direct help in arranging it. This scheme has proved popular and is being copied by a number of other charitable organizations.[68]

A number of commercial schemes have also been established to meet this need. One of these, known as the 'Funeral Expenses Plan', provides a free registration service. The company issues its members with a plastic card similar in size to the standard credit card. This instructs the next-of-kin to contact the company to find out the deceased person's wishes. The company also offers an assurance policy specifically geared to meet the costs of a funeral.[69] Another funeral plan has been developed by Age Concern in conjuction with an insurance company. A number of specific problems associated with arranging funerals are discussed later at 7.11.1.

7.9.1 INTESTACY

Where a person dies without having made a will, or where a will proves invalid, an intestacy arises. There were some 90,000 cases of intestacy in England and Wales in 1984.[70] It is not surprising, therefore, that the National Organisation for the Widowed and their Children claims that almost a half of all the cases with which they deal concern problems arising from an intestacy.[71]

Who inherits property on an intestacy, and in what proportions, is determined by the relevant statutory rules.[72] Where no one is entitled, the state acquires all the assets absolutely. Where a person dying intestate leaves a spouse but no issue, the surviving spouse inherits the total estate, unless the deceased had close relatives and the value of the estate is in excess of £125,000. Where there are children, the surviving partner is entitled to the first £75,000 only, plus a life interest on one-half of the rest. The other half will go directly to the children. It is often believed that the value of an estate will be below £75,000. This is because the benefit of insurance policies, and the value of the deceased's share in the matrimonial home are often forgotten. Sometimes, as the result of an intestacy, surviving spouses find themselves obliged to sell their home to provide for themselves.

The children of a deceased son or a deceased daughter of an intestate person will take the share in the estate which their parent would otherwise have received. Others entitled to inherit, apart from the spouse, children or grandchildren, include the parents, brothers, sisters, grandparents, half-brothers and sisters, uncles and aunts of the deceased, and their descendants. Where the total assets are worth less than £40,000, the surviving spouse inherits the whole amount.

7.10.1 DISTRIBUTING THE ESTATE

A will must normally be proved, that is, it must be produced by the executor(s)trix before the Probate Registry with a statement setting out the value of the estate and including a promise to administer it. Once probate has been granted, twelve months is normally allowed for settlement of the estate. Fees must be paid to the Registry proportionate to the estate's value. A solicitor's services are not always necessary in this context since the Registry will assist those applying for probate. A solicitor's advice may be needed, however, in distributing an estate should a will's provisions prove complex.

Where a person dies intestate, letters of administration directing an administrator to settle the deceased's estate, are normally required. The administrator will usually be the deceased's closest relative.

The fees which must be paid to obtain probate and letters of administration come from the estate itself.

7.10.2 STATUTORY NOMINATIONS AND SMALL ESTATES

Some statutes allow for disposal of certain assets by means of a written nomination operating at death. Examples of property which can be dealt with in this way include national savings certificates and funds in an industrial and provident society. The formal requirements for statutory nomination resemble, but are not identical, to those for making a will. The effect is essentially the same, since a nomination has no force until the nominator dies. If the nominee pre-deceases the nominator, the nomination fails.

Application to the Probate Registry is not necessary if the value of an estate is less than £5,000,[73] or consists of property subject to statutory nomination. Some statutory nominations are being phased out, however, and in any case, it is usually better to dispose of all assets by means of a will, since a statutory nomination once made, tends to get forgotten.[74]

7.11.1 FUNERAL ARRANGEMENTS

For many people there is stigma in not being able to make financial provision for their own funeral. They may also become anxious about the financial burden which could fall upon relatives or friends in meeting the costs. This worry is often very real, since the amount needed to pay for a funeral can be considerable. In 1984, funeral directors in various parts of Wales were asked by the Welsh Consumer Council to quote the price of a simple funeral. The average cost was £375.[75] It is not surprising, therefore, that meeting the costs of a relative's funeral is said to be a major cause of rent arrears.[76]

The only social security grant now available to meet funeral expenses is payment from the Social Fund. To qualify, the claimant must be responsible for arranging the funeral, although that responsibility can be delegated to someone else. The claimant must also be receiving income support or housing benefit. To qualify for the full amount, the claimant must have no more than £500 in capital, although the lump sum widow's payment of £1,000 is disregarded in this context. Capital above £500 must be spent before the DSS will make a payment. If, for example, the responsible person has capital amounting to £900 and the cost of the funeral is £425, the contribution from the DSS will be £25.

7.11.2 A funeral payment covers the cost of the following essential expenses: the cost of any necessary documents (such as the death certificate); the cost of a plain coffin; the cost of transport for the coffin and bearers plus one additional car; the reasonable cost of flowers; the undertaker's fees and gratuities; chaplain, organist and cemetery or cremation fees for a simple funeral; the cost of any additional expenses, not above £75, resulting from the religious beliefs of the dead person; the cost of transporting the dead person, either to his/her home, or to the undertaker's premises from any place within the United Kingdom; and the reasonable cost of *one* return journey either to arrange, or attend, the funeral.

It would seem from *R(SB)46/84*, (decided before the new social security provisions came into force) that 'necessary documentation' does not include press notices and that a 'plain coffin' does not necessarily mean the cheapest, but one that is simple and unadorned.

7.11.3 A funeral payment will be reduced by any sum received either from a charity or from a relative towards the cost of essential expenses. There should be no reduction where the charity or relative had contributed towards the cost of non-essential items, for example, a second funeral car. Moneys received from other sources, such as friends, burial clubs, occupational pension schemes, employers, or trade unions will be taken fully into account, irrespective of whether or not the sums were spent on essential funeral expenses. Claims on the Social Fund can be made even after the costs have been met, but only the proper form must be submitted (SF200). Where a claim is made by letter in the first place the appropriate form will still need to be completed. The claim dates from the day on which the letter of application was received by the DSS, providing the form is sent within a month of that date. Unless submitted within three months of the date of the funeral, a claim will fail if no good cause for the delay can be shown. It might be argued that a 'good cause' exists where the effects of the bereavement were to make the responsible person acutely depressed.

Wherever possible, the DSS will attempt to recover any payment it makes out of the deceased's estate. Where there is a surviving partner, however, the DSS must disregard the value of the home and any of the deceased's personal possessions. Personal possessions left to relatives must also be disregarded. A funeral payment is a grant and not a loan, and can be recovered by the DSS only if money is available to repay it out of the deceased person's estate. Money payable under a life insurance policy will be treated as part of the estate. Even where benefit from the policy is payable to the responsible person, that amount will be taken into account fully. In other words, not even the first £500 paid under the policy will be disregarded.

7.11.4 LOCAL AUTHORITIES AND HOSPITALS

District councils must arrange for the burial or cremation of any person who has died, or been found dead, in their area, if it appears that no other suitable arrangements can be made. The local authority may recover the costs of the funeral from the dead person's estate, or from any person liable to maintain the deceased immediately before his/her death. The authority must not arrange for a person to be cremated rather than buried where it has reason to believe that the deceased wished to be buried, even though cremation would be cheaper. Hospital authorities have a duty at common law to arrange for the burial or cremation of a deceased patient. This obligation is invariably carried out by the district council or London borough council of the area in which the hospital is located.[77]

7.11.5 Bereaved individuals may find it difficult to cope with funeral arrangements. Funeral directors are often a useful source of advice, assistance, and support in such circumstances. Members of the National Association of Funeral Directors pledge adherence to a Code of Practice which, amongst other things, requires members to give written estimates, and to ensure that information about social security benefits is made available.[78] Where payment for the funeral is dependent upon the receipt of a grant from the Social Fund, that should be made clear to the undertaker so as to avoid any misunderstanding.[79] It should also be remembered that useful advice and financial assistance may sometimes be available from other bodies such as trades unions, the various service and ex-service welfare organizations, such as the Royal British Legion or the Soldiers, Sailors and Airmen's Families Association (SSAFA), as well as from religious and charitable bodies.

7.12.1 FAMILY PROVISION

Where the provisions of a will, or the rules of intestacy, or a combination of both, fail to make reasonable financial provision for a deceased person's dependants, they can make an application to the court under the I(PFD)A 1975. Those who can apply are: the wife or husband of the deceased; a former wife or husband who has not re-married; the deceased's child (or any person treated by the deceased as a child of the family); and any dependant who immediately before the deceased's death was being maintained, wholly or partly, by him/her.[80] The I(PFD)A 1975 states that a person is to be treated as 'being maintained' if the deceased 'otherwise than for full consideration, was making a substantial contribution in money or money's worth towards the reasonable needs of that person'.[81] The effect of this provision is contrary to what many people expect. In order to succeed, an applicant must show that the balance of generosity was tipped in favour of the deceased. In other words, it has to be shown that the applicant was dependent on the deceased and not vice versa. In *Re Wilkinson [1977]*[82] the deceased had provided board and lodging for her sister who, in return, did some light housework, helped the deceased to dress, and acted as her companion. The sister's application under the Act succeeded since the judge took the view that she had been dependent on the deceased. The value of her services was outweighed by the value of the board and lodging which she had received. Although the Act requires the deceased's contribution to be 'substantial', the payment, in 1975, of £5 per week to a pensioner who had no other means of support was sufficient to satisfy the test.[83]

7.12.2 PROVISION FOR SPOUSES

As might be expected, it is spouses who apply most frequently under the 1975 Act[84] and provision for them is more generous than for other applicants.[85] Very substantial sums have been awarded on occasion. In *Re Besterman, deceased [1984]*[86] the husband had left the bulk of his £1 million estate to the University of Oxford. On making an application under the Act, his widow received an overall sum of £378,000. According to the court, a useful rule of thumb was to take, as the normal starting point, the one-third rule established in the leading divorce case of *Wachtel v. Wachtel [1973]*. (see para. 7.4.1 above) In other words, the widow would normally be entitled to at least one-third of the capital assets of the estate.

In the later case of *Re Bunning (deceased) (1985)*,[87] the court implied that a more generous test could be applied, taking into account the fact that it was no longer necessary to make provision for the deceased person. In other words, the court implied that more than the one-third rule in *Wachtel v. Wachtel* might be applied in some circumstances. In *Re Bunning*, the separation had been for the relatively short period of four years, whereas in *Re Rowlands (deceased) (1984)*[88] the application succeeded even though the separation had lasted 43 years. It seems clear that had the applicant, who was 90 years of age and living with a married daughter, been able to show unmet financial needs, she would probably have been awarded a more substantial amount than was, in fact, awarded. It was unlikely, for instance, that she would ever need to become resident at a private nursing home. Indeed, her future seemed secure.

In deciding whether or not to award reasonable financial provision, the courts will take into account the conduct of the parties. An applicant sometimes succeeds, however, even if he/she had acted badly towards the deceased. In *Re Snoek (deceased) (1982)*,[89] the widow could offer no explanation for her anti-social conduct - it was 'just for experience'. The court decided, nevertheless, that this behaviour did not quite cancel out her earlier contribution to the marriage, in managing the home for her husband, and in bringing up their four children. It decided, in the circumstances, that she should be awarded the 'modest' sum of £4,000.

Had the deceased proceeded with the petition for divorce filed a few years before his death, the outcome might have been different. Although ex-spouses who have not re-married can apply under the Act, it seems, from the precedent established by the Court of Appeal in *Re Fullard [1981]*[90] that they will succeed in limited circumstances only. The applicant and the deceased married in 1938 and were divorced in 1976. Both received legal advice. As a result, it was agreed that the wife should pay £4,500 for her husband's share in the matrimonial home, and that neither party should make maintenance payments to the other. The agreement was not embodied in a Court Order. The husband then took lodgings with an elderly lady who later inherited his entire estate. This consisted mainly of money which his ex-wife had paid him for his share in the matrimonial home. By the time of the application, Mrs. Fullard was of retirement age, but still working in order to pay off the mortgage she had taken out in order to buy her husband's share of the home. Nevertheless, her application failed. From this case, it would seem that former spouses will succeed only if at least one of three possible situations exists: first, that there was no proper settlement of financial matters on divorce; second, that there has been a significant change of circumstances between the date of the divorce and the death; or, third, that a continuing financial obligation existed, or that actual provision was being made for the applicant, which terminated on death.[91]

7.12.3 An example of the second of these situations arises where a substantial capital fund is unlocked by the death of the deceased. The late spouse might be very well insured, for example. In order to succeed, however, it would be necessary to show that the premiums had been paid before the divorce took place.[92] The third situation will be more common, although it is unfortunate, perhaps, that the courts place such emphasis on the need to show the commitment to have been long-standing. Financial vulnerability can be greater, the shorter the length of the marriage. Given the introduction of the clean-break principle by the MFPA 1984 (see para. 7.4.1 above) such commitments are likely to become less common. The 1984 Act allows the court, on application by either party, to bar the other party from making future application under the I(PFD)A 1975.[93] Before the introduction of this provision such arrangements were possible only with the agreement of both parties. The inheritance provisions can now be avoided even if there is no agreement between the parties, provided the court approves the requisite order.[94]

Following the decision in *Re Fullard*, it is now more difficult to obtain Legal Aid so as to make an application under the 1975 Act. The court also suggested that judges should abandon their previous practice of ordering that the costs of an unsuccessful spouse should be met from the deceased's estate, apart from exceptional cases. Applicants with weak claims should, therefore, be advised of the risks involved.[95]

7.12.4 PROVISION FOR CHILDREN

Neither a child of the deceased person, nor a person treated as a child of the family during the course of a marriage, need be a minor in order to apply under the Act. An elderly or middle-aged person can do so even though he/she was not treated as 'a child of the family' before becoming an adult. In *Re Leach (deceased) (1985)*,[96] a 55 year old social worker was awarded £19,000 from her step-mother's estate, although she was 32 at the date of the deceased's marriage to her father. A similar decision was given in *Re Callaghan (deceased) (1984)*[97] where the court placed considerable weight upon the fact that the deceased had apparently adopted the role of grandfather in respect of the applicant's children. The applicant had also given the deceased much care and support.

7.12.5 TIME LIMITS

An application under the 1975 Act must be made not later than six months from the date of a Grant of Probate or, in the case of intestacy, not later than six months from the date upon which Letters of Administration were taken out.[98] The court can use its discretion, however, to extend the time-limit in accordance with established guidelines.[99]

7.13.1 DONATIO MORTIS CAUSA - GIFTS IN CONTEMPLATION OF DEATH

An individual believing him/herself close to death, or contemplating a dangerous journey or activity, may wish to arrange beforehand for the transfer of property to be made to another person should death occur. In order to make a gift of this kind successfully, the following criteria must be satisfied: the gift must have been made in contemplation of death; the gift must have been delivered to the individual in question; the gift must have been conditional upon the death of the donor; and it must have been capable of passing as a *donatio mortis causa*. Some gifts, most notably of land, cannot be transferred in this way.[100]

Should a dispute arise, the burden of proving the validity of the arrangement falls upon the person receiving the gift, but evidence from the donee alone could be sufficient to establish its effectiveness.

7.14.1 THE FORFEITURE ACT 1982

Anyone found guilty of causing another person's death is usually prevented from benefiting under the will, intestacy, statutory nomination, or *donatio mortis causa* of his/her victim. The Forfeiture Act 1982 (FA 1982) modifies this rule with respect to manslaughter if it can be shown that justice requires it. *Re K (deceased) (1985)*[101] was the first case to come before the courts after the passing of the Act. A 62 year old widow, who had pleaded guilty to her husband's manslaughter, was allowed to inherit a life interest, valued at £412,000, in her husband's estate and a half-share in the matrimonial home, valued at £85,000. The deceased had subjected the applicant to frequent and unprovoked violence. Following a quarrel, she shot him. In reaching its decision, the court seems to have taken into account the conduct of both the offender and the deceased.

The question whether or not the provisions of the FA 1982 could be applied to a person found guilty of a so-called 'mercy killing' has not yet come before the courts.[102]

7.15.1 LIFE-TIME GIFTS

The practice of making life-time gifts is referred to here for two reasons. First, the courts are more ready to assume the existence of 'undue influence' where gifts are transferred during a person's lifetime than when they are made under a will.(see discussion at para. 7.8.6) Secondly, there may be tax implications. A detailed discussion of tax law is beyond the scope of this book but some of its features are discussed below.

7.15.2 CAPITAL GAINS TAX

Where assets, such as property, or shares, or other valuables are sold or given away, the transferor may have to pay Capital Gains Tax (CGT) should the real or notional gain arising from the transaction be above the annual exemption rate. Until the 1988 Budget this figure had risen annually with inflation. From April 1988, the exemption will be £5,000 per year. The gain is obviously notional where the asset is given away as a gift, but for tax purposes, it is deemed to have been disposed of at market value. From April 1990, it is proposed that married couples should be taxed independently on their capital gains, with separate annual exemptions, and so different rules will apply. At present, however, a husband and wife must share the one annual exemption.

It is not the value of the asset as such that is important, but the increase in its value between acquisition and disposal. Tax is paid on the difference between the price at acquiring it and value at disposal. Until April 1988, a flat rate of 30 per cent was levied on chargeable gains. From April 1988, however, the rate payable will reflect the individual taxpayer's rate of income tax. The tax rate will therefore rise to 40 per cent for higher rate taxpayers but drop to 25 per cent for standard rate taxpayers. Another change introduced in the latest budget will exempt capital gains made between 1965 and 1982. In other words, CGT will be payable only upon gains made after 1982.

7.15.3 Certain assets, such as a person's main or only residence, private cars, and savings certificates are exempt from CGT. Until the 1988 Budget, there was also an exemption for one other residence occupied by the dependent relative. The Budget abolished tax relief on homes provided for a dependent relative and the change will apply to all disposals after April 6, 1988. Arrangements made prior to that date, however, will continue to qualify for relief from CGT. To qualify, the property must be let rent-free and for no consideration, although the rules permit the dependent relative to be liable for the rates, and for the cost of repairs to the dwelling arising out of normal wear and tear. In this context, a 'dependent relative' means any relative of the tax-payer or his/her spouse who is incapacitated, by age or infirmity, from maintaining him/herself. It includes the tax-payer's mother, and mother-in-law if she is separated or widowed. For the exemptions to apply to a widower, he would need to be incapacitated. Only one dwelling can qualify for this exemption.

For the reasons given above, few family transactions are likely to give rise to CGT. A family transaction which may do so is an arrangement for the transfer or disposal of a family business on retirement. It is possible, however, to obtain relief from CGT even on transactions such as these, in certain circumstances. For it to be eligible for exemption, the transferor must normally be at least 60 years of age at the date of disposal (although he/she need not be retiring from the business). There is also an exemption on a transfer or disposal of a family business which arises because a person is forced to retire before the age of 60 on grounds of ill-health. The detailed requirements to be satisfied in establishing ill-health are set out in para. 3 of Sched. 20 of the Finance Act 1985 (FA 1985). It is not possible to appeal against the decision whether or not a person qualifies on grounds of ill-health. If either of the above conditions is satisfied, the maximum relief available on retirement is £125,000. From April 1988, half of any gain between £125,000 and £500,000 will also be tax free. In order to obtain it in full, however, the business must have been owned for ten years prior to disposal. It should be noted that ownership is broadly defined and includes, for instance, a share in a partnership. If the ten-year ownership condition cannot be satisfied, the amount of relief will be adjusted according to the number of years for which the asset was owned, the minimum period of ownership being one year.

7.16.1 INHERITANCE TAX

Capital Transfer Tax (CTT) was introduced in 1975 to replace estate duty. Whereas, estate duty was levied on the value of property upon the death of a person, CTT introduced a levy, subject to certain exemptions, on life-time transfers of property. The Finance Act 1986 (FA 1986) changed the name of CTT to Inheritance Tax (IHT) and, in relation to transfers made on or after March 18, 1986, reverted to the principle of charging tax on life-time gifts only when they had been made within seven years of the donor's death. Where a gift was made before March 18, 1986, but the person making it died on or after that date, the amount of tax payable will be no greater than it would have been had CTT continued. The 1986 Act, therefore, introduced a new category of potentially exempt transfers.

Transfers within the seven year period are now subject to a tapering charge. For example, transfers made between six and seven years before death are taxed at 20 per cent of the death rate, whereas one made within three years of death would be taxed at 100 per cent of the death rate. The value of gifts transferred during the seven years before death will be added to the value of the deceased person's estate. Where the total value is above the tax free limit, IHT is payable. The IHT tax-free limit is currently £110,000 (1988/89).

Exemptions and reliefs similar to those discussed in respect to CGT are also available. It should be noted, however, that with respect to the relief available for the transfer of business property, the qualifying ownership period is *two* years, not one. Technical procedures exist to deal with problems caused by ownership of a succession of businesses in order to ensure that no loss of relief occurs. In addition, gifts of up to £3,000 in any tax year are exempt, as are gifts made in contemplation of a marriage. For instance, a £5,000 exemption is allowed on gifts by one of the parents of a bride or groom, whereas grandparents can give £2,500 each, free of IHT.

The FA 1986 also introduced an important change to the law in respect to gifts with reservation which occur when the donor continues to enjoy some benefit from the gift. The most common example is where an individual transfers ownership of his/her house to another but continues to live there. Where such arrangements are made but the donor continues to benefit from the gift, then the whole value of it will be counted as part of his/her estate for the purpose of IHT. Where the donor no longer benefits from the gift, however, liability for tax depends upon whether the change in circumstances had occurred more than seven years before death. For example, where an elderly person who had previously transferred ownership of his/her home, later enters a residential home, there may be no liability for IHT. Where death occurs within the seven-year period, however, the amount payable will depend upon the number of years that have passed since entry into the residential home took place.

7.17.1 INTENTION TO CREATE LEGAL RELATIONS

There is a legal presumption that social and domestic arrangements do not create legal relations between the parties. The party wishing to establish the existence of a legal contract must present evidence to rebut the presumption. A factor which may weigh heavily with a court is whether or not the arrangements were spelled out in detail. In *Berryere v. Berryere [1972]*[103] a grandmother attempted to recover from her daughter money she had spent on bringing up her granddaughter. The grandmother had made it clear that she expected her daughter to share responsibility for the child. The daughter undertook to pay a regular sum each month for the child's maintenance. Only three payments were made, however, and nothing was then paid for some nine years. The court held that the presumption had not been rebutted in this instance and that the claim must fail. Legally binding contracts are possible between members of a family, nevertheless, as in the case of *Hagger v. de Placido* [1972].[104] In that case, the court recognized the existence of a contract between a 29 year old tetraplegic and his mother and brother who had undertaken to nurse him. Agreements by which grandparents care for their grandchildren might be treated in the same way but only where an intention to create legal relations was clearly established. One study of working mothers with children under five showed that no less than a quarter of the children were regularly looked after by their grand-mothers.[105]

7.17.2 LIVING WITH RELATIVES

The courts have been more prepared to presume a contractual intention where the agreement between the parties relates to joint residency. An example would be an elderly person moving to live with a son or daughter and his/her family, or vice versa. Households of this type are decreasing in number, at present, but might increase were it to become more customary to adapt property or build on to it to accommodate an elderly parent. In 1979, 13 per cent of elderly people in private households were living with relatives and no less than 29 per cent of women aged 85 or over lived with a son or daughter.

Difficult problems can arise in arrangements of this kind. In *Parker v. Clarke [1960]*,[106] a young couple sold their house and moved to live with elderly relatives on the basis of a promise, made in writing, that they would be left a share in the property. A later claim that there had been no intention to create legal relations was rejected by the court. It was held that the younger couple would not have taken the important step of selling their own home on the basis of a social arrangement only. The couple were successful in obtaining damages for the loss of a share in the house.

The more recent case of *Broughall v. Hunt (1983)* (unreported) illustrates some of the difficulties. This case involved a more common arrangement in that a 70 year old woman moved to live with her daughter and son-in-law. Her bedroom was in a new extension to the house, which was not self-contained, and to which she contributed £1,000. Much of the building work was done by her other two sons-in-law. Some years later the relationship broke down and she left. The court decided that she had a contractual licence to occupy the premises for as long as she wished, and that the licence had been improperly terminated by her daughter and son-in-law. She was awarded £1,500 damages (although, given the legal costs, the net benefit to her must have been minimal). Her daughter and son-in-law fared much worse, however. They faced having to sell their home in order to meet the estimated legal costs of £10,000, a reflection of the very complicated legal problems involved. An excellent discussion of the issues in *Broughall v. Hunt* and similar cases is to be found in a College of Law publication.[107]

Another point worth noting here is that where capital has been transferred, the courts may impute a trust giving the beneficiary a right to a share in the value of the property, as well as a right of occupation until it is sold. Rights created in this way could have the effect of blocking a future sale. Where no capital changes hands, however, an elderly person moving to live with relatives may have only a licence to occupy. Those contemplating arrangements of this kind would be well-advised to draw up an agreement establishing that a licence to occupy only is being created. This would establish the limited nature of the transaction and set out the period of notice required to end it. If an elderly person had exclusive occupation of a separate part of the premises, however, then a tenancy might arise.(see Chapter 3, at para. 3.5.2)

Where capital is transferred, it should be specified whether the sum in question is intended as a loan or as payment for a beneficial interest in the property. If a loan is intended, a charge under seal should be made on the legal estate, so as to give the person concerned protection similar to that of a mortgagee. If, on the other hand, a beneficial interest is intended then the best solution might be to use co-ownership as the basis of a trust for sale.[108]

Individuals contemplating joint residence would be well advised to consult a solicitor. They may feel some reluctance in doing so, since setting out the terms of the agreement in a formal document might seem like a declaration of bad faith. Formalising arrangements helps to protect both parties, however, and can also help foster mutual understanding, and allay suspicion about motives. Circumstances can change, often quickly and dramatically. Events such as divorce, redundancy, or death can render arrangements unworkable which were previously feasible.

7.18.1 IMMIGRATION

'Dependent relatives' can be admitted into the United Kingdom on the basis of rules established under the Immigration Act 1971 (IA 1971).[109] The primary requirement is for applicants to show they are without other close relatives in their own country to whom they can turn in time of need. Entry to the United Kingdom is possible under these rules even though close relatives remain in the country of origin but they are unable or unwilling to assist the dependent relative. These rules apply to three categories of persons: (i) widowed mothers and widowers, and parents of a person resident in this country, who are travelling together, and one of whom is at least 65; (ii) parents and grand-parents in other circumstances who have not remarried and more distant relatives; and (iii) parents and grandparents who have remarried. These provisions have resulted in complex litigation.[110] Useful advice in this context is available from the Joint Council for the Welfare of Immigrants.[111]

7.19.1 ELDERLY ABUSE

Evidence suggests that some 'old elderly' people are vulnerable to physical and/or mental abuse from those who care for them.[112] One estimate puts the number at risk as high as 500,000, but such claims have not been validated. Although not denying that abuse exists, other commentators feel that the extent of the problem is as yet unknown. They are critical of those who, on somewhat thin evidence, advocate the introduction of protective measures which might encroach upon the freedom of many elderly people.[113] One proposal is for the extension of s.47 of the National Assistance Act 1948 (NAA 1948) (see Chapter 4 at paras. 4.10.2 - 4.10.6) to encompass those allegedly being abused by their carers, and allow them to be compulsorily removed into care.[114] Another radical proposal is for the introduction of a provision similar to a care order which exists currently to protect children and young persons.[115]

7.19.2 Another problem relates to the way in which abuse is defined. A commonly quoted definition is that it involves 'the systematic maltreatment, physical, emotional or financial of an elderly person by a care-giving relative'.[116] It may take the form of physical assault,[117] threatening behaviour, neglect, abandonment, (for example, locking an elderly relative in a bedroom) or sexual assault. Elderly abuse is thus given a wide and imprecise definition.[118]

7.19.3 Where abuse is alleged, two forms of legal intervention exist. These consist of civil actions in tort alleging some form of trespass to the person, or criminal proceedings for assault. Trespass to the person consists of battery, assault, or false imprisonment. An assault can arise whenever a person has reasonable cause to fear that direct harm is to be directed at him/her. The tort of battery, however, requires actual, direct, and intentional application of force to the person.[119] The least touching of another person could constitute battery, although the everyday collisions of ordinary life are outside its scope. Battery can arise without real hostility in the perpetrator so long as the act is against the will of the plaintiff. An unwanted kiss, for example, or cutting hair without consent, or spitting at a person, could amount to battery.

False imprisonment is the infliction of physical restraint not expressly or impliedly authorized by law.[120] The tort cannot arise where a person consents to restrictions being placed upon his/her person, but consent cannot be implied simply because no resistance is shown.[121] A person can be falsely imprisoned without knowing it, for example, when asleep.[122] The tort does not arise, however, unless a person's freedom of movement and action has been restrained in every direction.

It is surprising, perhaps, that allegations of false imprisonment involving elderly people living in residential homes, or with relatives, are not more common, given recent scandals in some residential homes, and other evidence of restrictions placed upon elderly people. Claims are made, for instance, that elderly people living with relatives are sometimes locked up, confined in small rooms, and kept isolated from other members of the family.[123] One of the few cases involving an elderly person in an action for false imprisonment is reported here simply to illustrate some of the characteristics of the tort. A 72 old shopper was accused of shoplifting on the mistaken suspicion that she had stolen a greetings card. Her handbag was removed from her 'for a few minutes'. Following a 15 minute wait in an open changing cubicle she was taken to the local police station in a police van. She received £1,520 damages for false imprisonment, as well as substantial damages for trespass to goods because of the removal of her handbag.[124]

7.19.4 A characteristic of the three torts discussed above is that physical harm must have been directly threatened or inflicted upon the plaintiff. Where physical harm is caused indirectly, liability may arise under the so-called rule in *Wilkinson v. Downton [1897].*[125] The rule is sometimes referred to as the 'wrongful interference principle'. If someone were to shout at an elderly person descending a difficult staircase, with the intention of giving him/her a shock, that person might be held liable for any physical injuries which resulted, even though no direct force had been applied. An action might succeed even where there was no intention of causing actual physical injury, since the intention to cause shock may be sufficient to establish 'wrongful interference'. It should be noted, however, that no parallel criminal proceedings exist in this case. Another possible course of action might be in the tort of negligence if it could be established that the person caring for the elderly person had a duty of care towards him/her. The elements of this tort are discussed in Chapter 6 at para. 6.4.2.

7.19.5 Some actions are both criminal and tortious and can give rise both to prosecution and a civil action for damages. In general, it does not matter which proceedings are brought first, although the usual practice is for civil proceedings to be stayed until criminal proceedings have been completed. Some statutes, however, provide that criminal proceedings brought under them are a bar to future civil action. Section 45 of the Offences Against the Person Act 1861 (OATPA 1861) bars civil proceedings if, for example, summary criminal proceedings for common assault have been brought. The rule barring civil proceedings can be evaded, however, by the simple expedient of suing first and making a criminal complaint later.

The OATPA 1861 sets out a number of criminal assaults ranging in seriousness from common assault to assault with the intention of causing grievous bodily harm. The difference between the various forms of assault is beyond the scope of this discussion, but common assault warrants some attention. Common assault normally requires the victim, rather than the police, to initiate proceedings. It has been established at common law, however, that elderly and infirm people are to be treated as exceptions to this rule.

7.19.6 In *Pivering v. Willoughby [1907]*[126] an elderly woman who had suffered a number of strokes was assaulted by the niece who had moved to live with her. The court held that a great-nephew could institute proceedings on behalf of the victim on the grounds that 'if the person assaulted is so feeble, old and infirm as to be incapable of instituting proceedings, and is not a free agent but under the control of the person committing the assault, the information may be laid by a third person'. Many elderly victims of abuse may fall within this exception to the rule, in which case the police could initiate action on their behalf. This might assist those who are themselves reluctant to use the criminal law. Such actions might also overcome the problem that Legal Aid is not available for private prosecutions. Indeed, given these difficulties, there appears to be no good reason why the police should not shoulder the burden completely in the majority of cases and prosecute for assault occasioning actual bodily harm, particularly since such harm need not be serious. It could include, for example, an hysterical or nervous condition arising as the result of an assault.[127] Those found guilty of common assault can be required to enter into recognisance to be bound over to be of good behaviour.[128]

7.19.7 Some commentators have questioned the value of using the criminal courts for alleged cases of elderly abuse. It has been suggested that the police should be involved only where abuse is blatant and mercenary.[129] Magistrates, too, tend to treat such cases leniently.[130] It has also been suggested that involving the police may be futile because many victims will be reluctant to become associated with criminal proceedings. These are dubious arguments since, as indicated above, the police can shoulder much of the responsibility for bringing cases to court. Similar arguments were put forward in the context of domestic violence (see para. 7.6.1 above) but research has shown that the problem of getting victims to co-operate had been exaggerated.[131]

7.19.8 An advantage of using civil proceedings is that the burden of proof in criminal prosecutions is heavier than in civil actions since an offence has to be proved beyond all reasonable doubt. Substantial damages can also be awarded in a civil action. For this and other reasons, it has been suggested that civil actions for assault, battery, and false imprisonment may provide better remedies than criminal proceedings. There are precedents, however, which could prove helpful in criminal proceedings. In *R. v. Reigate Justices, ex parte Counsel (1983)*, for instance, it was held sufficient, in order for the court to infer actual bodily harm, for the victim of an assault to have suffered great pain, tenderness, and soreness even though no physical injury was discernible at the time of the hearing.[132]

There remains one compelling argument against an increased use of the criminal courts, however, in that many of the abusers are carers, themselves the victims of the general apathy of the community and, in particular, the welfare services towards them.[133] Many of those looking after the very old are themselves elderly and under considerable stress because of the responsibilities they shoulder.[134]

7.19.9 The Criminal Injuries Compensation Board can make *ex-gratia* payments to those who have suffered personal injury directly attributable to a crime of violence. Certain claims are excluded, such as those for less than £550 in the case of family violence. In practice, about half of all crimes of violence fall outside the scope of the scheme.[135]

7.20.1 THE MENTALLY INCAPABLE

As the numbers in the population of those aged 75 and over increase, so, proportionately, does the incidence of mental infirmity. Individuals who have become mentally incapable of dealing with their personal affairs may need to have their interests safeguarded. Two different legal procedures exist to protect the affairs of the mentally incapable. The first provides for the transfer of responsibility for the management of the infirm individual's affairs to another person, known as an attorney. Under the second procedure, an application can be made on behalf of a mentally incapable person for responsibility to be transferred to a specialized court.

7.20.2 *ENDURING POWERS OF ATTORNEY*

An ordinary power of attorney is a document by which one person (the donor) authorizes another (the donee) to act on his/her behalf. To be effective it must be signed by the donor, witnessed, and must be made under seal. It can then be produced to bodies such as banks and commercial firms as evidence of authority to act on the donor's behalf. A power of attorney of this kind, although useful in many circumstances, has the disadvantage of being automatically revoked should the donor become mentally incapable. Since 1986, it has been possible to make use of a new statutory power which overcomes many of the difficulties created by this rule. Under the Enduring Powers of Attorney Act 1985 (EPAA 1985), an enduring power of attorney (EPA) can be created. This has the advantage of not being affected by subsequent incapacity in the donor, as long as certain statutory procedures are followed should that occur.

7.20.3 *CREATING AN EPA*

An EPA can be validly created only by a donor with sufficient mental capacity to do so. In *Re K. and Re F. (1987)*, however, it was held that a valid and proper EPA could be created by a person who was already incapable of managing his/her affairs by reason of mental disorder. The test, apparently, is whether the donor, at the time when the EPA was executed, had the mental capacity to understand the nature and effect of creating the power, despite the existence of mental disorder.[136]

An EPA must also conform in its form with the Enduring Powers of Attorney (Prescribed Form) Regulations, 1987.[137] The Regulations provide, among other things, that the EPA must be executed by both the donor and the donee (although not necessarily at the same time) in the presence of a witness. Only individuals (other than minors and bankrupts) and trust corporations (such as the Public Trustee) can be appointed to act as attorney.

7.20.4 ONSET OF MENTAL INCAPACITY

If the donee has reason to suspect that the donor has become, or is becoming, mentally incapable, he/she must, as soon as practicable, take certain steps as prescribed by the Act if the EPA is to remain valid. 'Mental incapacity' is defined in the EPAA 1985 as inability in a person to manage his/her property or affairs by reason of mental disorder, as defined in the Mental Health Act 1983 (MHA 1983). It may not always be easy to determine a person's mental state. Since the donor's incapacity will, however, restrict the powers of the attorney should no action be taken, it can become important to act as swiftly as possible.

7.20.5 The first step is for the donee to inform the donor and certain of his/her relatives of the intention to apply to the Court of Protection for registration of the EPA. The relatives to be informed (in order of priority) are: husband or wife; children; parents; brothers and sisters, whether of the whole or half blood; the widow or widower of a child of the donor; grandchildren; children of the donor's brothers and sisters of the whole blood; children of the donor's brothers and sisters of the half blood; the donor's uncles and aunts of the whole blood; children of the donor's uncles and aunts of the whole blood.[138]
It is sufficient, in principle, to inform three relatives only, but, in practice, all relatives falling within a particular category must be included.

Entitlement to receive notice is waived where a person's name and address is not known and cannot reasonably be ascertained; or if he/she is believed to be under the age of 18, or mentally incapacitated; or where the Court has dispensed with the need to give notice; or where notice, in accordance with these rules, would otherwise need to be given to the donee him/herself. The purpose of giving notice in this way is to enable the relatives to object to the Court, if they so wish, against the registration of the EPA. It should be noted, however, that right of objection is not confined to the donor's relatives.

7.20.6 *APPLYING TO REGISTER AN EPA*

Application to the Court to register an EPA must be made in the prescribed form and must be accompanied by the document granting the original power of attorney, as well as the specified fee.[139]

Generally, the Court will register all EPAs which comply in form with the statutory rules. In two instances, the Court may even allow an application where a prescribed relative who was entitled to receive notice, has not been informed. These are circumstances in which it is either undesirable or impracticable for the attorney to give him/her notice; or where no useful purpose is likely to be served by doing so.[140]

There are circumstances, however, in which the Court will need to make further inquiries. They will be needed: (i) where a valid notice of objection has been received; (ii) where it appears that no relative of the donor was informed; and (iii) where the Court has reason to believe that inquiries might bring to light evidence sufficient to establish one of the grounds for objection set out in the Act.[141] The Court will then defer its decision until further inquiries can be made. Only if the Court is satisfied with the results of its inquiries will the EPA be registered.

7.20.7 *EFFECT OF REGISTRATION*

The effect of registering an EPA is that the Court of Protection has power to give directions on the management of property and the affairs of the donor, on the rendering of accounts, and on the keeping of records. It may also determine any question as to the meaning or effect of the EPA. Once registered, the EPA continues in existence until the powers of attorney are cancelled by the Court; or revoked, either automatically, or by an act of the donor or the Court; or by the attorney giving notice of disclaimer to the donor. It will be terminated automatically and by operation of law upon the death of the donor, and upon the death, mental incapacity or bankruptcy of the attorney.

7.20.8 THE COURT OF PROTECTION

The second procedure for protecting the interests of a mentally incapable person is to invoke the powers of the Court of Protection. The Court of Protection has considerable powers to act in relation to the property and affairs of a person suffering from mental disorder as defined by the MHA 1983. The statutory provisions are now contained in Part VII of the 1983 Act and the jurisdiction of the Court can be invoked by making an application on the grounds set out in the Act.

7.20.9 APPLYING TO THE COURT

Any person can apply to the Court to have a patient's property and affairs placed under the Court's jurisdiction on the grounds that he/she is incapable of managing his/her property and affairs by reason of mental disorder.[142] The person who applies is often a relative, but the director of a social services department, acting on behalf of a local authority, or a creditor, adviser or friend could also make the application. Where the patient is married, the Court normally requires proof that his/her spouse has agreed to the application being made.

The application must be accompanied by a medical certificate given by a doctor, who need not have particular expertise in the field of mental disorder. It must state that in the doctor's opinion, the patient is incapable by reason of mental disorder of managing his/her property and affairs. The grounds for that opinion must be given, as must the date upon which the patient was last examined; whether he/she is an informal patient or subject to detention under the MHA 1983; whether there is a previous history of mental disorder; whether he/she is dangerous to him/herself or to others; the state of his/her physical health and prospects for life; and the likelihood of his/her recovery.

7.20.10   An Affidavit of Kindred and Fortune must also accompany the application. This must set out prescribed details relating to the patient, such as his/her age, occupation or former occupation, nearest relative, and former residence. Other particulars must refer to the property owned by the patient and his/her income, present address and current commitments. Any debts incurred by the patient must be listed, including a statement whether or not the patient's income will be sufficient to meet them, and whether or not he/she is prepared, if necessary, to make use of capital for this purpose. The Affidavit must also state whether the patient has made a will, or executed a power of attorney. It should also propose the name of a receiver to act on behalf of the patient, and the name of a person to give a reference on the proposed receiver's suitability to act. A brief history of the patient should also be included.

7.20.11 Where the patient's assets are worth no more than £5,000, the Court can make a summary order without an application being made, and direct one of the Court's officers or some other suitable person to take particular action in relation to the assets. The Court can do this even where the estate is valued at more than £5,000 if it considered that no receiver needs to be appointed.[143]

7.20.12 NOTICE TO THE PATIENT

Notice that an application has been made to the Court of Protection on his/her behalf must normally be given to the patient, but this requirement can be dispensed with if the Court is satisfied that the patient is incapable of understanding the notice, or that the notice would injure his/her health, or for any other reason.[144]

If notice is given to the patient, he/she has seven days from its receipt, or up to the date of the hearing (whichever is later), within which to lodge an objection with the Court. The objection can be to the application as such, or to the recommendations and proposals which it contains. If the Court is satisfied that the patient is mentally incapable, the application is likely to be granted. If, however, the Court has doubts on this score, it may request one of its panel of Medical Visitors to visit the patient in order to examine him/her and prepare a confidential report on the patient's medical state. The Court will reach a decision on the basis of the report, and will inform the patient of its intention either to make an order, (but giving him/her the opportunity to produce further evidence in support of his/her objection), or, if the report states that the patient is capable of acting on his/her own behalf, it will set the application aside.

7.20.13   THE EFFECT OF AN ORDER

An order by the Court of Protection invests it with power to manage and administer the property and affairs of the patient. It may then do all that is necessary or expedient under s.95(1) of the MHA 1983: (i) for the maintenance or other benefit of the patient; (ii) for the maintenance or other benefit of members of the patient's family; (iii) for making provison for other persons or purposes for whom or which the patient might be expected to provide if he/she were not mentally disordered, or (iv) for otherwise administering the patient's affairs.   For this purpose, the Court is able to (i) control and manage the patient's property; (ii) sell, or deal or dispose of property; (iii) acquire property on the patient's behalf; (iv) make settlements or gifts to any persons mentioned in s.95(1)(b) and (c) of the Act; (v) make a will; (vi) carry on, by means of a suitable person, the profession, trade or business of the patient; (vii) dissolve a patient's partnership; (viii) carry out a contract entered into by the patient; (ix) conduct legal proceedings in the patient's name or on his/her behalf; (x) reimburse any person who has paid the patient's debts, or maintained the patient or members of his/her family, as well as providing for other persons of purposes for whom or for which the patient might have been expected to provide if he/she were not mentally disordered and (xi) exercise any power vested in the patient for him/herself or as a trustee or guardian, or otherwise.

7.20.14   APPOINTMENT OF A RECEIVER

Under s.99 of the Act, the judge hearing the application can appoint a receiver to carry out the Court's instructions in relation to the patient's property and affairs.   Usually the person appointed will be a close relative but should there be no suitable or willing relative, the Court can appoint the Official Solicitor, or the director of social services for the area where the patient is living, if that person is willing to act.   If the receiver needs to act outside the terms of authority which have been granted, he/she must return to the Court for further instructions.

7.20.15 There has been criticism recently of the way in which the Court of Protection works.[145] In particular, it has been suggested that it is over-centralized in London, and that this leads to geographical remoteness from many of the patients with whom the Court is dealing. In addition, some patients who are under the protection of the Court may have been placed there inappropriately. To prevent this, stronger safeguards may be required. More flexible procedures are also advocated so as to enable patients, where appropriate, to retain a degree of control even when under the protection of the Court.

7.21.1   LITIGATION AND INCAPACITY

A mental patient who is incapable of managing or administering his/her property and affairs cannot bring or defend an action in the courts. If he/she is under the jurisdiction of the Court of Protection, only the Court can act. Otherwise, where the patient is the plaintiff, applicant, or petitioner, the action must be conducted on his/her behalf by a 'next friend', and where the patient is the defendant or respondent, a guardian *ad litem* must be appointed to act. Any suitable person may act in this capacity, but it is often the Official Solicitor who takes on this responsibility.

Notes

1. CSO (1987) *Social Trends* at p.49; *Family Policy*, Issue No. 4, Winter 1987/88 (Family Policy Studies Centre).
2. *2 All ER 789*; see also Masson, J. M. (1976) 'Divorcing Mental Patients', *Fam. Law,* vol. 6 at pp.114-19.
3. *Smith v. Smith (1973)* 118 SJ 184.
4. *2 All ER 650.*
5. *Le Marchant v. Le Marchant [1977] 3 All ER 610.*
6. *Reiterbund v. Reiterbund [1975] 1 All ER 280.*
7. *Parker v. Parker [1972] Fam. Law 116.*
8. Judicial Statistics, Annual Report 1982, Table 4.11.

9. Matrimonial Causes Rules 1977, r.48(1)(a).

10. *R. v. Clarke [1949] 2 All ER 448.*

11. Matrimonial Causes Act 1973, s.23.

12. s.25(A)(1).

13. s.25(A)(2). On the relationship between maintenance and the level of state benefits, see *Ashley v. Blackman [1988] 3 WLR 222.*

14. *The Times,* April 22, 1975.

15. *1 All ER 56 CA.*

16. *15 Fam. Law, 123, CA.*

17. *1 All ER 829 CA.*

18. See Chapter 1 at para. 1.11.1.

19. See Powell, J. V. (1984) 'Pension Considerations on Marriage Breakdown', *Fam. Law,* vol.14, at p.187, where the issues are discussed.

20. ibid.

21. Matrimonial Causes Act 1973, s.24, s.25.

22. s.24(1).

23. *Warren-Gash and Another v. Lane (1984) 14 Fam. Law,* at p.184.

24. *Cooke v. Head [1972] 1 WLR 518.*

25. Domestic Proceedings and Magistrates' Courts Act 1978; Domestic Violence and Matrimonial Proceedings Act 1976.

26. *Vaughan v. Vaughan [1973] 3 All ER 449.*

27. See Griffiths, A. and Bhowmick, B. K. (1978) 'Sick role status and the elderly discharged from hospital', the *Practitioner,* vol.221 December 1978, at p.926.

28. Guardianship of Minors Act 1971, s.14A(1); Domestic Proceedings and Magistrates' Courts Act 1978, s.14(1); Children Act 1975, s.34(1).

29. Guardianship of Minors Act 1971, s.14A(2).

30. Adoption Act 1976, s.12(6).

31. *Re J [1973] 2 All ER 410; Re S [1975] 1 All ER 109; Re C(A Minor) [1988] 2 WLR 474, HL.*

32. *1 All ER 417.*

33. Domestic Proceedings and Magistrates' Courts Act 1978, s.8(3).

34. Children Act 1975, s.18.

35. *14 Fam. Law,* at pp.15-16.

36. ibid.

37. The so called Wednesbury principle: 'a person entrusted with discretion must, so to speak, direct himself properly in

law. He must call his own attention to the matters which he is bound to consider . . . Similarly there may be something so absurd that no sensible person could ever dream that it lay within the powers of authority'. *Associated Provincial Picture Houses Ltd v. Wednesbury Corporation [1947] 1 KB* at p.229.

38. Child Care Act 1980, s.2(3).

39. Magistrates' Court (Children and Young Persons) Rules 1988, r.17.

40. Legal Aid Act 1974 s.28(6A) as amended.

41. See *Money Care*, the customer magazine of the National Westminster Bank, June 1985 at p.26. Individuals experiencing difficulties on bereavement can contact the National Association for the Widowed and their Children, Cheill Road, Stafford, ST16 2QA.

42. *Money Care* op.cit., April 1985 at p.5.

43. A partner could, however, apply as a dependant for support under the Inheritance (Provision for Family Dependants) Act 1975. (see paras. 7.12.1-7.12.5).

44. The Law Society (1984).

45. Law Reform Committee (1973) *Interpretation of Wills* Cmnd. 5301; (1980) *Making and Revokation of Wills* Cmnd. 7902.

46. Mackay, R. D. (1983) 'Statutory Reform in the Law of Wills', *New Law Journal*, September 30, 1983 at p.861.

47. Administration of Justice Act 1982, s.18(3).

48. s.18(A).

49. Mackay, R. D. (1983) op.cit., at p.863.

50. See discussion at para. 7.12.2.

51. *Banks v. Goodfellow (1870) LR 5 QB 549, 565.*

52. *In the Estate of Bohrmann [1938] 1 All ER 271.*

53. *Parker v. Felgate (1883) 8 PD 171.*

54. See footnote 51.

55. See footnote 52.

56. *Hall v. Hall (1868) LR 1 P and D 481.*

57. *Wingrove v. Wingrove (1885) 11 PD 81.*

58. See Clark, I. B. (ed.) (1983) *Parry and Clark on the Law of Succession* (Sweet and Maxwell) at p.55.

59. *Allcard v. Skinner (1887) 36 Ch.D. 145.*

60. *Ch.D. 95.*

61. *[1929] AC 127.*

62. *Eckersley v. Platt (1886) LR 1 P and D 281.*

63. *Ministry of Health v. Simpson [1951] AC 251.*

64. Age Concern (1980) *Instructions for my Next of Kin and Executors upon my death* (Age Concern England).

65. Cremation Regulations 1965 S.I. 1965 No.1146, reg 7A.

66. Anatomy Act 1984, s.4.

67. McFarlane, S. (1984) 'Control of Anatomy: Anatomy Act 1984', SJ, vol.128 at p.507.

68. See *The Times*, September 1, 1984.

69. For further details, contact the British National Life Assurance Co Ltd, Perrymount Road, Haywards Heath, West Sussex. Also, Age Concern England provide a Funeral Plan in association with Chosen Heritage.

70. Figure supplied by the Principal Secretary of the Principal Registry of the Family Division of the High Court.

71. See *Money Care*, op.cit., June 1985 at p.26.

72. Administration of Estates Act 1925, as amended. See also Family Provision (Intestate Succession) Order 1987 S.I. 1987 No.799.

73. Administration of Estates (Small Payments) (Increase of Limit) Order 1984 S.I. 1984 No.539.

74. Clark, I. B. (1983) op.cit., at p.16.

75. Welsh Consumer Council (1984) *The Future of the Death Grant*, Working Paper No.6, at p.2. (WCC)

76. Oswald, R. (1985) 'Paying for Funeral Costs', *LAG Bulletin*, April 1985, at pp.57-8.

77. Public Health (Control of Diseases) Act 1984, s.46.

78. Ministry of Health Circular 13/49. For further information, contact the National Association of Funeral Directors, 57 Doughty Street, London, WC1.

79. Oswald, R. (1985) op.cit., at pp.57-8.

80. Inheritance (Provision for Family and Dependants) Act 1975, s.1(1).

81. s.1(3).

82. *All ER 221*. See also *Williams v. Johns (1988) 18 Fam. Law 257*.

83. *Re Viner [1978] CLY 3091*.

84. Oughton, R. D. (ed.) (1984) *Tyler's Family Provision*, (Professional Books Ltd) at p.51.

85. There are two standards of reasonable provision: the 'surviving spouse' standard and the 'maintenance' standard. Section 1(2)(a) of the 1975 Act gives spouses 'such financial provision as it would be reasonable in all the circumstances of the case for a husband and wife to receive, whether or not that

provision is required for his or her maintenance'.

86. *FLR 503.*
87. *15 Fam. Law 21.*
88. *14 Fam. Law 280.*
89. *13 Fam. Law 18.*
90. *2 All ER 796.*
91. For further discussion, see Oughton, R. D. (1984) op.cit., at p.185.
92. Prime, T. (1982) 'Ex Wife Ex Family', *12 Fam. Law,* at p.55.
93. Matrimonial and Family Proceedings Act 1984, s.8(1).
94. Inheritance (Provision for Family and Dependants) Act 1975, s.15.
95. Oughton, R. D. (1984) op.cit., at p.267.
96. [1985] *2 All ER 754, CA.*
97. [1984] *3 WLR 1076.*
98. Oughton, R. D. (1984) op.cit., at p.239.
99. ibid., at p.240.
100. Clark, I. B. (1983) op.cit., at p.21.
101. *15 Fam. Law 129.*
102. Williams, S. and Hepple, B. A. (1984) *Foundations of the Law of Tort,* (Butterworths) at p.148.
103. *26 DLR (3d) 764.*
104. *1 WLR 716.*
105. Bone, M. (1977) *Pre-School Need for Day Care* (HMSO).
106. *1 WLR 286.*
107. See Griffiths, L. and Gypps, G. (1986) 'Sharing a Home', in *Law and the Elderly,* (The College of Law).
108. ibid., at p.16.
109. HC 169 as amended by HC 503.
110. Scammell, R. (1987) 'Recent Developments in Immigration Law', *Legal Action,* November 1987 at p.13. See also *Immigration Appeal Tribunal v. Singh (1988) 18 Fam. Law 256.*
111. 115, Old Street, London EC1.
112. Eastman, M. (1984) *Old Age,* (Age Concern England); Kosberg, J. I. (1983) *Abuse and Maltreatment of the Elderly: Causes and Interventions,* (John Wright, Massachusetts and Bristol).
113. Traynor, J. and Haslip, J. (1984) 'Sometimes She Makes Me Want to Hit Her', *Community Care,* August 2, 1984, at p.20.
114. Cloke, C. (1984) *Old Age Abuse in the Domestic Setting - A Review,* (Age Concern England) at para. 7.16.

115. Select Committee on Ageing. *Domestic Violence Against the Elderly.* Hearings before the Sub-Committee on Human Services, House of Representatives, April 21, 1980 (US Government Printing Office, Washington DC).
116. Eastman, M. (1984) op.cit., at p.23.
117. For a detailed discussion of Eastman's definition, see Cloke, C. (1984) op.cit., at para. 4.8.
118. Age Concern (1986) *The Law and Vulnerable Elderly People,* (Age Concern England).
119. Fleming, John G. (1983) *The Law of Torts,* (The Law Book Company Limited).
120. Rogers, W. V. H. (1975) *Winfield on Torts,* (Sweet and Maxwell), at p.58.
121. ibid., at p.59.
122. per Atkin, L. J. in *Meering v. Grahame White Aviation Co Ltd (1920) 122 LT 44.*
123. Eastman, M. (1984) op.cit., at p.30.
124. *White v. W. P. Brown,* at York County Court, September 29, 1983, reported in Current Law 1983.
125. *2 QB 57.*
126. *2 KB 296.*
127. Maidment, S. (1978) 'The Law's Response to Marital Violence: A comparison between England and the USA', in Katz, J. M. and Katz, S. M. (eds) *Family Violence* (Butterworths, Canada) at p.113. See also *R. v. Miller [1975] 2 QB at 292.*
128. Justices of the Peace Act 1361.
129. Edwards, S. (1982) 'Granny Battering - a problem that doctors are failing to detect', *Medical News,* November 11, 1982 at p.17.
130. Griffiths, A. (1980) 'The Legacy and Present Administration of English Law: Some Problems for Battered Women in Context', *Cambrian Law Review,* vol.11 at p.31.
131. Dawson, B. and Faragher, T. (1979) *Battered Women Project: Interim Report,* (University of Keele).
132. *The Times,* December 27, 1983.
133. Millard, P. (1984) 'Views of a Geriatrician' in Eastman, D. (1984) op.cit.
134. Rossiter, C. and Wicks, M. (1982) 'The Future of Community Care', *Community Care,* September 23, 1982 at p.119.
135. Williams, G. and Hepple, B. A. (1984) op.cit., at p.5.
136. *Re K; Re F [1988] 1 All ER 358.*

137. S.I. 1987 No.1612.

138. Enduring Powers of Attorney Act 1985, Sched 1, paras. 1 and 2(1).

139. s.4(4).

140. Sched 1, paras. 3(2) and 4(2).

141. s.6(4).

142. Mental Health Act 1983, s.95.

143. Court of Protection Rules 1984 S.I. 1984 No.2035, r.7.

144. r.23(2).

145. Gostin, L. (1983) *The Court of Protection - a legal and policy analysis of the guardianship of the state*, (MIND).

INDEX

abuse of the elderly 302-6
accelerated procedure for admission into care 173-4
accommodation: and the elderly 70; duty to provide 70; duty to provide public sector residential 141; powers to provide 143-4; privately rented 86; public rented 73; *see also* dwellings, flats, houses, homelessness, property
Acheson Committee 205
'act of retirement' 24
adaptations for the disabled 98-9, 122-3
additional assessment duties 124-6
additional state pensions 29-30
admission to residential care 140-1; compulsory 172-4
adoption 277-9
adultery 266-7
Affidavit of Kindred and Fortune 310-11
after care 228-9
Age Concern 84, 86, 285, 287
age: eligibility (unfair dismissal) 10; 'normal retiring' 8; of retirement 1-2, 8-9, 25; pensionable 2, 8, 24-5, 35-6
Agencies Benefits Unit (ABU) 219
agoraphobia 38
Agricultural Wages Boards 3
Allocation Joint Committee (AJC) 200, 210
allowance: attendance 39-43, 116, 159; domestic assistance 127; invalid care 43-5; mobility 36-9; personal (in residential care) 146-7; severe disability 35
ambulance services 220
annuities 18, 99
appeals against FPC decisions 245-6
appliances for disabled 120-1
'applicable amount' 46, 51
Approved Social Worker 175
arthritis 35
assault 303, 304-5
assessment: of ability to pay 146-8; of needs for disabled 124-6
assets, disposal of 152
assignment of a tenancy 76-7

Association of County Councils 144-5
attendance allowance 39-43, 116, 159
Attendance Allowance Unit (AAU) 43
Attorney, Enduring Powers of 307-9

bankruptcy 154
Barclay Committee 179
battery 303
benefits *see* social security benefits
blindness 35, 38, 41, 168
'board' 158-60
boarding-out schemes 108, 113-16
body, disposing of one's 286-7

'capability' 9
capacity: mental 283-5; test 34
capital: assessment of 148-9; disregard 171; limit (HB) 56;
    limit (IS) 48; transfer of 301
Capital Gains Tax (CGT) 296-8
Capital Transfer Tax (CTT) 298-9
car allowance 37
care: order 302; personal 158-60; private domiciliary 128;
    reasonable standard of 259-60; 'regular and substantial' 44
carers 127
Category A, B, C, D pensions 23
Centre for Policy on Ageing 129
charging for local authority services 126-7
chiropodists 217-18, 258
Chiropodists Board of the Council for Professions
    Supplementary to Medicine 258
Christian Scientist homes 167
Citizens Advice Bureaux (CABx) 197
codes of practice 157-8
cohabitees 47, 89, 279
cold weather payments 54-5
community care, definition 108-9
Community Care Grant (CCG) 53, 54
Community Health Care Services 196
Community Health Council (CHC) 203, 239-40, 243-4, 251
community nurses 196, 258-9
Community Nursing Service (CNS) 211-12, 255
community pharmacists 208

loans: budgeting 53; crisis 53
local authorities: assessment procedures 146-51; charging for
    services 126-7; duty to handicapped 118-21; duty to provide
    residential accommodation 141, 143; homes 138, 140,
    154-6; hospitals and 290-1; housing 70-1, 93-4, 122
Local Government Commissioner, *see* Ombudsman
lodgers 77-8
lump sum (pensions) 17

magistrates' court, financial provisions 273-4
maintenance 271-2, 273-4
marriage breakdown 266
meals provided by District Councils 111
Medical Officer (Complaints) 252
Medical Services Committee (MSC) 241-6
mental disorder 163-4
Mental Health Act Commission (MHAC) 256-7
mental incapacity, onset 308
Mental Nursing Homes 163-4
mentally disordered persons 143, 221-2, 256-7, 310
mentally incapable 306-7
Merrison Committee 199, 202-5, 207-8, 216, 262-3
misconduct, professional 257-8
mobility allowance 36-9
money purchase pension schemes 17
mortgage interest payments 53, 83
mortgages, interest-only 82

National Association for Patient Participation 247
National Association of Health Authorities (NAHA) 163, 254
National Association of Funeral Directors 291
National Health Service (NHS): charges for services 209;
    chiropody 217-18, 258; complaints about 235, 239, 253,
    259; dental care 213-15; drug prescription 206; entitlement
    to services 193-4; general medical care 198-9; hospitals
    218-19; invalid cars 37; nursing homes 156; ophthalmic
    services 215-17; primary health care 196-7; private sector
    arrangements 195; referral 209; residential accommodation
    141; tribunals 248
National Institute of Social Work (NISW) 84
national insurance contributions: classes 21; Class 1 18, 21,
    29-30, 33; divorced couples 272; reduced rate 18, 21, 28

Trustee, Public 307
trust property 48-9

unfair dismissal *see* dismissal
unmarried couples 47, 89, 279
Unregistered Residential Care Homes 160-1

vicarious liability 261
violence, domestic 274
voluntary organizations: definition 110; district council
    employment of 111
'vulnerability' 70

wages councils 3-4
wages protection 3-4
Wagner Committee 137, 138, 161, 166, 171, 179, 182
water rates 82
welfare, extended duty to promote 118-20
welfare provisions 109-10
Welsh Consumer Council 289
Welsh Office (WO) 251
wheelchairs 121
widows/widowers: intestacy 279-80; pensions 19, 29
wills 279-80; depositing 285; living 225-6; making 280-2;
    providing 288; provision for children 294-5; provision for
    spouses 292-4
women: discrimination against 20, *see also* Equal Pay Act and
    Sex Discrimination Acts (in Table of Statutes); working age
    1-2
work *see* employment
wrongful interference 304

Youth Training Scheme (YTS) 179